WHAT PRICE TRUTH?

Raymond Gilmour

Copyright © Raymond Gilmour 2015

This book is sold subject to the condition that it shall not, by way of trade or otherwise, be lent, resold, hired out, or otherwise circulated without the publisher's prior consent in any form of binding or cover other than that in which it is published and without a similar condition including this condition being imposed on the subsequent publisher.

The moral right of Raymond Gilmour has been asserted.

ISBN-13: 978-1507584750
ISBN-10: 150758475X

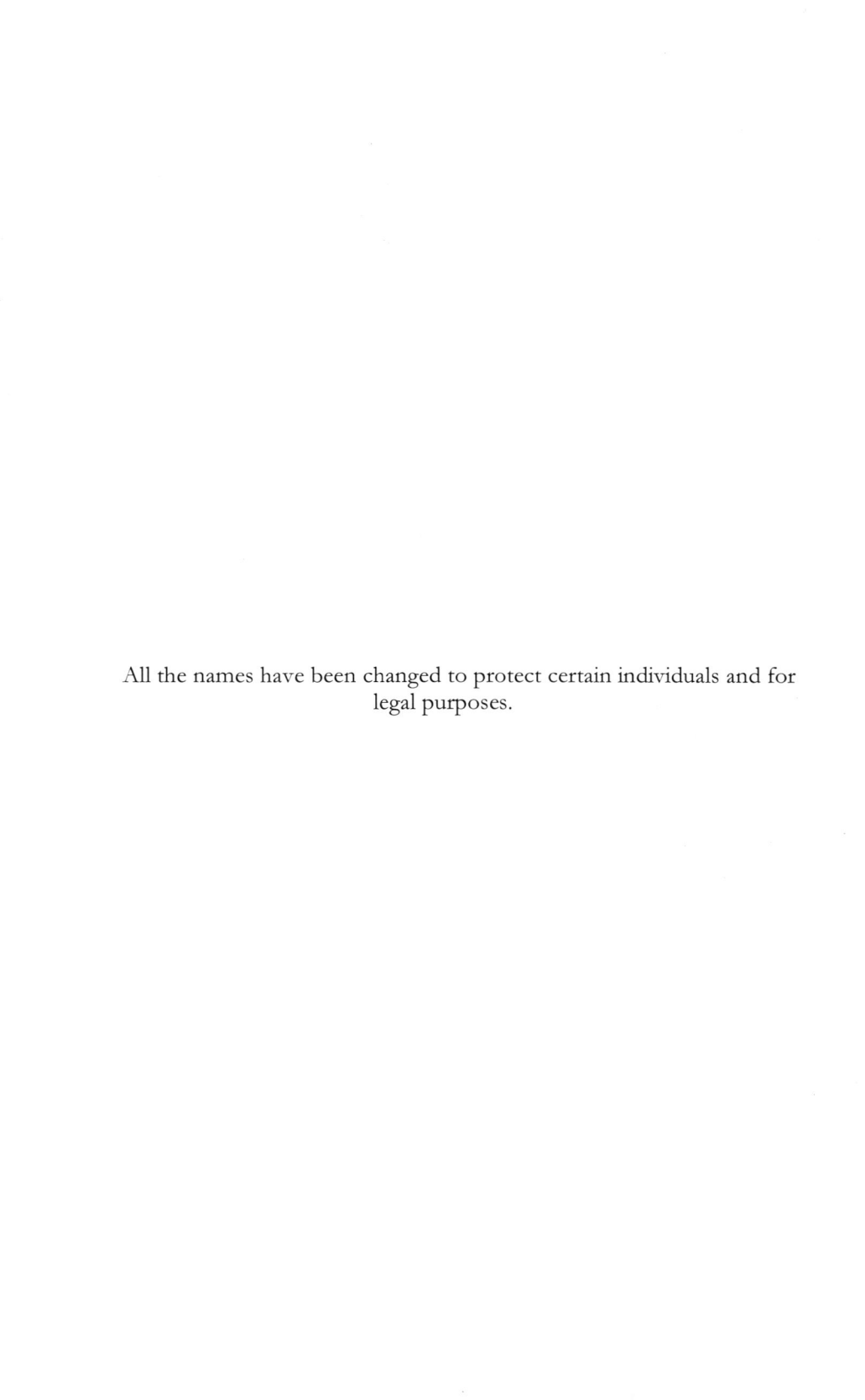

All the names have been changed to protect certain individuals and for legal purposes.

CONTENTS

ACKNOWLEDGMENTS	i
PROLOGUE	1
CHAPTER 1	6
CHAPTER 2	23
CHAPTER 3	35
CHAPTER 4	52
CHAPTER 5	70
CHAPTER 6	82
CHAPTER 7	105
CHAPTER 8	113
CHAPTER 9	128
CHAPTER 10	142
CHAPTER 11	156
CHAPTER 12	166
CHAPTER 13	187
CHAPTER 14	204
CHAPTER 15	218
CHAPTER 16	229
CHAPTER 17	242
EPILOGUE	250
APPENDIX	252
OTHER PUBLICATIONS	256

ACKNOWLEDGMENTS

To Ken Wharton former member of HM Forces The Royal Green Jackets Regiment now turned author to whom we owe our gratitude for his outstanding contribution to this book. To Chris Barnes George Cross former member of the Royal Ulster Constabulary (RUC GC) for his excellent investigation work and covert interviews with Raymond Gilmour.

To Joseph Magee for his perseverance and his extensive research. And finally last but not least to all the Close Protection members (ANON) who provided much needed protection to all involved in the production of this work.

PROLOGUE

The hotel bar was packed. The smell of sun tan oil and sweat mingled with beer and tobacco smoke as the tourists took their midday break from the beach. They'd escaped the horrors of Christmas with relatives for a holiday in the Cyprus sun, and didn't seem to be having too many regrets.

There were two guys at the far end who were different from the rest. I'd acquired an instinct for danger over the years in Derry, and these two guys were definitely wrong. One was dark and swarthy, wearing a crumpled white linen suit. The other was sandy- haired and as pale as only a newly-arrived British-or-Irish tourist can be. He'd gone for a cheap department store's idea of casual leisurewear – polyester short sleeved shirt and trousers in shades of pastel green. I half-recognised him, but I couldn't remember from where.

Their drinks sat untouched on the bar in front of them. They exchanged little conversation, speaking occasionally in low tones, lips barely moving. When a tourist pushed his way to the bar along side them, the pale one stopped in mid-sentence and didn't continue until the tourist had picked up his drinks and gone.

My unease could have been just paranoia; they weren't looking in my direction and might only have been discussing a business deal. But when I glanced at the big mirror behind the bar, I was sure. They were studying my reflection intently. Our eyes locked for a fraction of a second, then I let my gaze move on around the bar, trying to look as natural as possible. My heart was pounding and the hairs on my neck were beginning to rise.

I scanned every other person in the room, looking for any suspicious signs, no matter how faint. There were none. As far as I could tell, all the rest were just holiday-makers. I turned to face the bar again, keeping my expression neutral and disinterested – just another bored holiday-maker killing time. I saw enough in that glance to be pretty sure that the pale guy was not carrying a gun, but the other's shapeless suit could easily have concealed one.

Even in the confused aftermath of a shooting, however, they would be unlikely to run the risk of trying to escape from a crowded bar with only one handgun between them. It seemed more likely that they were checking things out, before they, or another hit team, returned after dark. I waited for a few seconds, trying to get my breathing under control and slow my thumping heart. Then I told my minder, Mike, "don't look now, but I think those guys are after us. The far end of the bar: the swarthy guy, Middle Eastern type, and the guy behind him. I recognise him from somewhere."

Mike straightened up, yawned and stretched, glancing along the bar as he did so. Then he picked up his drink, took a swallow, smiled as if he was about to crack a joke and said, "You're imagining things."

I laughed, as if we'd got to the punch line, but my tone was deadly serious. "No, I'm not. I'm telling you, I know him."

"You're sure?"

"Do you want to wait until they pull out a fucking gun? I am sure."

"All right."

We left our drinks on the bar and walked out. Mike turned and called out, "thanks, see you later," to the barman as we left the bar giving him a chance to clock if the two men were behind us. They stayed where they were initially, still watching us in the mirror, but as we reached the door, I saw a movement out of the corner of my eye. They'd got up from their barstools and turned to follow us.

As soon as we were in to the lobby and out of sight, we raced for the lift. "Not our floor," Mike said, "they'll watch the lift to see where it stops."

I jabbed the top button. There was an agonising pause before the doors creaked slowly together. Through the narrowing gap, I saw the pale man appear around the corner and then hang on his heel for a moment as he saw the door closing.

We got out at the top floor and ran down three flights of stairs to our own. I held open the door from the stairwell while Mike checked that the corridor was clear.

"My room," he said. "They might have your number."

"What about Lorraine and the kids?"

"I'll send Jeff. Lisa's already down there with them. We'll put you all in my room with two of us on guard."

"What if there's a bomb?"

"We'll have to take that chance." I'll get on to the army guys, but until they get here, we're safer staying put than bolting. We don't know how many of them there are… or where they are."

We dived into Mike's room, slamming the door and drawing the curtains. Mike sent Jeff haring down to the beach, then got straight on the phone, making a series of calls to the army and to the Special Branch back in Northern Ireland. Jeff was back inside five minutes, having shepherded Lorraine and the kids through the hotel kitchens and up the service stairs, with Lisa scouting ahead to make sure it was safe.

The children were crying, confused and frightened by the tension and urgency on our faces. Denise was whimpering and clinging around Lorraine's neck, while Raymond just retreated to a corner of the bedroom and sat down on the floor, refusing to speak or look at any of us. Lorraine didn't speak either, but the look that she gave me over Denise's shoulder said more than enough. There was the same unspoken plea in her eyes as always – give it up, come back to Derry, it will be all right – but it was now tinged with hatred for what I had brought upon my family.

We sat in the room, the silence hanging heavily on us, until six plain clothes Army Intelligence guys arrived from Akrotiri three-quarters of an hour later. Their news wasn't calculated to relax us.

"We got a tip-off that a known IRA man and three PLO suspects entered Cyprus two days ago," one of them said cheerfully. "We've been searching for them, without success, but it looks like you have done our job for us. We were wondering what they were up to."

The IRA had bought a lot of weapons from the PLO over the years, and as long established and trusted business partners, the Palestinians had obviously been recruited to help with the hit. The IRA's public enemy number one – me – was getting the full, five star treatment.

The Army had called in the Cypriot Special Branch and the hotel was sealed as they searched the public areas, but the two men were no longer there. The police and army searched every room with sniffer dogs hunting for guns and explosives, but found nothing.

The senior army officer came to see me in Mike's room when they'd finished the search. "We will be moving you to the army base at Dhekelia tonight, just to be safe. We've got armoured transport and an escort already on their way; they should be here in about two hours. Meantime, sit tight. We've got a guy with a camera stationed outside the hotel. He'll be photographing everyone who comes in or out or goes anywhere near the place."

"Oh, great," I said. "I'll get killed and the RUC gets a commemorative photograph."

"There is not much else we can do. We're not authorized to carry guns in this part of Cyprus." You saw the furious, incredulous look in my eye and added, "We searched the hotel thoroughly and we've got the area saturated with men."

"Unarmed men," I said flatly.

"Er...yes." He gave me a nervous glance and then said hastily, "Right, we'll leave you to it ... Mike, a word."

He and Mike disappeared into the corridor for a whispered conversation. As the rest of the group filed out, one of them hung back for a moment, turned to me and said hurriedly, "I'm with MI5. When all this is over, give me a ring. I'll try and get you some work in a similar line." He scribbled his number on a slip of paper and handed it to me. As soon as he'd gone, I threw it away – I'd seen more than enough of that kind of work.

We sat in our room for over three hours, not speaking, alone with our thoughts as each minute dragged by interminably. Finally the armoured vehicles rode up outside. Mike and the soldiers made their preparations, then we were hustled down the stairs and out through the kitchens. The vehicles were parked about twenty-five yards from the door, surrounded by a cordon of soldiers who were doing their best to hold back a large crowd of holiday-makers, drawn by the commotion.

As soon as I took in the scene, I grabbed Lorraine and the kids and pulled them back inside.

"What's the matter, Ray?" Mike asked.

"What's the matter? There are about three hundred people milling about out there. How do we know the hit-men aren't among them somewhere?"

"You've got wall-to-wall army here. It's perfectly safe."

"Is it? Then why don't you prove it? You're about my build – put my jacket over your head and then run out to that armoured car. If we don't hear any shots, we'll be right behind you."

I held my jacket out to him, but he didn't take it.

"Don't be daft, Ray," he said nervously.

"What's the matter? Not quite as confident as you cracked on? You could always get Jeff or Harry to do it instead." I glanced around. Both of the others had taken an involuntary step backwards.

"It looks like there are no volunteers, Mike, so I guess it has to be you. If you're so sure it's safe, then prove it. If you're not, then make sure it is safe before you ask me, my wife and kids to step out into the open.

He stood motionless for a moment, then took the jacket I was holding at arm's length and draped it over his shoulders. As he stepped out into the yard I called sharply after him. "Mike!"

He froze and turned back to face me. "Yes?"

"Nothing – I just wanted to be sure they had time to get you in their sights."

Even in the shadow cast across his face by the coat, I could see his eyes blazing with anger. He turned and ran across the yard to the armoured car. There were no shots, just mutters of curiosity from the crowd.

I turned to Lorraine. "I'll go next. Don't come out with the kids until I'm inside the armoured car. It's me they want, but they won't be fussy about hitting you as well if you're nearby."

I took a deep breath, and then ran out of the door and across the yard. As I clambered into the armoured car, I could see Mike still glowering at me in the gloom.

"Now you know what it feels like every single time I step out of a door, Mike. It's not pleasant, is it?" He didn't answer.

A moment later Lorraine and the kids were hurrying to join us. We were moving soon afterwards, rumbling down the road in an armoured convoy that trailed dust behind it for miles. The kids weren't remotely excited by the soldiers - they'd seen plenty of them around Derry. They huddled close to Lorraine and sat there silent and watchful as the convoy ground down the deserted roads and pulled to a halt inside the wire of the army base at Dhekelia.

We were safe for the moment, but it was a very temporary respite, for I knew the IRA would never give up. Sooner or later they'd catch up with me again. When they did, I'd be dead.

CHAPTER 1

I grew up in the Creggan, a run-down, post-war council estate in Londonderry – known as Derry in republican circles, to erase the hated imperial connection. The council painted the rows of pebble-dashed terraced houses every few years in pastel shades of mauve, yellow or lime-green, but the walls were quickly stained again with the ever- present damp. High up on a bleak hill above the town, the cold and wet were always with us. On the few winter days when the wind didn't blow, smoke from a thousand chimneys would drift slowly down through the still, lifeless air and lie across the Bogside like a grey prison blanket.

There was a great view from the Creggan. We could look down to the Craigavon Bridge and right across the river to the Waterside, but it was almost the only good thing about living up there. The streets were filthy and there was rusting iron beds and burned-out cars in the alleys at the back of the houses. Every morning there were ashes blowing through the streets and smell of smoke on the wind; it was like the morning after Bonfire Night every day of the year.

The gardens behind the disintegrating concrete fences were mostly unkempt, and the public spaces, like the stretch of grass across the road from our house, were minefields of broken bottles and bits of scrap metal, further scarred by the burned, bare circles left by countless fires. Some of the houses were as filthy as the streets. There was one in particular, Ogie Barrett's, on Rinmore Drive, which stank like a public toilet. It reeked so strongly it would make your eyes water when you walked past.

There was a straight route down from the Creggan to Derry's other Republican ghetto, the Bogside, which was half a mile away down a hill.

The road to the Bogside ran down past the large, disused BSR factory. The army had taken it over as a base, but there were riots every day that they were there and in the end they moved out, leaving nothing but a burned, battered wreck of a building behind.

Eighty or ninety per cent of the people on the Creggan were unemployed, for like the Bogside, the estate was almost exclusively Catholic, and the Protestants kept all the decent jobs for their own boys. There were scarcely any Protestant areas until you went across to the Waterside, on the other side of the River Foyle, although there were some mixed areas around Templemore, down by Shantallow.

Derry has changed now, but in those days the whole west side of the town was very dirty and derelict. A lot of the places around Brandywell, the area near the Creggan and Bogside, had been burned out or knocked down and the shops boarded up, especially the shops at the Creggan, where most of the Provie-Provisional IRA – activities took place.

The shops that were still open all had steel shutters, but after a few years of the Troubles there weren't that many left: a paper shop, a launderette, a butcher and a hardware store. There was also a doctor's surgery in the Sinn Féin Centre. At the end of the row, surrounded by iron railings, was the Telstar Bar, an IRA Bar. There were also shebeens owned by the Provies at the back of the houses and blocks of flats, and sheds fitted out with slot machines and pool tables, which would rake in money from us kids.

Above the shops were flats with balconies, but eventually all the flats became derelict and were boarded up too, because when the IRA were not using them to shoot at the army, the army were using them to spy on the IRA. Some of the derelict places were also used as squats by kids going wild and sleeping rough after walking out – or being thrown out – of their family homes.

Beside the shops there was a little row of houses and an alleyway – Little Lane – running up to the Creggan Heights, with another row of shops and flats on the other side. A zebra crossing led down to the chapel, where there was a big green with the Holy Child Primary School, where I went as a kid.

At night it was pitch black on the Creggan, for all the street lights were smashed and would be broken again as quickly as they were mended. We kids played terrible tricks in the dark, putting bottles on top of walls and tieng them with thread to the fences on the other side. As people walked down the road the bottles would be pulled off the wall, exploding like gun shots as they hit the ground.

We used a crueller refinement down at the town centre shops on

Saturdays. We bought packets of caps from Woolworth's – big ones, twelve to a packet – and laid a few on the ground. When a policeman walked by, we stamped down on the caps and laughed ourselves silly as he dived for cover, thinking he was under fire. We could have been shot ourselves if the policeman had been trigger-happy, but those were the dangerous games we played.

If the Creggan was grim, we could quickly escape over the fields and up to the moors. We used to walk up the road – "up the country", as we called it – and over the border with the Free State to a little shop, where we would buy cigarettes and sweets. There was a small forest of conifers surrounding Killea reservoir a few fields away. We would sit by the reservoir skimming stones, or walk over the heather moor and peat bog to the Stone Man – a cairn of stones on top of Holywell Hill. Every person who climbed to the top would add a stone to the pile. If you were courting, you also went up to the forest by the reservoir. The only alternatives were to go for a walk round the estate or stand by the Creggan shops; without money there was really nowhere else to go.

Even though there were barriers at the army base on the border at Piggery Ridge, we used to just walk past them. The name wasn't a comment on the army, there actually was a piggery up there. Dominated by two look-out towers, the base was an ugly mess of concrete and corrugated iron, dumped in the middle of the green fields. There was only one entrance, guarded by massive concrete blocks to prevent anyone driving straight at the towering, green steel gates. Helicopters flew in and out constantly, their rotors clattering, and there was a sound of firing every day as the soldiers practised their shooting.

Even before the army built the camp, there were guns going off, for the IRA would often use the area for target practice. Going up the road one day when I was about eight or nine, I saw a line of about twenty IRA guys firing at targets. I found a little white cat cowering in the hedge that day; it had been shot through the paw with a .22. I carried it home and nursed it back to health, but it disappeared a few weeks later. I hoped it had simply found a better place to live, but the chances were that it had either been run over or killed for sport.

You could see the base at Piggery Ridge from our house, a draughty, two storey terrace in the middle of a row on Balbane Pass, in the Creggan Heights. The only heat came from a coal fire in the living-room, and the kitchen, living-room, toilet, bathroom and three small bedrooms had to accommodate thirteen people, for I was the last of eleven children.

When I was fairly young, I slept in my Ma and Da's room, but later on I shared a bed with a couple of my brothers. Things got a bit less crowded by the time I was three or four, when my brothers began to get married, or went to England to work or lived in other places. From then on, the whole family was rarely all at home at once, although my brothers would come back for a visit from time to time. I was almost burned to death one night when one of them fell asleep smoking in bed. I woke up along side him to find the whole room filled with smoke and the bed smouldering.

I was very unhappy as a child and never liked our house; it always had a bad feeling about it. One of the few really happy memories I have of the place is of the occasional days when my father had gone down to get his dole money, and brought home hot, freshly baked baps for us, from the little baker's at the Creggan shops. In a home that was perpetually poor and often torn by violence, there was nothing in the world to match that simple treat.

My mother, Bridie, originally Bridget Burns from Dublin, was a formidable character. She was short and very stocky, with dark hair, occasionally dyed red or blonde, and though far from a tyrant, she had a voice that could stop a speeding child in its tracks. She ran the home with iron discipline, reinforced by frequent cuffs to the ear. Yet despite that strong personality, raising all eleven of us on virtually no money put her under so much stress that she was often in and out of mental hospital. She was always worrying about money, and if my Da wasn't around, she would take out her frustrations on me and my sisters instead.

My father, Patrick was tall and thin as a rail. He could eat like a horse and still would not put on any meat, and when he was sober, he was a mild, meek, mouse of a man. He'd spend most of his time sitting in an armchair, reading cowboy books and comics and chain smoking untipped Park Drive. They were really strong, but he'd smoke as many as he could get his hands on, which killed him in the end. He'd usually sit around until about eleven in the morning, then go out just to get out of my mother's way.

They'd met during the war, when they were both working in munitions factories in Coventry. They got married and came to live in Londonderry, my father's home city, after the war, but from then on he was out of work a lot of the time. That wasn't altogether his fault; everyone was unemployed around the Creggan. There was virtually no work for anyone.

Sometimes he got bits of work with the council, but they never lasted long. He went back to England a few times with my uncle, who lived down the lane. They worked in construction, but the jobs never lasted more than a few months and they would be skint again as soon as they got back home.

I felt sorry for him in many ways, because he'd no qualifications and could only labour or do menial work. An unskilled, unemployed Catholic man in Northern Ireland had no future at all. And like so many in Derry, when he could drink, he did drink.

When he was drinking, he wasn't a pleasant man to be around. He was normally very quiet and placid, but when he got his dole money on a Friday, he'd go out, get drunk and then come home and take out his frustrations on my mother and the rest of us in outbursts of drunken, violent rage.

Most Saturday nights he'd again go out and come home drunk. He'd argue with my mother and sisters, and if my big brothers were there, they'd fight with him just because he got so annoying and aggravating in drink. He would start mouthing off and they'd tell him, "be quiet or else you will get a good pasting," and then all hell broke loose. The rest of the family didn't look forward to Saturday nights at all, because four or five people were always shouting at once and the fists and boots were flying.

My Ma would go round to one of her friends' houses most Friday and Saturday nights just to keep out of the way, and because I was the youngest, she'd usually take me with her. When we got back, my father had often locked us out of the house. We had to sit on the freezing pavement outside the front door for hours and hours, shivering with cold, until my father either woke from his drunken stupor or finally decided to let us in again.

Often we'd have been better off staying on the pavement, for being inside the house when my father was the worst for drink was not the safest place to be. He beat my mother regularly, while I cowered behind the sofa, crying and begging him to stop. One night he frightened her so much that she jumped out of the bedroom window to get away from him. She hurt her back so badly that she was in traction in hospital for several weeks. We had to go and stay with my eldest sister Patricia – Patsy – down at Fern Park, round Shantallow, who looked after us until my Ma was well enough to come home.

I don't really remember Patsy at home, for she married and moved out when I was very young, but we spent weeks at a time at her house later on, for she also had to look after us all on several occasions when my Ma was taken into mental hospital because everything had got on top of her.

Patsy was always very strict and straight with us, but it was a relief to get away from the Creggan for a while and stay in a nicer area. It was as close as we ever got to a holiday in my childhood, for the only other times I got away were to visit my mother's family in Dublin. We stayed in a three-bedroomed flat, as crowded with kids as our own home, but it wasn't the Creggan and that was good enough for me.

My other sisters, Kathleen, Geraldine and Dympna, were all nice, well-mannered and well-behaved – "good Catholic girls", as my Ma would have approvingly say. When they grew up, they all got jobs in shirt or denim factories. They brought their wages home and gave my mother whatever they could afford. They were the main bread winners in our house; there was always more work for women than men in Derry.

I barely knew my eldest brother, Patrick – Paddy. He left Derry for Liverpool when he was fifteen, the year before I was born, and only came home once or twice in all the time I was there. My mother took me to visit him in Liverpool twice, but both times she got into furious arguments with Paddy and his wife and we went back to Derry on the next boat.

Unlike Paddy, my brother Harry stayed around Derry. He was a bit of a funny man, always cracking jokes, but he could be serious when he had to be. I idolised him. He had a job as a window-cleaner for a while, but like most of the lads from the Creggan, he was not adverse to a bit of thieving on the side if the chance presented itself. Two of my other brothers, Johnny and Dessie, were also into the same things.

My Da used to punch and beat them in the hall to try and make them stop, but the more he punched them, the worse they seemed to get. Johnny was about six foot two and built like a brick shithouse, but he always seemed quite childish and immature. He married a Protestant woman whose mother was a staunch loyalist and very anti-Catholic, even though her daughter had married one. Johnny's brother-in-law was even less tolerant. He'd actually been tried for the murder of two Catholics in the South of Ireland, though he was eventually acquitted. In the circumstances, it was perhaps not surprising that Johnny, like my mother, was bad with his nerves and was in and out of the mental hospital on a number of occasions.

Desmond – Dessie – loved practical jokes and would do anything for a laugh. He was always playing tricks to scare my mother and sisters, like turning off the electricity at the main box. When they went to see what had happened, he'd jump out of the cupboard or from behind the stairs and scare the shit out of them.

Harry had also been very lively and jokey, but his character was changed overnight by tragedy. He'd married Marie Meenan, a girl from a very Republican family in the Bogside, but their first child died at birth. He was absolutely devastated and never really recovered. I still remember the funeral and carrying that pathetic little white coffin down to the grave. The hole was barely big enough to bury a dog.

Johnny, Harry and Dessie, had all been in the army cadets in their teens. I can remember them bulling their boots up and setting off for parade with their berets on and their green uniforms immaculate. I'd never seen anything as fine in all my life. The other two soon lost interest, but Dessie was hooked on the army and joined up when he was sixteen.

My Ma and Da originally forbade it, scared of what might happen to him; kids from the Creggan just didn't join the British army. They finally relented after Dessie whinged, sulked and moaned for days. He became a bandsman, playing a trumpet in the Royal Irish Rangers.

He'd signed up for ten years, but things started to go wrong after three or four years and he deserted. When they caught him, they put him in the guardhouse for a few months. Eventually he bought himself out of the army and moved to England, where he married a Liverpool girl. He came home a few more times after that, but on the last one he was threatened by some IRA men, who told him that because he'd been in the British army, he'd be murdered if he ever came back to Derry again. He never did.

My next brother Gerald – Gerry – was a strange boy. He'd been a sickly child, forced to live on a special diet and bullied a lot at school. When he grew out of his health problems, he made up for his own miserable childhood by beating and torturing my sisters and me.

He and his friend Paul Doughty from next door were bullies of the worst kind. When he grew up, Doughty joined the IRA and was in Long Kesh when the prisoners rioted and burned their sheds. He almost lost his sight in one eye because of the beating he took from the army when they regained control, but I've no sympathy for that tosser. I can remember too many occasions when he and my brother beat up my sisters and me and tried to make us to drink their piss.

My Ma and Da always went out on Saturday mornings. As soon as they were out of sight, Paul and Gerry would lock us in the pantry and make us stay there for hours, only letting us out to give us another beating. Gerry also forced me to keep my school dinner and bring it home after school so that he could eat it. If I didn't, he beat me again.

He eventually went south to Dublin and became a tele-communications engineer for the GPO. We didn't see a great deal of him after that, which was no loss at all as far as I was concerned.

My other brother Eugene was a bit of a tearaway. He used to knock around with these guys called the O'Briens, well-known criminals from the Creggan Heights. They'd go down to the town at night, break into places and thieve things, but they never broke into anywhere on our estate; you didn't shit on your own doorstep. Even so, Eugene was reported to the IRA and threatened by them, and eventually he too left for England.

My Ma always did the discipline on the younger ones like my sisters and me, but my Da really used to go to town on the elder boys. Until they got old enough to fight back, he'd often stick the boot in really heavily on them, giving them a good kicking under the stairs, while we sat in the kitchen, avoiding each other's eyes. I always pressed my fingers into my ears to try and block out the noise of his thudding boots and my brothers' cries and groans.

My Da sounds an ogre, but I suppose he didn't know any better; it was just the way he'd been brought up as well. Nor was his behavior unique to our house, for the whole of the Creggan seemed to be like that. Blokes would come back from the pub on Friday nights and knock their wives about, and they would just have to take it.

The wives knocked the kids about in turn. I hated school and we all used to bunk off lessons constantly, but whenever my Ma found out I got a thrashing. She was a very strong disciplinarian, but she also protected the weak and the underdog. If there were any riots going on and she saw someone getting hurt, it didn't matter if they were the neighbour's kids, adults, police or soldiers, she would stick up for them. She stopped many a riot in our street and at the Creggan shops, and not just by kids. She would face down big men as well, shouting at them, "you should be ashamed of yourself," and giving them a good old slap around the face.

She reserved the hardest slaps for her own children if she caught us joining in the stonings and riots which went on most of the time. The four o'clock riot – as soon as the kids got out of school – happened so regularly that photographers from the local papers would be hanging around every day waiting for it to start. Riots normally happened spontaneously and didn't need organising but if the IRA wanted to create a diversion, somebody would be sent to get the kids wound up to start a fire or something.

I threw stones with the best of them, but I drew the line at petrol-bombing, although plenty of the other kids were willing to do it. The IRA men would bring in milk-crates full of petrol bombs and stash them in the alley or around the back of a block of flats, ready for the kids to throw when the riots started.

They'd also teach us how to make them ourselves. I can remember one teenage Provie volunteer giving a nonchalant lecture to a group of us saucer-eyed kids. "Sure, they're easy to make," he said, revelling in the attention. "Get a beer bottle or a milk bottle – milk bottles are best – fill it with petrol and make a fuse from a bit of old rag soaked in petrol. If you can't get any, you can use paraffin instead, but petrol's the best. Now the really important thing is not to throw it too soon. When you've lit it, count to three before you throw it and it'll explode as soon as it hits yer man. That's what we want, isn't it?"

A lot of the kids nodded their heads shyly or said "aye", their eyes shinning, but I felt sick at the thought and had nightmares for weeks. I'd see anonymous people smothered in flames, and although I tried to beat them out with my hands, they'd just burned brighter. Then through the flames I'd see the faces of my brothers, blackening and cracking. I'd wake screaming and crying, drenched in sweat. My ungrateful brothers would just curse and punch me for waking them up and I would lie their sobbing until my mother came in and comforted me.

Despite the nightmares and my mother's warnings, I'd still often go with the older kids down to Aggro Corner on William Street and throw stones at the soldiers. Even my brother Dessie, who was in the army himself, would throw stones at them when he was home on leave, just for a kick.

The Orangemen also came in for their share of stones during the annual summer marching season. There'd be long columns of Prods in dark suits, white gloves and bowler hats, with orange sashes around their necks. At their head were the bands and posturing drummer-boys beating out a tattoo as they marched through the streets.

Whenever their route took them past Catholic areas, they were separated from us by a wall of green-uniformed RUC men, all facing us with their backs to the Prods. The Orange anthems – "The Sash" and "The Green, Grassy Slopes of the Boyne" – blared out from the bands, every word a provocation, while the marchers looked warily to the right and left as they strolled through behind them.

The reply was never slow in coming. An arm or two came out of the middle of the crowd and the first stones flew, black against the sky. Then there were fusillades, most bouncing on the tarmac, but a few striking home, sending Orangemen reeling as the stones thumped into their chests or sent blood spurting from gashes on their faces. At each hit there were cheers from the mob and the volleys of stones would redouble.

The bands kept playing and the Prods kept step as best they could, responding to the stones with jeers and taunts as their defenders, the RUC and the hated B-Specials held the line between the sides. Extra police, waiting in the side-streets in riot gear, advanced towards the crowds, batons waving as rocks bounced off their shields.

As the Prods marched on out of range, there was a rattle of rubber bullets and the muffled crack as gas canisters went off. As one, the crowds would turn and run, a few kids still hurling stones as they retreated, leaving streets strewn with rubble and the whiff of CS gas in the air.

We'd look on stoning the Prods or the army as a bit of a laugh at the time, but when things started getting serious, the laughter quickly stopped. My mother never found it funny at all. She loathed the IRA, abhorring the violence and killing that was their trademark, and she never shrank from expressing her opinions. Others voicing such views were stoned or even burned out of their houses, and it says much for the respect – and fear – that she inspired among her neighbours and their children that she remained unmolested even after British troops moved in.

In 1969 a two-day riot – the Battle of the Bogside – erupted during the annual Apprentice Boys march. As the Protestant marchers passed the edge of the Bogside they were met by hail of stones. Police and Orangemen broke ranks and charged into the Bogside. Fighting and rioting quickly spread, and the invaders found themselves attacked with rocks, bricks, bottles and iron bars. Showers of missiles were also hurled from the roofs of the tower blocks.

After two days of rioting, British troops were sent in to restore order but though they were welcomed at first, the Creggan and Bogside quickly became no-go areas for them. They stayed that way until Operation Motorman in 1971, when the army bulldozed the barricades and broke in.

It was strange, alien territory to the Brits, a sprawling warren of slum housing, with broken windows, shattered doors and torched buildings on every side. The streets were littered with rocks and broken glass and the tarmac was scarred where hijacked cars had been burned out. Every piece of waste ground also housed a burned-out rusting wreck. In the drab vista of grey stone and smoke-stained red brick, the only bright colours were those of the Irish Tricolour – green, white and orange – claiming ever pillar box and lamp standard for Mother Ireland.

There were Irish flags and murals of Easter lilies painted on the gable ends along side warning slogans: "BRITS OUT", "IRA", "YOU ARE NOW ENTERING FREE DERRY". The only one missing was "ABANDON HOPE ALL YE WHO ENTER HERE".

After the barricades were smashed and hauled away, the army came in mob-handed to take control again. There were army patrols everywhere, backed by hundreds of big Saracen armoured vehicles in curious yellow desert camouflage.

They rumbled through the streets day and night with grim-faced rifle men, their faces darkened with boot polish, peering along with rifle barrels poking out of the slits at the front and back. Hundreds of older IRA men and sympathisers were rounded up and taken away for questioning, but most of the young activists were missed. The random and increasingly brutal sweeps and searches by the army and the constant frisking and body searches on people as they walked around the streets, polarised the Creggan even more. My brothers would come in boiling with rage after being stopped and searched as many as four times in a single journey down into the town.

House-to-house searches were the biggest cause of anger, however. Army Saracens screeched to a halt at either end of the street in the middle of the night, while soldiers and Police battered at our front doors, first with rifle butts and then, if the answer was too slow, with axes and sledgehammers.

Women and kids rushed outside, blowing whistles and banging dustbin lids to alert the neighbours, and an angry crowd would start to form, held back by a circle of tense, twitchy shoulders clutching transparent plastic riot shields. RUC men, each protected by a personal bodyguard of soldiers, moved among the houses using sniffer dogs to search for explosives.

Everyone was turned out on to the street and stood huddled in blankets, jeering and cursing at the soldiers as they went through our homes, smashing and destroying everything. They even prised up the floorboards to look for weapons. There was the constant sound of locks being forced, wood splintering and glass breaking, as they turned each house upside-down.

Often the troops left empty-handed, but occasionally there would be a shout from one of the soldiers, emerging from a house with a trophy – a balaclava mask, a sack of weedkiller used to make primitive bombs, some batteries and electrical wire or a few rounds of ammunition. All were wrapped in plastic evidence bags to preserve the fingerprints and forensics.

The usual suspects were lined up and taken away for questioning, and finally the soldiers climbed back into their Saracens and disappeared into the night, the engines belching out a cloud of stinking diesel fumes as the residents yelled the last defiant round of abuse. There was silence for a moment, broken rapidly by cries of rage and despair as they saw the state of their homes.

Whether anything was found or not, known Republicans and IRA members had their houses absolutely ransacked. They'd find their crockery and ornaments smashed and even their family pictures torn up. It was brutal, unnecessary stuff and only served to fuel the hatred that so many felt for the Brits.

While the Army were met elsewhere with abuse and volleys of missiles, however, they got a very different reception at our house. When the Saracen parked right outside our back gate, my Ma asked the soldiers if they wanted a cup of tea.

"We don't want to get you in any trouble, Missus," said a soldier, jerking his head at the twitching curtains of our neighbours.

"I don't give a fuck about them," said my Ma. "You're a human being like anybody else." She served up the tea in her best china and I carried it out to them.

A couple of the neighbours started on at her, yelling, "you soldier doll bastards!"

My mum gave as good as she got telling them, "shut the fuck up or I will rip your fucking heads off."

The neighbours were a bit wary of my Ma to start with, for she was southern Irish, and they knew not to mess with southern women. Despite her origins and her Catholic faith, however, she had no Republican sympathies. She knew what it was like to live in the South and, as she repeatedly told us, it was very hard then, without all the subsidies that the British Government pumped into the North. "If the Brits pull out," she would say, "there would be no more subsidies and life for everyone up here will get even harder … and God knows, it's hard enough as it is."

There were furious arguments between my mother and father over the IRA. My father was an armchair supporter of the Provisionals. He sat in his chair with his cowboy comics muttering, "at least the Provies are defending us from the Brits."

My mother rounded on him, yelling, "it's not the Brits we need defending against. It's the fucking Provies."

Her attitudes also brought her into fierce conflict with many of the people in our neighbourhood, none more so than Danny Gillespie, who lived in the same row of houses. His son was a well-known IRA man, but my mother hated Danny the most, because he became an instant staunch Republican after Operation Motorman, though he'd been in the British army himself for twenty years. I can even remember him coming up the road in his uniform. She called him a turncoat and everything under the sun, while he called her a pro-Brit bastard.

Most Catholics hated the RUC even more than the army. Members of the Royal Ulster Constabulary were all Protestants, keeping the best jobs for themselves as usual, while we got nothing. Our house was probably the only one on the Creggan where they wouldn't be greeted with a mouthful of abuse. They were often on our doorstep, for despite my father's attempts to kick some morality into my elder brothers, they were in constant trouble for breaking and entering and stealing things from shops. Two of them were sent to Borstal for it. When I got a bit older, I was into the same sort of thing myself. Also everybody was; it was the only way for anyone from the Creggan to make any money.

The RUC came round in their cars, which were black in those days and said, "bad news, Mrs Gilmour, we've got two of your boys down at the station."

While they talked to my mother inside, one of the policemen kept me amused by taking me out to the car, giving me his hat to wear and letting me play with the controls and even operate the siren. Uniquely among the kids on the Creggan I grew up with friendly feelings towards the RUC.

When I was a kid, most people on the Creggan – apart from my mother – had much more confidence in the IRA than the RUC. The Provies presented themselves as the true protectors of the Catholic population, and for a while they were believed. There was a lot of solidarity with them, but when the deaths, torture and knee-cappings started to happen, people began thinking a bit harder about things. Neither the Stickies – the Official IRA – nor the Provies did themselves any favours with the local people and the majority supported them through fear rather than conviction.

A mate of Dessie's in the Royal Irish Rangers, a guy called Michael Best, was taken away by the Stickies one night and tortured badly, just because he was in the army. Dessie took me to see the body before the funeral. I peered over the edge of the coffin at the first dead body I had ever seen. His face was wax-like covered with thick make-up, and he was dressed in his best Sunday suit, but his hands had been left exposed and untouched. There were cigarette burns all over the backs of his hands. Some of his nails were missing altogether; others were hideously split, scorched and scarred.

"He wasn't even a Brit, he was one of our own," whispered Dessie, his voice breaking with emotion. "They put lighted matches down his nails and tore some of them off with pliers. They did other things to him as well, awful, terrible things."

"What did they do?" I asked, with the insatiable curiosity of a child, but he just shook his head as the tears rolled down his cheeks.

We learned the realities of life in Derry very young. I may not have been old enough to fully understand the world around me, but I could sense the fear that ruled the Creggan without being told. Running down the alley behind our house one day, I ran in to a local IRA man, sending him sprawling. The fear and anxiety in my father's voice as he helped the man up, dusted him down and then back-handed me to the ground in punishment, groveling his apologies until the man was out of sight, told me more than any words about the power of the IRA.

The streets of the Creggan had never been leafy lanes, lined with quaint cottages and peopled by apple-cheeked children and smiling grannies. The Creggan was windswept and dirty, the people were shabbily-dressed, pinched, poor and grey-faced. All we had was a tribal solidarity, upon which the IRA fed like a leech.

In the days before Operation Motorman everyone knew who was in the IRA for they made no real attempt to conceal their identities. I would go down to the Creggan shops and see guys, neighbours of mine, in balaclava helmets, carrying guns and stopping cars.

As more and more of them got lifted by the army, they became much more cautious, but even when unstated and unseen, their menace was understood by everyone from the youngest to the oldest. The film *The Godfather* was released shortly after Motorman, when my brothers sneaked me in to see it at the Rialto, I didn't need to have the parallels pointed out to me. The Creggan was in the grip of the IRA just as surely as a Sicilian village ruled by the Mafia, and the IRA's punishments were every bit as vicious.

We all grew to take guns and shootings for granted, for there was the sound of gunfire and explosions every single day and night. Even the pigeons became nonchalant about it. Some took off momentarily at the sound of a shot, others remained unruffled, barely pausing from preening their feathers or pecking at scraps in the gutter.

The humans were more worried than the pigeons. If a car back-fired, everybody would duck or hit the deck. It was second nature, and more often than not, the explosions were for real. We would hear the crump of a bomb going off and look out to see the dull red glow of a fire, sparks flickering upwards on a column of black, oily smoke.

Bombs went off down the city centre so often that it almost ceased to exist. At one stage only twenty of the centre's hundred-plus big shops were still open. All the rest had been completely destroyed or had shut down for repairs to bomb damage. There was scarcely a pane of glass in tact in the whole city centre. Virtually every window was boarded up and the shops that were open kept their lights burning all day, even in high summer.

As usual, the destruction provoked furious arguments in our home. My mother lamented the endless bombings, which continued even after the Army surrounded the city centre in a ring of steel. "The Germans didn't do as much damage to Coventry in the war as your brave IRA boys are doing to Derry," she shouted at my father one day. "What the fuck is the point of destroying our own city?"

My father's rejoinder, "it's not our city, it's their city," only served to make her more angry.

Gunfire was so much a part of the background to our lives that we all became experts, easily telling the hollow rattle of rubber bullets and the high crack of an Armalite with a heavier bang of the army's assault rifles. We showed off our knowledge every time we heard a shot: "SLR."

"Nah stupid, Armalite."

Walking down to the shops one afternoon, I saw two cars pull up. Eight men got out very quickly and hurried round to the boot of one of the cars. They lifted out rifles with big banana magazines and took them into the flats.

The weapons could have been the ones used a few weeks later, when three schoolfriends and I were caught in cross-fire between the IRA and the army. We were just turning up towards the Creggan, into Little Lane, the alleyway that led on to the back of the shops, when we heard shots and saw bullets striking sparks off the walls. We ducked into one of the entrances to the flats. They were bricked up, but there was just enough room to get in there and lie flat on the ground. My best friend's little brother was with us and he crying with fright.

The army returned fire to the IRA, but when they saw us in the doorway, a soldier was sent to try and calm us down. He sprinted across the alley, his boots striking sparks from the ground as he ran "just keep your heads down until the shooting stops and you'll be fine," he said, in an almost impenetrable Geordie accent. He patted our heads and gave us each a Polo mint.

I gazed shyly up at him as he crouched beside us, apparently unconcerned by the bullets still ricocheting off the walls. We stayed there for about ten minutes after the shooting had stopped and then the soldier told us, "right it'll be ok now, get yourselves off home."

For the next few weeks, whenever we played IRA and soldiers by the reservoir, I pretended to be that Geordie infantryman as we mimicked the movements of the army patrols we saw every day. Three soldiers face forwards and one back, all turning their heads constantly from side to side, scanning the streets, the windows and the roof-tops for any sign of danger.

Not long after that, again coming home from school, another gun battle broke out right in front of me. I threw myself flat on the ground. Looking ahead, I could see the bullets flying across the darkened sky; the IRA had obviously bought some tracer. Heavy rain began falling, but I stayed face down until the shooting stopped, then got up and scrambled into a doorway. I waited for a few more minutes until people began moving up and down the street again and then walked nervously on up the hill.

A body lay in the gutter, covered with a red blanket. Soldiers stood guard on every corner, their rain-soaked capes shining as sleek and glossy as crows' wings. The blanket, the only splash of colour in the drab, grey street, was darkened by the rain to the colour of blood. I stared at the mound under the blanket for a long time, until a soldier gruffly moved me on.

Another night I was sitting in the house with my father when firing started up outside. One round hit the back wall of the house, knocking a big chunk of concrete, about the size of a dinner plate, off the wall. It sounded as if the house had been hit with a sledgehammer.

My Da shouted, "Get on the floor," and we lay there under the table and watched the tracer rounds zapping across the backs of the houses. A few minutes later we heard a dull thud as a bomb exploded, setting the place rattling on the sink and the bare light bulb dancing a jig at the end of its cable.

As I looked out of our window one afternoon, I saw a few guys go into a house on Rinmore Drive and set up a mortar in back garden to fire at the army camp on Piggery Ridge. They rigged up some lengths of what looked like drainpipe, braced with timber. There was flash and a roar like a rocket taking off as each one fired.

As soon as the last one went off, they ran through the house, across Rinmore Drive and down to their own houses again. By the time the army patrols came round, turfing people out of their houses while they searched, the same guys just stood out in the road with their neighbours, the picture of injured innocence.

One day I got home from school to find my bedroom window broken by a ricochet. A squashed, misshapen bullet lay on the floor. My Da stuffed some rags into the hole in the window. Stiffened by the frost that night, they rattled against the glass like bony fingers as I lay awake, too scared to sleep. I kept the bullet in my pocket for weeks, proudly showing it to all my friends, and was heartbroken when I lost it playing by the reservoir one day.

Not long afterwards, a soldier was shot down at Fanad Drive. As soon as we heard about it, my mates and I ran down to have a look. As usual, after the shooting had stopped and it was safe to go outside, a few nice people had gone to do whatever they could for the victim; a few of the other sort just spat on him as they walked past.

As army helicopters clattered overhead, the soldiers and police went through the usual motions, cordoning off the area, carrying out a house-to-house search and taking statements from those living nearby – though there were never any witnesses.

After the body had been taken away, the people who lived in the nearby houses went out to wash the blood from the streets. Most people tried to keep the little patch of ground outside their house immaculate, despite the broken glass littering the pavements and the ashes and rubbish blowing constantly through the streets. Cleaning up the blood was partly just being house-proud, like sweeping the path and donkey-stoning the front steps, but it was also probably an attempt to erase all trace of the deed itself. We were all good Catholics after all, and good Catholics just didn't hurt people. The blood was a constant mute reproach; a man was killed here and you did nothing to stop it. They didn't want blood stains on their doorstep pointing an accusing finger at their door, because the Good Lord might come and strike them dead that very night.

In addition to the gun battles, there were regular IRA punishment shootings as well, which almost invariably took place behind the Creggan shops. As you went down the lane from the Creggan Heights there were high walls on either side, but part of the walls had been knocked down to give easy entry to the area at the back of the shops; it was handy for dragging in people for shootings that way.

Facing the backs of the shops was a high wall punctuated by gateways, though the wall screened the view from the windows of the houses. The area was surfaced in crumbling tarmac, smothered in broken glass, tin cans and shards of broken metal and wood. Old cars littered the area, stolen, smashed up and burned out. Despite the dereliction – and the danger from IRA men – we kids would often meet there on Sunday and gamble the money we had been given for the Church collection baskets, pitching pennies against the wall.

Shootings and knee-cappings would happen day or night, there was no specific time. Walking with one of my brothers down by the Creggan shops in broad daylight one afternoon, I heard two gunshots from behind the Sinn Féin offices. I was agog to see what had happened, but my brother, older and wiser, dragged me away. All the men and women around us averted their gaze, keeping their eyes downcast. They knew better than to interfere as the IRA – police, judge and jury – knee-capped some petty thief or burglar.

Some victims of the IRA were even less culpable. An old Stickie guy, Gerry Cannon, made the mistake of trying to be a good neighbour to an old man in a flat in Rinmore Drive. The next-door neighbours told him that the man wasn't answering his door and hadn't been for a few days. Gerry climbed in through the window, but when he switched on the light, a bomb exploded, blowing his leg off. The Provies had taken the old man to the Republic and booby-trapped the flat, hoping to catch out an RUC patrol when neighbours reported his disappearance. It was Gerry's misfortune to get there first.

CHAPTER 2

Knee-capping or worse was a punishment that could easily have befallen me and my friends, young though we were. We used to go round the houses asking if there were any jobs that people wanted doing, in exchange for a few biscuits or a couple of bob. We were walking up towards Piggery Ridge one day, past an old cottage at the side of the road, and I knocked on the door. An English woman answered it, "Hello." I said, "We're just seeing if you have any jobs you want doing."

She thought for a moment. "Yes, there is some wood round the back that we want cutting up. We'll give you a shilling each."

We were delighted and went straight round to make a start. Her husband, a big man with dark hair and moustache, came outside as we were working away and started chatting to us. He asked us our names and where we came from, and then began asking us if we knew this or that man from the Creggan. Being young and naïve, we thought nothing of it and were answering him quite truthfully.

"Hang on a minute," he said, and went back inside, re-emerging with a pile of photographs.

We were all saying, "Oh yes, we know him and him."

He countered with more questions. "Where does he live? Where is he at the moment?"

Gradually, painfully slowly, it began to dawn on us what was going on. They were obviously British agents, who could not believe their luck in having these garrulous local kids drop right into their laps. We finished cutting the wood, collected our shillings, and went back down the hill in an awkward silence. We were not so young that we did not realise the enormity of what we had just done. Finally I broke the silence. "We'd better not say anything about this to anybody."

There was a series of nods and murmurs of agreement. The young English couple in the cottage near Piggery Ridge disappeared shortly afterwards. But they were never mentioned again, for even ten-year-old Creggan kids know that touting is a capital offence in the eyes of the IRA.

The Provies did not have the monopoly on senseless violence, however, as Bloody Sunday was to show. A big Civil Rights Association march was planned for Sunday, 30th January 1972. Twenty-six thousand families were already taking part in a rent and rates strike, and the barricades smashed in Operation Motorman had gone back up, once more turning the Creggan and the Bogside into no-go areas for security forces.

The previous weekend there had been another march and demonstration outside Magilligan camp, where many suspected IRA men were being interned. After the crowds threw rocks and bottles, paratroopers used volleys of rubber bullets to disperse them. The bad blood spilled over into the following weekend, when the same soldiers were once again used against the demonstrators.

Fearing more trouble, my Ma had taken us over to my brother Johnny's place at Kilfennan in the Waterside, a staunchly Protestant area, to keep us out of the way. We saw the march on television. It was supposed to begin in the Creggan and end at the Guildhall, but the police and army, having decided that halting it altogether would be impossible, erected barriers to prevent it reaching the town centre. The march began peacefully but when the crowd reached the army barriers at Aggro Corner, there were insults and taunts and stones were thrown. It was just a normal day in Derry, but shortly before four o'clock the familiar pushing, shoving, shouting and stoning turned into something more horrible than I'd ever seen in my life.

Four or five Pigs – armoured cars – suddenly raced along William Street into Rossville Square. Paratroopers piled out of them and began firing their rifles into the crowds. Three men fell to the ground immediately, one writhing in agony, with blood spurting from his leg. The others, teenagers, lay still, already dead. As the thousands of people turned and ran or dived for cover, the soldiers kept firing. Some people put their hands above their heads, one waving a white handkerchief, but the Paras fired at them too and they fled or fell to the ground.

I saw Bishop Daly leading two guys carrying a body past the 7:20 Bar. The bishop was holding a white handkerchief above his head, half-crouching and wincing as the guns fired. The army blocked his path, but a big guy, so wound up he didn't seem to care if he was shot, shouted furiously at them, the veins standing out in his forehead, until they let the bishop through. When the shooting finally stopped, crying men and women manhandled the bodies of the other dead and injured into cars to drive them to hospital.

The British soldiers had simply fired indiscriminately into the crowded streets, as if every Catholic was the enemy, not just the IRA. We watched in stunned, disbelieving silence. Still just a kid in a world suddenly turned upside-down I kept tugging at my mother's sleeve asking her what had happened, what it meant, but she couldn't speak and just sat there with tears trickling down her cheeks. I kept thinking, *This hasn't really happened, everything will be all right tomorrow.* But I knew it wouldn't.

Like all Creggan kids, I'd grown up taking for granted what would have seemed like a nightmare almost anywhere else. We used to play IRA men and soldiers, running in and out of the alleys past men armed with real guns without a second look, and we threw stones at the soldiers as if it was just another game.

Now the games were over. Thirteen people had been shot dead and another seventeen wounded. The Paras later claimed that they'd been fired on first and had had nail bombs thrown at them, but that claim was flatly contradicted by every eye-witness, including the English journalists covering the march.

Of the dead on Bloody Sunday, seven were still in their teens. Among them was my cousin, Hugh Gilmour. His name had been read out in the list of dead on the television news that night, but we were so stunned that we hadn't taken it in, and didn't find out until we got home a couple of days later.

That single incident changed the whole atmosphere of the city. When we went home, the Protestant gangs were already starting up and we had to walk past one group of vigilantes. These were not kids, they were mature men and women, all dressed in bush hats and camouflage jackets, with masks over their faces.

They were standing in a group across the road from my brother's house, around an old car, battering it with hurley bats and baseball bats and making a terrifying noise. They knew that we were Catholics and were jeering and taunting, shouting "Fenian bastards" at us.

My mother, her voice cracking with tension, told us, "Don't speak or look at them, just keep walking." She pulled me in close to her as they began pelting us with stones. Two hit my mother and one gashed me above my eye.

I was quivering with fright, sure that we were going to be killed. I had never seen such hate; they were inhuman, like wild animals. I wanted to break free of my mother's grip and run for my life, but she tightened her grasp on my shoulder and hissed urgently, "Just walk. If we try to run, they'll be on us before we have got fifty yards."

My scalp was prickling with fear but though every instinct told me to run, I obeyed my mother. As we kept walking, fewer stones were thrown and the noise gradually died down behind us. We still didn't look back and didn't feel really safe until we'd crossed the Craigavon Bridge back into Catholic territory.

It was my first real experience of the vicious tribal warfare that was to become just another part of life in Derry. I quickly had to learn the lesson that religion could be dangerous to your health. Going to my brother's house a few weeks later, I was stopped by two fifteen-or sixteen-year-olds who asked me, "What's your religion?"

I had to take a hasty guess. "Er, Protestant."

It turned out to be the right answer, but another time I got it wrong. Three of us had been down the circus in the Brandywell – safe Catholic territory – and were walking out of the back, when two guys and a girl came up to us.

"What's your fucking religion?"

"We're Catholics – are you not?"

They were not. They punched us and made us get down on our knees and say, "Fuck the Pope," and all that sort of thing. I just couldn't understand why anyone would want to do that.

Bloody Sunday drove many of my contemporaries into the arms of the IRA or the INLA, but my mother's beliefs were too deeply ingrained in me. Despite my horror at the army murder of my cousin and the other innocent civilians, I was equally horrified by the violence of the IRA. The thought of all violence and killing simply turned my stomach.

When I tried to steer clear of the Troubles, others proved willing recruits, among them my best friend, Colm McNutt, who lived four doors away from me. Even though he was two years older, we were inseparable. He was a hero to me, brave to the point of rashness, and there was no dare he wouldn't attempt, his keen blue eyes sparkling with mischief.

We would play over by the reservoir, day after day, jumping across from bank to bank of the stream, seeing who could jump the farthest, climb highest up a pine tree, run the fastest or swim the farthest out across the reservoir. When we played soldiers, Colm would make the most marvelous wooden rifles. I would just chop the twigs off a small branch and call it a gun, but Colm would carve his carefully out of wood, sanding it down and painting it in black and green camouflage, until it looked exactly like the real thing. He was also great at building forts out of scrap wood in his back garden.

He was only five feet four inches tall, with a thatch of firey red hair and freckled skin, but he had such charisma that he could twist people around his little finger. Later on, he always had a string of good-looking girlfriends, which was another cause of my admiration for him, but I was not alone in that, for all my peers looked up to him. The only people immune to his charm were the army and the IRA. He had a gob on him and a quick wit and would dish out cheek to army patrols or IRA men alike, and then be off sprinting down the road, his laughter taunting them as he ran.

That reckless streak got him into trouble. The Provies twice tied him to a lamp-post outside the Sinn Féin office at the Creggan shops, shaved his head, covered him in tar and threw a bag of feathers over him, while the usual rent-a-mob laughed and jeered. After a while, the crowd tired of the sport and drifted away, and an ambulance came to take him to hospital to scrape the tar off him.

Only Colm's youth saved him for a more extreme punishment for hooding, for the Provies had a strict rota of punishments for "anti-social behaviour." For his first offence you would get a warning, second time you would get a beating and the third time you would be knee-capped.

Two or three Provies held the victim face down on the ground while another put a gun-barrel behind the man's knee. When he pulled the trigger, he blew the victim's knee-cap off. For obvious reasons, people would never obligingly hold still while this happened and it wasn't unusual to hear of victims of knee-capping who'd been shot anywhere from the calf to the thigh. If they were very lucky they got away with a flesh wound instead of a shattered knee-cap, but people also died after botched knee-cappings. One Derry man bled to death after a shot went through the artery in his thigh.

My brother Harry was one of the lucky ones. One night he came home with armfuls of bottles of booze, which he hid under the armchairs in the sofa. When I asked him where they came from, he just winked, put his finger to his lips and gave me a conspiratorial smile.

He didn't get away with it. A couple of weeks later he was grabbed by the IRA and taken round the back of the Creggan shops. An IRA man shot him in the leg, and though the shot missed the knee-cap, they blew a hole in his calf. When he came home from hospital, he showed us the stitched-up holes in his leg: a neat round one where the bullet had gone in and a bigger, jagged crater where it had exited.

From that moment on, I felt nothing but hatred for the people who'd dared to do that to my big brother. I wanted to do something about it, but what could a kid like me do against the IRA? They say that the Irish have long memories. I kept my anger inside; I never did forget, I never will forget and in the end I found a way to take my revenge.

Johnny was also knee-capped by the IRA. They shot him in both knees, supposedly for molesting the young child of the woman he lived with at the time, though none of us really believed that. I went to the Altnagelvin Hospital to see him and sobbed all the way home afterwards. It was one other debt to the IRA that had to be repaid.

A lot of my friends were knee-capped, and at one stage the IRA went completely overboard about it; someone was being done almost every day. One of my friends was actually knee-capped four times and still he didn't stop hooding. Even though he was on crutches, he still kept breaking into places and stealing things.

Girls and women were never knee-capped they were regularly tarred and feathered. Soldier dolls – girls who went out with soldiers or were even seen talking to them in the street – were tied to lamp-posts. They had hot tar or red lead paint poured over them and a pile of feathers from old pillow dumped on top. As a farewell gesture, the Provies hung a card round their necks inscribed "SOLIDER DOLL" or "WHORE." If their heads hadn't already been shaved by the Provies they'd be cropped by the hospital staff as they tried to get the tar off them.

The punishments were always carried out by whoever happened to be in the local Sinn Féin office at the time. If you were going to be shot, they would take you round the back and do it; if you were going to get a beating, they would take you in to the Sinn Féin Centre and give you a good pasting with fists and boots, iron bars or hurley bats.

Some people – a minority – approved of the IRA's barbaric methods of law enforcement. The majority did not, but dared not say anything about it for fear of being burned out of their homes. People who knew one another fairly well might talk freely within the confines of their own four walls, but talking about the IRA outside was not a very wise thing to do. Everybody had to go to work or to school or to the shops and everywhere you went, eyes were watching and ears were listening.

Tarring and feathering did not daunt Colm, however. When I called at his house afterwards, he opened the door, rubbed his hands over the red stubble on his head and said, "What do you think of the new hairstyle, Ray? Pretty good huh?"

The army also tried to sort him out. We used to run around taking the piss out of the army patrols together and there was a certain amount of banter both ways, but they hated Colm, because he gave them so much lip. He was always embarrassing them as well, nicking their hats and running away, and even stealing the magazines from their guns. He was so quick that he would nip in, unclip the magazine and be away before they even realised what had happened.

We took on the of magazines he stole to a friend's house in the Beechwood area and took all the rounds out of it. They were big rounds, from something like a .303. I had never seen live ammunition before and rolled one around in my hand, horribly fascinated, thinking, *These actually kill people.*

The soldiers could never catch Colm, for he was far too quick for them, but they knew who we were and inevitably took revenge for the indignities they had suffered. I was thirteen, Colm fifteen. We were walking up the country one day, planning to go and buy ten cigarettes at the shop over the border and then smoke ourselves dizzy by the reservoir.

An army patrol rumbled past in a Saracen and as usual we gave them a gobful of cheek. They stopped and as we turned to run back down the hill, we saw another Saracen behind us. Several heavily-armed Scots Guards jumped out, but we hurdled the hedge and took off across the fields. They made no attempt to chase us, but our escape proved to be only temporary.

At five the next morning army jeeps and Saracen's screeched to a halt outside my house. There was a pounding on the door and I heard the soldiers shouting my name. I dragged myself out of bed, pulled on a shirt and trousers and went downstairs. The soldiers - Scots Guards – arrested me and told me they were taking me to Piggery Ridge. I stood there shivering with fright, for I had heard so many bad things about the place – guys being taken up there and given kickings, even guys not coming out again.

There was pandemonium in the house, with my mother and father shouting at the soldiers, but they half-dragged, half-carried me outside. The commotion had brought most of our neighbours out into the street and they stood with quilts and blankets draped around their shoulders, yelling sleepy abuse at the soldiers.

The Scots Guards ignored them and threw me into the back of one of the Saracens. I squealed as the sharp metal sill bit into my shin. Four soldiers got into the back with me, one stamping his boot down on the back of my neck, grinding my face into the floor. I lay there with the smell of cold metal in my nostrils, twisting my face to one side.

The soldiers looked even more frightening hunched over me in a confined space, their battle-dress festooned with gas masks, truncheons and rubber-bullet guns as well as the automatic rifles strapped to their wrists.

"Why don't we just shoot the humphy bastard?" a soldier said in a thick Glaswegian accent.

"No, lets tell the Provisionals he's been touting and let them do it for us," said another.

There was a burst of braying laughter. I shat myself with fear, which only provoked the soldiers even more.

"You filthy, stinking little twat," said a third, kicking me with as much force as the restricted leg-room would allow.

The Saracen ground its way up to the top of the hill, bounced over the speed bumps – put in to stop IRA men firing bursts at the sentry as they roared past in a hijacked car – and swung in through the steel gates of Piggery Ridge. We stopped abruptly and the door of the Saracen was flung open. One of the soldiers grabbed me by the hair and threw me out of the back. I crouched on the ground, but he booted me in the ribs, yelling at me to get up.

"Watch out Georgie, you'll get shit on your boots." There was more hyena laughter. I stood there trembling, thankful only that Colm hadn't seen this humiliation.

It was freezing cold and pouring with rain, but they made me take my shirt off stand to attention in the yard. A few minutes later, another Saracen rumbled in through the gates and Colm was kicked and shoved across to stand beside me. I felt better with him there, but I was still shaking with fear and Colm, though full of his usual bravado, was white as a sheet.

"Not so clever now, are you? Not so brave?"

We said nothing. I was too frightened to speak and for once even Colm didn't have a wisecrack ready. I looked fearfully from one soldier's face to another. There was hatred in every one.

Suddenly my legs were kicked from under me and I took a crashing fall onto the concrete. Colm landed beside me a second later and once more there was a burst of derisive laughter from the soldiers.

Colm winked at me as we lay facing each other in the dirt, but before I could draw much comfort from that, rough hands seized my arms. They dragged me inside one of the buildings, into a small room, bare but for a wooden table and a single hard-backed wooden chair. They tied my hands behind me and lashed my legs to the legs of the chair with nylon rope.

Two fat plain-clothes men came in and leaned against the back wall, while two of the soldiers slouched against the table. The third, a sergeant, walked towards me and without warning booted me in the shins. Pain seared through me. I cried out, but the only answer was the sergeant's steel toe-capped boot, kicking my shins and stamping down viciously on my insteps. I could feel blood trickling down my shins, soaking my socks.

He paused for a few moments, allowing the pain to subside to a steady throbbing ache, and then again booted me in the shins. The pattern repeated, over and over again. The pain came in waves, building to an agonising crescendo then fading back, only to build to an even higher peak. Finally he stopped and walked round behind the chair, out of my sight. There was the rasp and flare of a match and smoke drifted over my shoulder as he drew on a cigarette. I held my breath and waited, every muscle tensed rigid, my scalp pricking and cold sweat trickling down my neck.

Nothing happened. In the silence, I could hear the sergeant's boots squeak faintly as he shifted from foot to foot and from the adjoining room, there were cracks and thuds as the other soldiers punched and kicked Colm. He didn't cry out, but I could hear him grunting and his breath whistling between his teeth. There was a brief pause, then a volley of abuse from him, quickly silenced.

I sat motionless, scarcely daring to breathe, the pain in my shins and feet slowly subsiding to a dull, throbbing ache. The sergeant still stood unseen behind me and I didn't dare turn my head. My neck muscles kept twitching, anticipating the next barrage of blows. I had heard the sergeant drop his cigarette and grind out the butt with his foot. I glanced up at the two soldiers in front of me, still sprawled against the table. Their eyes were hooded, impassive, but as I watched them, their gaze shifted to look over my shoulder and a smirk spread across their faces. There was a swishing sound as the sergeant swung his baton and then a blinding flash of light inside my head.

I slumped to one side and must have lost consciousness for a few moments, but I was roused by the sergeant dragging me upright by my hair and kicking me again on my bruised shins. "Right, you wee shit. That's just a taste of what you'll be getting next time if you don't do as these men say."

One of the plain-clothes men lumbered to his feet and walked over to face me. "You know the IRA men around the Creggan, don't you?"

I was slow to respond and got another savage boot in the shins, this time from him. I nodded, my eyes streaming.

"Right. Every time you see them going to someone's house or driving off together, or you hear any talk or rumours about jobs they have done or jobs they are going to be doing, you tell us about it. Get us good information and you get a few quid; do it badly and you'll get a beating that will make this seem like a school picnic. Understand?" Without waiting for an answer, he kicked me in the shins again.

I nodded again hurriedly. At that moment I would have agreed to assassinate the Pope, if it would have stopped the roaring in my ears and the pain shooting through my body.

"Meet us underneath the bridge at eight o'clock on Thursday. Now fuck off."

"What about my friend?"

He cocked an ear towards the thuds and grunts still coming from the next room. "It sounds like he's still busy, doesn't it? You fuck off now, if you don't want another kicking."

The two soldiers untied the ropes and I staggered to my feet. They marched me off the post, giving me a farewell boot in the arse that sent me sprawling in the dirt once more.

It was already light. I limped down the road until I was out of sight of Piggery Ridge, then climbed the earth bank and hid behind the hedge. I took off my trousers, wincing as they ripped the congealed blood away from my shins and started them bleeding again. I threw away my soiled underpants and cleaned myself up as best I could, then dragged my trousers back over my legs, already a mass of livid, purpling bruises. I lay down on the cold, damp earth behind the hedge and sobbed my heart out.

A few minutes later, I heard Colm coming down the hill. I hastily dried my eyes and scrambled back over the hedge, for I didn't want him to see my underpants and know that I'd been crying. He was limping badly and his lip was swollen and split, but when I hissed, "Colm, are you alright?" he was full of his customary bravado.

"Of course, it'll take more than a few Brit bastards to do for me."

"Did they try to get you to tout?"

"Aye. I told them I would, but there's no fucking chance of that. I'd sooner shoot myself, if I can't shoot those bastards first."

"But I'm scared, Colm."

He looked hard at me and then dropped the bravado, realising what an effort it had taken for me to admit my fear. "Look, Ray," he said gently, "I was scared of them too, but I wasn't going to let them see that."

"But if we don't do what they want, they'll lift us again."

"They've got to find us first and even if they do, the worst they can do to us is give us another hiding. If you start touting and the Provies find out, it won't be a hiding you'll be getting, it'll be a bloody nutting – a bullet in the back of the head. Now come on, let's see your war-wounds."

I rolled up my trouser legs and showed him my shins.

"Sure, they were only teasing with you," he said, laughing. Just then, one of the Saracens went rumbling past, the Scots Guards yelling derisively at us. Colm stiffened and was about to give them a mouthful, when I laid a restraining hand on his sleeve. "Not now Colm, let it go this once."

He smiled at me, winked and ruffled my hair. "All right then, just this once."

When I got home, my mother spotted the bloodstains on my trousers straight away. "What happened? Did the soldiers do that?"

"I fell over."

"Take your trousers off."

I hesitated.

"Take your trousers off or I'll give you the back of my hand."

I had had enough of that for one day; I took off my trousers.

"Mother of God, will you look at this?" said my mother. "Patrick, come here."

Sighing, my father put down his comic, prised himself grumpily out of his armchair and come through to the kitchen. He stared at the purple bruises welling up on my legs for a minute. "Did the soldiers do this?"

I shook my head.

"Tell me or you will get another thrashing." He grabbed me by the collar and cuffed me across the ear, which was still ringing from the blow with the baton.

"The soldiers did it," I sniveled. "They took me and Colm up to Piggery Ridge and beat us up. They told me I had to tout for them."

"Did they, begod? We'll see about that. Put your trousers on and get your coat."

"Where are we going?"

"You'll find out."

My Da dragged me round to Martin McGuiness's house and made me repeat my story. When I'd finished, McGuiness smiled his chilling smile. "You did right to tell us this, Ray."

The next morning he fronted a press conference, announcing the army's attempts to recruit kids as informers. The following day there was a big piece in the Derry *Journal*, headlined "ARMY TRIES TO GET YOUNG MAN TO INFORM."

I was delighted with my new-found fame, but scared stiff of the likely reprisals if the Scots Guards got hold of me. For the next few weeks I stayed well away from Piggery Ridge and ducked down a back alley at the first sign of an Army patrol or the sound of a Saracen coming up the road. Perhaps fearing more bad publicity, the Scots Guards didn't make a repeat visit to our home.

Colm and I were even firmer friends after our shared ordeal, but later that year, not long after his sixteenth birthday, he left Derry, going South and volunteering to join the Irish army. I missed him terribly, but didn't see him for over a year, until he suddenly reappeared in Derry, a deserter on the run.

His army training had taught him how to handle and fire weapons, however, and his hatred of the Brits burned even more brightly. He was desperate to fight against them, but he wouldn't join the Provies, for he hated them for what they'd done to him. When his sister married Pat Tohill, whose brother, Joe was in the IRSP at the time – the political wing of the INLA, as Sinn Féin is to the IRA – Colm got to know him very well and was soon recruited into the INLA.

He wanted me to join too, but though I knew all the guys he was involved with, I wouldn't join them. Much as I liked Colm, I was not going to get involved in terrorism. Petty crime, though, was a different manner.

CHAPTER 3

Like my brothers before me, I started thieving as I grew up. When I was fourteen, two friends and I dogged off school and went over to the Glen, a Protestant area by Rosemount. We climbed over the garden wall of a big house and broke into it through a window. We couldn't find any money, but we helped ourselves to food and drink and stole a few ornaments.

We never saw anyone but we'd obviously been spotted, because the women who owned the house phoned our school. As the only three to have missed school without a note that day we were prime suspects, and after a grilling from the headmaster we owned up to it.

Knowing what a thrashing we would all get from our parents, never mind what the RUC would do about it, we decided to run away from home. We went down to Letterkenny and stayed there for a couple of days, but someone who knew one of the lads tipped off his parents. A delegation of very big and very angry brothers and cousins came down to take us back to face the music.

When I got home it was my turn to endure one of the rights of passage of all the Gilmour sons, being punched and kicked black and blue under the stairs by my Da. After that, still sniveling, I was sent down to Strand Road Police Station to see what the RUC had in store for me.

It was the first time I'd ever been inside a Police Station, and my initial impressions were not good. They obviously thought the best way to steer me away from a life of crime was to frighten it out of me, and a couple of big, bad-tempered RUC men gave me a good slapping around and then put me in a cell for a few minutes. I sat on the lumpy mattress staring at the cold, stone walls and the iron-barred door and howled.

When they let me out, they took me back upstairs and sat me in an interview room. "Wait hear," growled one of them before they walked out, leaving me on my own. After a couple of minutes, two other policemen, Special Branch men wearing plain clothes, came in to talk to me.

One stood at the back, and took no part in the conversation, gazing at me with ill-concealed dislike. The other sat facing me at the table and began to chat. He was swarthy with jet-black hair, a roguish grin and piercing blue eyes. He had a black, bushy moustache and a chin as blue as Richard Nixon's – I could almost see the stubble growing as I watched him. He didn't seem like a policeman at all, and didn't talk to me like one. It was as if we were just a couple of mates, passing the time of day. He said his name was Pete, and I took to him right away.

He asked me a few questions about the break-in and I answered him as truthfully as I could. Then he turned the conversation to myself. Did I like living on the Creggan? What were things like at home? Wasn't it tough being the youngest of all those children? What did I do in my spare time? Did I throw stones at the soldiers like the others?

I looked up sharply at him, wondering if he was trying to trap me, but he just laughed and said, "Sure I did it myself a few years ago, but that's not something I'm keen to tell my bosses about now."

I relaxed again and we chatted some more, with Pete still probing, but not in a way that put my back up or alarmed me. "Tell me, Ray, what do you think about the IRA?"

"They knee-capped two of my brothers."

"I know, I'd heard about that."

I paused, surprised and flattered that he'd taken such an interest in my family. "Then you'll know how I feel about the IRA. I hate them."

"Do you hate them enough to try and stop them knee-capping and killing other people?"

I looked at him suspiciously, back on my guard. "I'm no tout."

"I never thought you were. But we all have to take sides in a situation like this, Ray. People who look the other way when someone is beaten with a hurley bat or shot through the knee-caps, or in the back of the head, are helping the IRA just as much as those who throw petrol bombs for them."

I hesitated, unsure what to say.

"Anyway, I'll leave you to think about that," Pete said. "If you're ever passing and fancy a chat, I'm usually here. I won't show you out myself.

You don't want to be seen in public in my company, people might think you were touting." He chuckled and turned to go.

"Pete."

He turned back and waited.

"The house we broke into …"

"Oh, that. You'll get an official caution, but we'll be taking no further action this time. Take the hint, though, and don't do anything like it again. If there is a next time – and I sincerely hope there won't be – you won't be getting off so lightly." He winked and strolled out, followed by the other guy, who didn't even bother to look at me. A moment later a uniformed policeman appeared and led me to another room to receive my formal caution.

The warning did some good, for I didn't break into any more houses, though it didn't stop me from throwing stones at the soldiers after school every day. I thought a bit about the other things Pete had said, but then pushed them from my mind. There was time enough for that later on - for the moment there were girls to be chatted up, illicit cigarettes to be smoked and school to be dogged off whenever possible.

I might have forgotten about Pete altogether had I not had another enforced meeting with him a few weeks later. This time I'd done nothing wrong. Some INLA guys had fired at an RUC patrol and there'd been a round-up of known INLA members. Colm was lifted, and as "one of his associates" – as the RUC men put it – I was also pulled in for questioning. They lifted ten or twelve of us altogether, re-assuring us, "It's purely a matter of eliminating you from our enquiries."

I was sitting in an interview room waiting my turn and feeling pretty sorry for myself when Pete stuck his head round the door. "I heard you were in, Ray, what have you been up to this time?"

"Nothing."

I caught his quizzical look.

"No, really. They've lifted loads of us. They are on about some INLA shooting, but it's nothing to do with me."

"I'm glad to hear it." He looked at his watch. "Look, Ray, I'm sorry, I've got something on and can't stick around. See you some other time. Don't forget what I said to you last time."

He disappeared again, but I felt much better just for seeing a friendly face in there. I had to wait another fifty minutes before the uniforms got round to interviewing me, but it was soon over with. They asked me if I knew Colm and I said I did, but hadn't seen him for ages. I played dumb to all their other questions and after a few minutes they let me go. They didn't get enough to pin anything on Colm either, for I saw him on the street the next morning.

I was spending more and more time dogging off school, for the good weather was coming on and I wasn't old enough to leave officially that summer. There didn't seem much point in sitting around in a dusty classroom. I wasn't taking any O'Levels, there wasn't much point. As soon as I left school, I joined the only long-term career available to people on the Creggan: I signed on the dole.

The only official paid employment I was to enjoy was on the Free Enterprise Scheme, as it was then called, a kind of government job-creation scheme. I worked on metalwork at a factory in the Springtown Industrial Area of the Buncrana Road, but at the end of my six- month scheme, like all the other lads, I was dumped straight back on the dole.

I did have a few unofficial jobs as well. I earned a couple of quid on the side working at the community centre on Friday nights, along with a few mates. We just checked off the numbers on winning bingo cards, tidied the place up and picked up the glasses. I also did a bit of labouring with the boyfriend of one of my sisters. He was a bricklayer who worked on the lump – no tax, no forms, no questions asked. I got an odd two weeks' work here and a month's work there with him, otherwise all I had was my weekly giro.

Unemployment only increased the temptation to turn to petty crime, but I soon fell foul of the police again after getting involved with a guy called Noel Kavanagh, one of the biggest hoods in Derry. I thought he was the bee's knees, a real hard man. One day he asked me if I would be interested in robbing a post office with him. My blood started pounding at the thought, a mixture of excitement and sheer naked terror. I said, "I dunno, how do you do that?"

"We'll buy a toy gun, a replica from Woolworth's, dye it black and use that," said Noel.

I agreed to it, scared witless at the prospect, but desperate not to lose face with him.

We met at his house for a rehearsal. Noel produced the replica gun, two green camouflage hats and two ridiculous red and white woollen masks: people wouldn't be hurt, but they might die laughing at the sight of us. I was to keep everyone covered, while Noel did the actual robbery. The gun didn't look terribly convincing to me, but Noel airily waved away my fears. "Don't sweat it. The old biddies in there'll be shitting themselves that much, we could rob the shop with a potato."

We walked down to Rosemount and stood just round the corner from the Park Avenue Post Office while we scanned up and down the road.

"Right," said Noel. "All clear, here we go."

We masked up and marched in, Noel leading the way. I tagged nervously behind, thinking, *Oh God, get me out of this.*

It was a scruffy, dingy place. There were racks of the sort of greeting cards that only your aunts and grandmothers would ever buy for you and some assorted stationery, mainly envelopes, brown paper and string. The post office counter was at the back, dispensing sweets and cigarettes as well as stamps and postal orders. It was separated from the rest of the shop by glass screens and a locked door. The postmistress was standing behind the counter and there were two customers.

Noel marched up to the counter and barked, "Nobody move, this is a stick-up. Now open the fucking door."

There was a gasp of shock from the girl standing near the greeting cards as I waved the replica gun around. I looked at her and nearly died on the spot; she'd been in the Legion of Mary with me when I was a kid, and we'd been to all these endless Holy, Holy meetings together.

Relax, Ray, I thought to myself. With this mask on, she won't know you from a hole in the ground. The other customer, a woman of about sixty, had been carrying on a monologue from the moment we entered.

"Away, you should be ashamed of yourselves," she shouted, "taking our money."

Completely unfazed by the gun, she reached out and pulled my mask off. The girl's eyes widened in surprise and I could tell she'd recognised me instantly.

The stick-up was rapidly turning into a cock-up. "For Christ's sake, let's get out of here," I yelled, but Noel was busy arguing with the postmistress. She was still refusing to open the door by the counter, despite all his bluster and the threat of a gun.

Finally, in a fury, he kicked the door off its hinges. "Now where's the fucking money?"

The women showed him the safe and he pushed her out of the way and grabbed the cash. We ran out of the shop and up the hill, cutting through alleys and backstreets until we got back to Noel's house, where we hid the money – a hundred pounds – under the floorboards.

We arranged to meet to divide the spoils the following afternoon, but I went home full of dread, knowing that I was bound to be lifted by the police. Nothing happened that day, but the next morning I watched from my bedroom window as the RUC Land Rover drove agonisingly slowly up the road. I was willing it to stop elsewhere or drive on past, but I knew in my heart exactly where it was heading.

My mother opened the door to the policemen, greeting them like old friends and saying, "What is it this time?" There were a few moments of muttered conversation and then I heard her say, "No, not Raymond, surely?"

She called me down. "Do you know why these Officers are here?"

I hung my head but said nothing.

She sighed. "God help you when your father finds out."

Then she stood aside as the police arrested me and took me out to the car. This time I would not be trying on their hats and playing with the siren. I kept my eyes averted from my mother's reproachful gaze as we drove off.

They took me down to Strand Road and began questioning me. I denied any involvement in the theft for six or seven hours, even though they kept telling me, "We know you did it. You were recognised."

I knew I'd done it too, but I wasn't going to admit it if I could help it. Eventually I cracked.

Then they wanted me to name my accomplice. "Who did it with you? It was Noel Kavanagh, wasn't it?"

I admitted that too, in the end.

While they went up to Noel's and found the money under the floorboards, Pete and the other Special Branch man who had interviewed me after the house break-in came in to talk to me again. Once more the other one, Stuart, stationed himself at the back of the room and ignored me, while Pete sat down and started chatting as if we were two old mates.

"Bit of bad luck for you yesterday, Ray. We were over near Park Avenue when the call came in about the robbery. We drove around and saw you and Noel Kavanagh come running out of an alley. I said to Stuart, "Looks like a starter for the robbery. Didn't I, Stuart?"

Stuart nodded still not speaking.

"But we thought we would leave the uniform boys to come and get you in the morning."

Pete then changed the subject and we talked for a while about football, girls and TV programmes, before he came to the point. "Well, Ray, I don't think we are going to be able to get you off this one with just a warning."

He scratched his head and looked around the room, as if searching for a way out for me. "Look, Ray, you're an intelligent guy so I'm not going to beat around the bush with you. You're now at the point of no return. You've committed a serious crime. You're in trouble with the RUC and you'll be in trouble with the IRA as well when they get to hear about it. You're mixing with some bad company. People like Noel Kavanagh and some of those INLA guys you've been hanging around with are already beyond help. They're in too deep. You're not … yet, but if you don't sort yourself out now, there will be nothing that I or anyone else can do to help you.

"Do you really want to end up the way some of your friends – and your brothers – have wound up, knee-capped, in gaol or even dead?"

He paused and let that sink in, rolling a paper-clip between his fingers.

"Well, do you?"

I said, "No," in a very small voice. Perhaps I wasn't quite as big and tough as I thought.

"You know what they got themselves into and how it finished for them. You should do the smart thing before it's too late, but it's up to you, no-one else can make that decision for you."

He again fell silent for a few seconds and then, having pulled me down, he set about building me up again.

"I've been impressed with they way you handled yourself during interrogation," he said, still abstractly rolling the paper-clip between his fingertips. "And with your coolness under pressure."

It was partly flattery, but his next question showed it was also true. "What are the chances of you working for us?"

"You mean as a tout?"

"No, I mean as a police agent."

"What's the difference?"

"An informer is usually someone already involved in terrorism, saving his own neck by ratting on his mates. An agent is someone working under our direction and control to infiltrate and subvert terrorist organisations."

"Like an undercover Policeman?"

"Exactly."

I kept silent, thinking hard about what he'd said.

"We'd be very appreciative – in every way," said Pete, "an you'd be helping to save lives."

"How appreciative, exactly?"

He smiled. "If you did well for us, it would be more money than your Da's ever seen in his life, or you're ever likely to in yours."

If a solider had been making the suggestion, I'd have told him to get lost, for the battering I'd taken from the Scots Guards was still fresh in my memory. If Pete had tried to blackmail me or strong-arm me, he'd also have got the same response. But this was different.

Even though I'd only met him a couple of times before, Pete was treating me as an equal – always flattering to a teenager – and I already felt I could trust him completely. The thought of the money was also a very powerful attraction to a sixteen-year-old kid with no qualifications and no prospects whatsoever. I was still too young and naïve to know or care about the short life-expectancy of agents and informers, and the thrill of working under cover was almost as compelling as the cash.

I was tempted to say yes straight away, but I hesitated and eventually said, "No, I can't."

He didn't push it hard, just shrugged his shoulders, smiled and said, "Think about it and let me know if you change your mind. If you want to chat about it any time, here's my number."

He scribbled it on a piece of paper. "It'll be best if you memorise it and then throw the paper away. I don't want that number falling into the wrong hands." He winked and had handed me back to the uniforms and walked out of the room before I'd thought of a reply.

My mind was racing as I was taken down to the cells. I lay down in my bunk and stared at the ceiling for a long time, turning what he'd said over and over in my mind. The more I thought about it, the more I wanted to do it. The money would certainly come in handy, but I was also driven by the sheer excitement of the thought of working undercover. Still I hesitated, however, finally deciding to wait until after my release before committing myself.

If I'd agreed straight away, I might have saved myself a taste of prison. The next morning Noel and I were refused bail and sent on remand to the Crum – Crumlin Road Prison, Belfast. We were taken up there is a police van, handcuffed together, and heard the big iron gates clang shut behind us with a sound that had an awful finality.

We got out and were taken to Reception. "Just like a hotel," breathed Noel, nudging me in the ribs.

We were given our Prison numbers and then checked in all our belongings. We handed our clothes, shoes, wallets and watches over the counter to a warder who chanted an inventory to the clerk: "…shoes, black, size eight, toes slightly scuffed. Shirt, blue denim, 15-inch collar, tear on right sleeve. Black plastic wallet, containing a five pound note. Yale key. Cotton handkerchief, white …"

Everything disappeared into a plastic bag which was sealed until our release.

I felt small and vulnerable standing naked under the harsh lights, surrounded by stone-faced warders. The feeling grew stronger as we were given a rudimental medical – chest, eyes, cough – and an internal search. A pig-faced warder snapped on a pair of plastic gloves and jammed his fingers into my arse, searching for hidden contraband. The humiliation was complete.

After we dressed in our prison clothes, we were taken down a steep flight of stone stairs, cupped and worn from a century of use. At the bottom was a long dank tunnel. Bulkhead lights, their metal cages rusted to paper thinness, cast weak pools of yellow light. The walls of the tunnel ran with moisture and the air was foetid and heavy. The smell was so strong that I could taste it at the back of my throat. I hesitated a moment, gulping lungfuls of the fresher air at the bottom of the stairs, but the warder shoved me in the back and I began to walk through the tunnel, gagging on the stench.

"Stop." The warder unlocked an iron door and shoved me into one of the overnight holding cells; stinking, filthy, freezing holes in the ground, alive with cockroaches. As I lay on my bunk, staring into the darkness, I could hear them scuttling across the floor and even feel them on the bed. In the morning I shook a cockroach out of one of my socks.

After a sleepless night, we were brought up into the main hall. A queue of other prisoners stood waiting at each of the big iron gates leading to A, B and C wings. The jangle of heavy keys as the warders opened the locks and the clash of iron and steel as the doors and gates were banged shut again was continuous from dawn till dusk. I was put on to A3 wing – the third floor up. The walls were painted a dingy yellow and the steel doors were a dull, dark red, the colour of blood. The stairwell at each level was covered with wire mesh, to stop prisoners throwing things – or themselves – over the balconies.

My cell, built originally for one, now shared by three, was less filthy and cockroach-infested than the holding cell in the basement but only just. There was a window, but the glass was opaque, cracked and blocked by iron bars, and it was set high up in the wall. The cell was furnished with three iron beds, a table and one chair and a bucket in the corner – the only toilet facility for three men banged up together from six at night until eight the next morning.

Using the prison toilets was not much better. You knocked on the door and said "Can I go to the toilet, Mister?"

The cubicles had no doors and the warders would just stand there staring at you, while you tried to take a shit. The first couple of times I couldn't do it at all, but in the end, like everyone else, I stopped caring.

On our first morning we made the acquaintance of Liam Hanrahan and Mickey "Flash" McFarlane, who were very high up in the IRA. It was not a pleasant meeting – for us at least – for they gave us a taste of the punishment that the IRA reserved for hoods. We were called out wing by wing for exercise in the prison yard. When we got down there it was absolutely packed with prisoners, all shuffling along in an endless circle.

Noel and I were standing in the middle of the yard, looking around nervously, when Hanrahan and McFarlane walked over to us. Hanrahan had a pair of prominent buck teeth and spoke through his nose. He was like a six-foot-two version of Bugs Bunny, but his eyes were hooded and cruel and it was obvious that this was going to be no joke. McFarlane was similarly tall and burly and had reddish hair, greying at the temples. "You Kavanagh and Gilmour?"

We nodded.

"We want a word. Go in the bogs over there and wait for us."

We walked over to the toilets with leaden feet. I was not reassured to notice that the guards in the watch towers at either side of the yard were studiously looking the other way. The toilets were absolutely filthy, a single-storey brick building, looking and smelling as if it had been built in the Middle Ages and never cleaned since. There were two urinals and a wash-basin that looked as if it was often used as a third, and two cubicles at the far end of the room.

Noel had time for a wisecrack while we waited. "The good news is they're probably not going to rape us. The bad news is that they're going to beat the piss out of us instead."

A moment later Hanrahan and McFarlane and a few other IRA men appeared in the doorway. They put one of us in each cubicle and began interrogating us, punctuating the questions with a few punches to the guts and to the head.

"What did the police ask you?"

"How long were you held there?"

"Did they ask you to tout?"

They kept running between the cubicles, comparing answers. Finally they were satisfied. The interrogation was over, but the punishment was about to begin. There was no word, no warning, they simply laid into us as if their lives depended on it. Hanrahan kneed me in the balls and I doubled up in agony, gasping for breath. He battered me around the head and then dragged me upright by my hair and head-butted me in the face. Blood spurted from my nose and mouth as my lips split wide open. I fell backwards, sprawling against the wall, with my head in the trough of the urinal.

The acrid smell of urine brought me round like smelling-salts. I lay still for a moment with the sweet taste of blood filling my mouth then Hanrahan was on me again, booting me across the room, kicking my balls, my guts, my chest, my head. I curled myself up like a woodlouse, trying to cover my groin and my head with my hands, but that only seemed to provoke him more and he rained in kicks and blows from all angles. Two savage boots in the kidneys sent pains stabbing through me like a knife.

He stood over me panting with exertion as I lay curled across the doorway of one of the cubicles. Then he grabbed me again, jack-knifed one arm up behind my back and forced me into the cubicle, ramming my head face-downwards into the stinking toilet bowl. He pulled the chain, keeping my arm forced between my shoulder-blades so that I couldn't move. Water gushed around, over and into my mouth and nose. I gagged and choked, swallowing more water and flailing helplessly, unable to breath and panicking as the water kept swirling around me; my head jammed in the bowl, stopping the water from escaping. There was a roaring in my ears and my lungs felt as if they were bursting.

Finally the pressure eased on the arm forced up my back and I dragged my face clear of the water, coughing and retching. I heard McFarlane's voice saying, "Easy, Liam, don't kill the little gobshite."

Hanrahan grunted and put one more boot into my kidneys as I lay there draped across the toilet bowl. Then he stepped back. I slumped sideways on the floor.

"Listen up, the pair of youse," said Hanrahan. "Stay out of the protection area. Go in there and you may keep away from us, but the boys'll be waiting for you when you're released." Then he spat on the floor and they walked out.

Noel and I were still lying there when the guards came to find us at the end of the exercise period. They showed no surprise and offered no help, just saying "Get back to your cells."

I lay down on my bunk and gave myself up to the pain. Compared to this, the hiding I had taken from the Scots Guards was nothing. What the IRA lacked in military precision, they more than made up for in enthusiasm. Eventually I fell asleep, but woke too stiff to move, with every muscle screaming. When I tried to piss I was in agony, and when it finally came the urine was stained with blood. I also had violent diarrhoea – probably as a result of my dunking in the toilet bowl. I was too scared to ask for the doctor, but over the next few days, the pain gradually lessened.

Another IRA man, Brendan "Shorty" McNally from Derry, was in the same landing as me. We slopped out together, dumping the stinking buckets of piss and shit from our cells down the chute every morning before getting washed. If I'd have expected sympathy from him I was to be disappointed. "You've had a valuable lesson, Ray," he told me. "Stop your hooding, you're hurting your own people. Save your energies for fighting the real enemy, the Brits."

If anyone was hurting our own people, it was the IRA, but I was not going to risk another beating by answering him back. "You're right," I told him. "I've had some time to think about myself in here, and I'll be doing things differently when I get out."

The same speech must have been made by about a million prisoners before me, but Shorty acted as if he was hearing it for the very first time. "That's it, Ray. Good lad."

It took more than a few pious phrases to appease Liam Hanrahan, however, and until our release Noel and I were always at his beck and call, running after him like dogs.

In exercise the next day, I saw that the Provies could use subtlety as well as violence. A priest in a black coat went over to another new prisoner, took him to one side and asked him for his confession. The man began to give it, but after a few minutes the priest suddenly turned his back on him and yelled to the prisoners in the yard, "He's not been touting, but he's been shagging his neighbour's missus." Then he ripped off his dog collar and his black coat to reveal his prison clothes.

There was a burst of laughter from the IRA men, who had all been in on the joke. On that occasion that was all it was – a joke – but things could have been very different. The Provies regularly used false priests to get confessions, and if they contained any hint that the man had been touting, he would be executed.

With my bruises still fresh from Hanrahan's beating, a career as an undercover police agent did not seem such a brilliant idea after all. I kept thinking of all the potential pitfalls. What if I get into the INLA or the IRA? What if I'm caught? I'll end up with a black bag over my head, well-tortured and dead. I tried to forget the idea altogether, but it kept coming back to me. I lay awake night after night when I was in the Crum, thinking, *Should I do it, could I do it, would I do it?*

After a few weeks on remand, we were given a two-year suspended sentence and released. I'd already decided that I wanted to see Pete again and talk some more, but I couldn't have avoided a meeting even it I'd wanted. One of the conditions of bail was that I had to sign in once a week at the police station.

The first time I went down there to sign, I was told to wait and then taken through to a room at the back. I wasn't too surprised to find Pete waiting for me.

"Were you expecting me, by any chance?"

He smiled. "If you come in for one thing, it's good from our point of view, because then we can have a discreet chat without attracting attention. Now then, have you thought anymore about what we talked about last time?"

"Yes, I've thought about it a lot."

"And have you come to any decision?"

I played for time, pulling back from the brink. "No, not yet."

"In one way I'd have been disappointed if you had. Any fool can take a leap in the dark, but a good agent always thinks things through before he acts. And I'm sure you're going to be a very good agent ... if that's what you decide."

I coloured a little, pleased even though I knew he was flattering me.

"How long have I got?"

He gave a broad smile. "As long as it takes. It's a long process, Ray, a confidence-building exercise. I want you to think everything through before you commit yourself. There has to be complete trust between us and it has to be two-ways. It just doesn't work if it's only one-way. There may come a time when your life depends on me or my life depends on you. That's quite a responsibility for anyone, let alone a kid from the Creggan. Think you can handle it?"

I glanced up sharply, but once more he was grinning broadly, taking any sting out of his words.

I grinned back. "Of course I can... if that's what I decide to do."

"That's it, Pete said. "Sure you're getting the hang of it already."

We both laughed and I left to walk home in great good spirits.

Back home, the idea that Pete had planted kept eating at me until finally I gave in. I gave him a ring at the police station and asked to meet him again the next time I went in to sign for my bail. I was just sixteen years old when I began working as an RUC agent.

When we met I told him straight away that I wanted to do it.

"Great, Ray, but you've already made your first mistake."

"What's that?" I asked suspiciously.

"You should have asked how much you'd be paid first. Now I know you want to do it, I needn't offer you as much."

He held a straight face for a moment, then burst out laughing at my crestfallen expression "it's all right, I'm just rattling your cage. You'll not grow fat on it to start with it. We don't pay a regular amount until you've proved your worth, but you'll get a few quid for each tip-off and a bonus if it leads to arrests or seizures of weapons. Once you have shown your worth it, however, you'll find that we are very generous indeed."

We shook hands to seal the deal and then Pete got to his feet ready to leave. Slightly surprised, I asked, "When should we meet to start things off?"

"Soon enough, but before we get to that, you have to do a lot of thinking and a lot of planning. That applies not just to that first meeting, but to every single one you ever go to. You must always think the whole thing through in advance; how you should prepare yourself, how you should travel, how to make sure you're not being followed, what you should say if you happen to meet someone who knows you unexpectedly."

"And will you teach me all that?"

"Of course, it's all part of the service. I won't even charge you for the advice."

We arranged that Pete would never contact me because of the risk of blowing my cover. Instead I would ring him daily and we would meet two or three times a week, usually up the town, by the fountain. It was a Protestant area where I felt reasonably sure that no Creggan eyes would be on me.

Pete would pick me up in his car, though it wasn't always easy to spot. He changed his car every year, but it was also re-sprayed a different colour every couple of months and the number plates were different almost every time he picked me up. He had a set of a dozen false plates in his garage and would change them every few days. The IRA always had people looking out for strangers. If the same car was spotted cruising through the Bogside or the Creggan too often, it might be met with a bullet the next time.

When Pete had picked me up, we'd often go down to the site of Fort George on the Strand, parking behind the hedge, about twenty yards from the road. My sister lived nearby, giving me a good alibi, but I never needed it. In all the years I worked as an agent, no one ever spotted us together.

He had a handgun in his glove compartment, a Walther PPK, which he later traded in for an even heavier calibre Magnum .357. I was always pestering him to let me handle the gun, but even the idea of it gave him heart failure and he wouldn't let me anywhere near it.

For the first year or so, I simply phoned Pete when I saw IRA or INLA men in groups or heading off in cars and passed on any gossip I had heard, but before long he began to pressure me to become a member of the Irish National Liberation Army. The INLA was the military wing of the Irish Republican Socialist Party, which had been formed in December 1974. The INLA came into being at the same meeting in a secret session after many of the delegates had already gone home.

Many of the INLA's new recruits were disenchanted ex-members of the official IRA – the Stickies. Within two months a full-blown feud was going on between the INLA and the Stickies, fueled by INLA members stealing weapons from Stickie arms dumps. There were many deaths and scores of wounded before a truce was called. By then the Stickies were no longer a serious threat to anyone, but the INLA's feuding with the Provies was only just beginning.

Until Pete began pressuring me, I'd never had the slightest intention of joining any republican organization; I knew what my Mum would say and do if she ever found out I was involved with them. When my brother, Harry, did find out, not long after I joined the INLA, he came straight home, dragged me out of bed and gave me a good kicking, telling me, "you get out of it now or I'll break your neck."

I did leave for a few weeks, but was soon involved again, for I was already hooked on the adrenaline rush of it. The excitement was the main attraction in the early stages, because the money was very modest, just £10 or £20 for each of piece of useful information.

At Pete's instigation, I'd finally become a member of the INLA in 1978. I was working at the Spring Town training centre at the time and often got a lift home from work with Dave Dwyer from Glenowen. He came to the Cash-and-Carry next to the training centre every afternoon to buy stock for his shop in Beechwood Avenue.

I knew he was a member of the INLA, for he had talked about it on his way home, and had even asked me to join. One night towards the end of November, as we were driving home in his Volvo, he asked me again. I'd been non-committal before, but this time I told him I was ready to do it.

"Great. There is a meeting tonight in Connelly House. Come there at seven and I will introduce you."

Chamberlain Street was windswept and deserted as I made my way to Connelly House just before seven. I knocked on the door and was taken upstairs to a big room, painted a garish yellow and furnished only with two small settees and a low, square table. A few other members were already there and Dave introduced me to them: Davy Geraghty, Frank Slasher Riley, Donal McBride from Broadway, Robert McDonagh from the Creggan and Joe Tohill from Harvey Street. There was no initiation ceremony or oath of allegiance to swear, I was simply introduced and that was that.

At the end of the meeting, Dave Dywer turned to Tohill and said, "might as well get Ray to work straight away."

Davy Geraghty and I were then told to go to Faith Hodge's flat at Carranbane Walk, to pick up some ammunition and timing devices being stored there and deliver them to a car waiting just across the border.

We caught the bus down to the Shantallow shops and walked up to Carranbane Walk. When we reached the flat, Faith opened the door to us, dressed in a pink pull over and blue jeans. She was a good-looking woman in her late twenties and her flat was clean and smart, newly wall-papered and with a new three-piece-suit. Davy was highly impressed, nudging me in the ribs with his elbow and muttering, "I could do worse than get my feet under the table here," in a staged whisper that could have been heard in the next-door flat.

Faith gave a faint smile and let us into her bedroom, sparking off a fresh wave of excitement in Davy and a few innuendo's, which were about as subtle as a bomb going off. Faith, her smile a little fixed by now, rebuffed him with a curt, "I doubt you're man enough," and pointed to the built-in wardrobe. "The stuffs in there."

Davy opened the door. The wardrobe was bulging with clothes and he gazed stupidly at them for a minute, until Faith pointed to a plastic bag on the top shelf. As Davy lifted it down, the bag burst and the timers and ammunition cascaded all over the floor. All three of us were down on our hands and knees, scooping it up. Davy shoved the timing devices into the pocket of his coat and asked Faith for something in which to put the ammunition. Faith rummaged around for a minute and produced an old pair of tights.

"Christ, Faith, have you not got a bag?" said Davy.

"No, I haven't."

"Oh, alright then, give us the bloody tights."

We stuffed the ammunition, and about thirty or forty rounds of all different types, into one leg of the tights, then left the flat heading along Carranbane Walk and up the road that leads to the border. We passed the "Dragon's Teeth" laid across the road just past Mickey Henry's breakers yard and crossed into the Free State. Two men were sitting in a blue Mazda car, parked at the side of the road, waiting for us. The car was an INLA staff car I'd often seen parked outside Connelly House.

Mickey Montgomery was in the driver's seat, with Patsy O'Hara alongside him. They were both prominent Republicans, and Mickey was the OC (Officer Commanding) of the Derry Brigade. We exchanged a few words as Davy handed over the ammunition and the timers and then they turned the car around and drove back the way they had come. We watched them go, then walked back over the border and down into Derry.

CHAPTER 4

I quickly dropped into the INLA routine, hanging around the IRSP book shop in Connelly House in Chamerlain Street, where INLA members always got together, and carrying out whatever jobs the unit had for me. I saw Colm there often. He was delighted when I told him that I had joined the INLA, but he would have been considerably less pleased had he known the real reason for my change of heart.

As a junior member my INLA jobs were mostly menial duties, picking up guns and ammunition for the real hard men who were going out to do the actual shooting. That suited me very well, however, for I had no wish to point a gun at anyone.

Many of my supply runs were to or from the weapons dump in Callum Roskell's coal shed at his flat in Hyde Park. After one INLA meeting on a freezing December night, Callum and I were sent down to the Castle Bar in Waterloo Street to pick up a remote-control device from Davy Geraghty. When we got there, we found Davy sitting right at the far end of the bar looking as wired as an electric chair.

He pushed a plastic bag across the table to us. "If you left a bomb at the Guildhall, you could sit in Connelly House and blow it up with this." Then he was up and out of the door, without another word.

Callum and I went up to Hyde Park, but before we stashed the bag in the coal-shed, we took it into Callum's kitchen and opened it up. Inside the bag was a metallic blue box with two antennae sticking out of it.

"Look at this little beauty, Ray," Callum said, his eyes shining with excitement. We played with it for a few minutes, twiddling the control knobs like two kids with a Scalextric set, then packed it away in its bag then hid it in the coal-shed. While we were inside the shed, Callum reached up on top of the door-frame and then pressed cold metal into my hand. I looked down.

"It's a .38, Ray," he said eagerly, "but be careful how you handle it. I'ts been filed down and it's got a hair-trigger."

I almost dropped in my anxiety to get rid of it. Callum reluctantly stashed it back on top of the door-frame and locked the coal-shed door.

Two days later I was back at Callum's flat with a grenade and two blocks of TNT. I'd been told to go to Johnny O'Rourke's house in Gartan Square to help him move the stuff. When I got there, he took me round to the back of the house and pulled the grenade, wrapped in a plastic bag, out of an open drain near the back door. The TNT, wrapped in plastic and sealed with black, waterproof tape, was sitting under a roof-tile and a crumbling breeze-block in the corner of the yard.

I stagged him – scouting ahead for Police or army patrols – up to Callum's with the stuff and once more we had a look at it before we put it in the coal-shed. The grenade was Russian-made and looked like a small green pineapple with a silver tip about an inch and a half long. Even Callum couldn't get too excited by the two featureless slabs of TNT, however, and after a couple of minutes he put the stuff in the shed and Johnny and I went home.

There was some risk, but not much, in moving the explosives and guns around town. Within our community we could move fairly freely, certain that in an emergency we could knock on almost any door and shelter until an army or RUC patrol had gone. Sometimes willingly, more often reluctantly, impelled as much by fear as any strong sympathies, people would let us use their houses as refuges and then we would slip away when the danger was past.

Slasher Riley, Robert McDonagh, Donal McBride and I were on our way to a job in the Brandywell one night. The plan was to wait for an army Land Rover driving up the Lone Moor Road and then Slasher would toss a grenade into the back of it when it went past. He'd shown me the grenades before we set out. They were the same Russian-made type I'd seen at Callum Roskell's flat.

We'd tried to hijack a car but it was pissing with rain and the car we chose, a cream Volkswagen wouldn't start. We pushed it down Southway and managed to bump-start it, but the engine cut out again almost immediately. We fiddled with the engine for a while, but then gave up in disgust and walked on down towards the Lone Moor Road, rain trickling down our necks.

Southway had always scared me since I was a kid. It was known locally as the Coach Road because of an old story about a headless coachman who some people claimed to have seen riding by, driving his ghostly horses into the night. We all scoffed at the tale, but just the same none of us liked walking alone down Southway, especially after dark.

Slasher and Robert were carrying grenades in their pockets. Donal had a .38 and I was carrying a little .32 revolver. We were walking in pairs down opposite sides of the road checking up and down for army patrols and less earthly presences, when Slasher suddenly stopped dead and said, "Listen! What's that?"

I was ready to turn and run for it before the headless coach man came to get me, when I heard the noise of two jeeps suddenly screeching to a halt at the bottom of the street. We couldn't see them, but we heard Brit voices shouting as the army patrol spilled out of the jeeps. We panicked a bit, ran through some gardens and knocked on the door of a house. A woman we had never seen before answered it.

"Is it all right if my friends and I wait in your house until the army has gone?" said Slasher.

She peered over his shoulder towards the street and then nodded. "Come in."

We sat and drank tea with her and her husband for an hour, while army patrols moved up and down the road outside. It was obvious that the couple were far from pleased with their uninvited guests, but they weren't foolish; they knew that reprisals would inevitably have followed if they'd have refused us entry or betrayed us to the Army. Eventually the patrols disappeared. The man stepped outside to make sure the coast was clear and we then left by the back door. Robert and Donal went first and Slasher and I followed a couple of minutes later.

As we came out into the street, I could see Donal and Robert almost at the bottom of Lone Moor Gardens. Just then I heard shouting. Donal and Robert tossed the grenade and the revolver over a wall as the army jeeps came roaring round the corner. We ducked into a garden and watched as they were surrounded by soldiers, who handcuffed them and taped bags over their hands to preserve the forensic evidence. They then hustled them into the back of the Land Rover and drove off at high speed. The rest of the soldiers set up a check-point and began searching the street, so we slipped back the other way and went home.

I phoned Pete to tip him off about the grenade and he contacted the army. They'd missed it in the initial search but went back again and found it at the second attempt. Slasher called for me the next morning to go back and look for the grenade and the revolver. We found the gun, but, strangely enough, the grenade had disappeared.

Working undercover in the INLA was not that difficult, even for an apprentice agent like me. Despite a ruthless attitude, some blood-curdling rhetoric and some high-profile successes, the INLA was never as formidable an organisation as the IRA, and it was deeply penetrated by RUC agents, some at a much higher level than a mere volunteer.

One guy came up to me one day and said, "Hello, Ray. How are you doing?"

"Fine."

There was a long silence as he stared at me, saying nothing.

"Is there something wrong?" I asked.

"Yes, there is. There have been a few things going wrong with jobs you've been involved in recently…I've got a feeling you're informing."

I nearly died. The moment that I dreaded had arrived. At any moment I would be surrounded by INLA men, bundled into a car and driven off. After a few days of torture, over the border in a safe house in the back country of Donegal, I would be shot in the back of the head and my body dumped as a warning to other touts.

I felt faint and his voice seemed to be coming to me from a long way away. I kept what grip I could, but my denial, "No, no, you're wrong, I wouldn't do that," sounded pitifully weak even to me, and my pale face and trembling hands were as good as a signed confession.

He kept questioning me, asking why I thought certain jobs had gone wrong, and I kept stammering out my unconvincing replies as he toyed with me, a cat with a mouse. Finally he gave me an enigmatic smile, and sent me on my way. "That's all, Ray, for now at least."

I walked home, starting at every shadow and diving down side-roads and alleys at the sound of any car, and then lay awake for hours, my nerves twitching even at the routine, familiar sounds of the night. When I at least fell into a fitful sleep, I was instantly jolted awake, bolt upright and pouring with a cold sweat of pure terror by a coal collapsing noisily in the grate downstairs. I lay back in the dark, my heart thumping, and did not fall asleep again until it was already light outside.

I lived in fear for two days, constantly looking over my shoulder and expecting to be picked up, shot and dumped in a ditch at any moment. Finally, I called Pete and asked for an urgent meeting, but when I told him what had happened, he said, "no, he's only pulling your leg," and started laughing.

I was not amused. "What the fuck are you laughing about?"

"He wouldn't tell me, but I soon worked it out for myself. My tormentor was also an undercover agent. Sadly he died in a shoot-out a couple of years later.

At the next INLA meeting in Connelly House, Dave Dwyer and Joe Tohill had big news for us. There were to be simultaneous bombings of the Allied Irish Bank in Racecourse Road and the Bank of Ireland buildings at Shipquay Street, Sackville Street and Greenhaw Road.

A stunned silence greeted the news. It was broken by Davy Geraghty, who piped up, "What the fuck are we after bombing Irish Banks for? Are there no Brit Banks we could blow up?"

Tohill smiled indulgently. "They may be called Irish Banks, Davy, but they're backed by British money and it's the Brits who are running them."

There were no further questions. We met the next day and we were divided into teams for the job by Joe Tohill. I was paired with Neil McMonigle, which didn't fill me with confidence, for he was a dangerously unstable and reckless character.

Tohill then gave out the orders. McMonigle and I were to hijack a car in Shantallow and then drive it to the Collon Bar on the Buncrana Road, where Vincent O'Reilly would be waiting with two grille bombs – designed to hook on to the railings outside the banks. We were to do the banks on Greenhall Road and Racecourse Road.

We travelled out to Shantallow on the bus. McMonigle stared straight ahead, scarely speaking.

I tried to crack a joke – "I bet James Bond doesn't travel by bus when he's on an assignment" – but McMonigle just turned his cold, unsmiling stare on me for a moment and then went back to his study of the back of the driver's head. I took the hint and kept quiet the rest of the way.

We got off not far from the Collon Bar and walked into a half-built new housing estate to find a car. As we walked along, I spotted a short length of pipe lying by the side of the road and slipped it into my coat pocket.

A blue Ford Escort van was parked by one of the houses. We walked in and found its owner standing in the kitchen, smoking a cigarette.

McMonigle didn't waste words. "INLA. We want your car."

The man looked us up and down. He was powerfully built and didn't look like he was going to let go of the keys without a fight. I moved the piece of pipe around in my pocket. When he saw what looked like a gun barrel pointing at him, he had the keys out of his pocket and into

McMonigle's hand in record time.

"You'll get your van back later. Don't report anything to the police."

He nodded nervously and we strolled outside. McMonigle got into the driver's seat and started the engine. It spluttered and finally started, but it ran as rough as guts and after driving it around for a few minutes we dumped it on the other side of the estate and walked over to Devlin's supermarket, looking for a car that wouldn't break down half-way through the job.

By now it was four o'clock and we only had a few more minutes before the rendezvous with Vincent O'Reilly. Luckily there was a green medical supplies van parked outside the chemists. The driver was carrying boxes into the shop. I put my hand back in my coat pocket and pointed the pipe at the driver as he came outside.

"INLA. We want your car."

Once more the pipe worked its magic and we drove off with the van-driver sitting terrified between us. We dumped him a couple of miles up the road and then drove to Messines Park, close to the Collon Bar.

We sat in the bar for two hours waiting for O'Reilly, but he never showed up. In the end

I tossed the van keys away over the hedge and we split up and headed for home. I never found out why Vince didn't turn up, but it was the only part of the plan that went wrong, for I heard on the news that night that the other two banks in Sackville Street and Shipquay Street had been bombed.

The INLA's successful operations were punctuated by strings of jobs that went wrong. That was only partly because of agents and informers betraying their plans, for the calibre of both the INLA members and their equipment was pretty poor. We were also given only the most rudimentary training. The one training camp I attended quickly degenerated into farce.

As usual I was hanging around Connelly House with Slasher Riley and the rest of the guys one morning, when Joe Tohill appeared and asked if any of us would volunteer to go on a training camp somewhere in the South. "It's a bit of a rush job, lads. There's a camp set up and a few Belfast men going. They need some Derry men to go as well."

"What, to show those Belfast twats which way to point a rifle?" Slasher sneered.

Joe gave a mirthless smile. "Right, come on, who's on for it?"

Neil McMonigle and I were the only two to volunteer. Tommy told us to go home and get some heavy clothes and then meet him in Willie Kelly's Bar. When we got down there, he bought us a pint, gave Neil £30 to cover our expenses and then told us to catch the Dublin Express bus from the Foyle Street depot. "When you get off the bus, there'll be a man waiting for you."

"How will we know him?"

"You won't, but he'll know you."

By the time we arrived in Dublin it was dark. We got off the bus and stood waiting as the rest of the passengers struggled off with their bags and disappeared. We were hanging around for ten minutes before a tall, fair-haired man detached himself from the crowds standing listlessly around the platforms and came over to us.

"Are you from Derry?"

"Aye."

"Come with me."

He led us out of the bus depot and over to a battered car parked in a side-street. We got in and he drove us out of Dublin, taking the road south past Dun Laoghaire and down to Wicklow. Along the way he told us a little about himself, but not much. He was originally from Belfast and had come south after escaping from the Crum. He wouldn't tell us his name and when I tried to ask him a bit more about himself, he just shook his head and changed the subject.

When we got to Wicklow, he pulled up outside a ramshackle stone building on the outskirts of town and took us up the echoing staircase to a one-room flat on the top floor.

The room was sparsely furnished: a cooker, a sink unit, a wardrobe, an iron-framed bed with no mattress and a pile of grubby sleeping bags dumped in the corner. The bathroom was on the landing, shared with the other flats. God knows what they made of the procession of men trooping in and out of the toilet all weekend.

After half an hour's desultory conversation we heard footsteps on the stairs and the three Belfast INLA men walked in. They were all stockily built, about five foot eight inches tall and dressed in jeans and jackets, but one of them, called Rooster, stood out because of his shock of red hair.

The tall Belfast man then stood up and briefed us. "You'll be getting trained in the use of an AK47 rifle and some other weapons. I'll be showing you how the AK47 works here tomorrow and then the day after we'll be going up into the Wicklow mountains for a shoot-off. I'll also be teaching you the rudiments of bomb-making – how to make a complete circuit."

We went out and got some fish and chips to eat, had a few beers and then kipped down for the night. I huddled down in one of the sleeping bags on the bare boards and eventually fell asleep despite the snores from a couple of the others and irritable mutterings from Rooster, who talked continuously in his sleep.

The next morning Rooster failed to live up to his name, being the last one awake. We had a spartan breakfast of tea and white bread scraped with margarine and then got down to work. The tall Belfast man produced an AK47 from the wardrobe with a flourish and demonstrated how to use it. He opened out the black folding butt of the rifle and then showed us the trigger, and the cocking piece and the safety catch.

There was no magazine and no ammunition, but he showed us where the magazine fitted and told us we'd be able to fire the weapon when we went up into the mountains. "We've other weapons up there as well that you'll get a chance to use."

Our next lesson was how to construct a bomb, making a complete electrical circuit using a cheap watch, a couple of pieces of wire, a battery and some superglue. In place of explosive, he used a small torch bulb. He made a tiny hole in the watch-face by the figure 12 and pushed one end of the wire through it, fixing it with a dab of superglue. The wire was connected to the battery and when the hand reached the hour it completed the circuit and the bulb lit up, indicating that the bomb had gone off. He then took it apart again and got each of us to make a complete circuit a couple of times before he pronounced himself satisfied.

He then showed us some detonators, laying out about fifty of them on the floorboards. We picked them up and examined them as he lectured us in how to use them. By early afternoon he'd exhausted his repertoire and we sat around aimlessly for another hour or so, then we had little tins of beans for our tea and set off down the town for a serious drinking session. The Belfast men were prodigious drinkers, but even when pissed they maintained their traditional mistrust towards Derry men. They all sat in one group, leaving me with only the taciturn Neil McMonigle for company. It was a long night.

The next morning it was hosing down with rain. Our instructor, struggling to shake off his hangover, took one look at the weather and told us that we couldn't go up in the mountains for a shoot-off because there'd be snow up there. I couldn't believe my ears. It was hard to imagine the British Army calling off a training exercise because the weather wasn't very nice.

Instead of the shoot-off, our instructor sat us down in a circle around him, like a primary school teacher with a class of kids, and read us a story. The book was *The Informer*, the true story of a man who'd spied for the Brits, which certainly captured my attention. I wasn't sure if our instructor was reading it to us as a warning to watch out for informers or because he simply couldn't think of anything else to do.

By lunch time the three Belfast men had had enough of story time, and after a near-mutiny, our instructor put away his book and we all trooped down to the pub for another marathon session. Much later we settled down to another night on the floor, and in the morning McMonigle and I were driven back to the bus depot for a return journey to Derry.

If that was a sample of INLA training, it was a miracle they ever managed any successful operations at all. In truth, there weren't many, at least in Derry. My INLA unit was hopelessly compromised, undone by agents and informers and by its members' own carelessness and incompetence. Many of the people in the unit, like Neil McMonigle, Patsy O'Hara and Mickey McMonigle, were to die, most of them in shoot-outs with the army and police.

Neil McMonigle was killed after he and another INLA man tried to hold up an SAS guy on a Derry street. McMonigle had a rifle and his companion had a pistol, but the soldier pulled out his own gun and shot both of them. McMonigle was hit in the head and died instantly, the other man survived after being hit in the shoulder.

I couldn't shed any tears for most of the INLA guys, and if ever a person deserved to die, it was Neil McMonagle. He was using the INLA for his own ends and would have shot anybody. They didn't have to be police or army, if they rubbed him up the wrong way, he'd shoot them. He just didn't care.

If the deaths of the INLA terrorists like McMonagle left me cold, though, there was one that almost tore me apart.

The INLA were planning to rob the Maybrook Dairy down in Shantallow, and, as usual, I tipped off Pete. On the day of the job, Colm McNutt, Hessie Phelan and I went up to the Dunloe Bar, which was the IRSP bar at the time. Joe Tohill met us there and gave Colm a Webley revolver to hijack a car for job, warning him that it wouldn't fire. The firing-pin was damaged, and even if it had worked, there were no bullets for the gun. "It's just for show anyway," said Joe. Showing a weapon was usually enough to persuade a driver to hand over his car.

I wanted to help Colm with the hijack, even though I wasn't directly involved in the Maybrook job, but he took Hessie Phelan instead and went over to the William Street car park. Disappointed, I hung around on the street with Charlie Power and Neil Quinlan. Colm and Hessie went over to an old, red Hillman Hunter, with a black vinyl roof. A guy was sitting in the driving seat. He was wearing a snorkel jacket and had curly, bushy hair. I'd recognise him anywhere, even today.

Hessie and Colm bent over, talking to him. He got out, a big guy, over six feet tall. Hessie got behind the wheel and Colm walked round to the other side. The guy had probably done something to the car, because Hessie couldn't get it started. While he was struggling with the ignition, I saw the guy run round to the passenger side.

Colm had tucked the Webley in his waist-band and was lowering himself into the passenger seat when the guy booted the door shut on his head. He fell out onto the ground and the guy stood over him, shooting him several times as he lay there. I was paralysed, rooted to the spot, the hairs on the back of my neck standing on end.

Hessie got out of the car and ran. The guy pointed the gun at him but I don't know if he fired; I was in too much shock. Colm got up and staggered a few paces across the car park and I thought, *Thank fuck, he's not that badly hurt,* but then he slumped to the ground and lay still. The guy who'd shot him ran back around the driver's side of the car again. He pointed the gun directly at us as we stood by the bus stop across the street but then got in the car and sped through the car park and off up William Street. We ran to Colm, carried him into the flats and phoned for an ambulance, but it was too late. There were no last words or tearful farewells. He just lay there cold and dead, as a pool of blood slowly congealed like a dark halo around his head.

The INLA had a big funeral for him, with Charlie Parr, Tom Pitman and I among the colour party. We changed into paramilitary uniform – black berets and dark glasses – at Mickey Montgomery's house and went down to the chapel. We stood by Colm's coffin and walked with his cortege down to the cemetery, as an army helicopter hovered overhead. Police photographers snapped us from a safe distance as well. Spying on burials was a two-way business, for the INLA and IRA also tried to photograph police funerals, hoping to identify Special Branch men, though Pete told me that for that reason they rarely went to funerals, even of close colleagues.

We formed up around the grave, near the grey slate monument to the dead of *Óglaigh na h'Éireann* – the Provisional IRA. We stood to attention, looking down over the ranks of grave stones to the dull grey roofs of the Bogside, breaking in waves against the rock of the city walls.

The priest murmured a few graveside platitudes and Colm's mother and sisters wept and wailed. Then I helped to lower the coffin into the black, dank earth and stood stiff and unseen as the relatives sent handfuls of soil rattling onto the coffin lid. From the corner of my eye, I saw the sexton peering out from his shed, impatient for the last mourner to leave before he filled in the hole.

There were no guns and no volley of shots over Colm's burial place at the time, though some INLA men went down to the cemetery the following night and fired a few rounds. We just turned and walked away, leaving Colm to his last rest. He was not alone in death, for the surrounding gravestones were engraved with eulogies to dead martyrs of the Republican cause.

The *in meroriam* columns of the local papers were also filled with them: "Dear Ireland, Take him to thy breast, the soldier who died for thee; within thy bosom let him rest among the martyrs sanctified." "In this supreme hour the Irish Nation must, by the readiness of its children to sacrifice themselves for the common good, prove itself worthy of the august destiny to which it is called."

Grieving parents might have taken some consolation from the belief that there sons' deaths served a higher purpose. Numb with my own grief for my boyhood friend I could see no purpose at all in his death, only a cruel waste of a life.

I'd never really considered that I might be compromising his safety by working for the Special Branch, but now it was too late. My best friend had been shot dead, killed by the people I was working to help. I cried my eyes out in Pete's car that night. I was sure that the information I had passed on had been the cause of Colm's death, but Pete shook his head.

"We'd certainly staked out the Maybrook Dairy, but we were looking to catch them in the act, not kill them before they'd even got there. We didn't pass any information on to the army – we wanted the credit for this operation ourselves. We don't often share intelligence with the army; sometimes it seems as if we are fighting each other as much as the terrorists."

He gave a mirthless smile and then pulled himself back to the subject. "Look, Ray, it was just bad luck that Colm tried to hijack a car with an SAS man in it. The irony is that he wasn't even there to watch the INLA guys. He was laid up in a rest period from another job. It was pure misfortune that of all the cars around, Colm should have chosen that one."

I wanted to believe it, but was still unconvinced. Sensing my hesitation, Pete tried again. "I told you before, there has to be absolute trust between us. I swear to you that the RUC had no involvement whatsoever, direct or indirect with Colm McNutt's death. You have to believe that."

He held my gaze until I nodded. "Good. Now I'm sorry that you've lost a good friend, but let's not kid ourselves, the path that Colm chose to follow has only one end. He was a terrorist who went on the streets armed with a gun, and he paid the price for it."

"But the gun wasn't loaded; it didn't even work."

Pete gave me a world-weary smile. "And the solider is supposed to put his own life at risk, just in case the gun might not be loaded?"

"Colm didn't die in a fair fight, Pete. It was cold-blooded murder."

He shook his head. "That's what the IRA and INLA are involved in, Ray: cold-blooded murder."

In the end, I allowed Pete to reassure me about my own part in Colm's death – partly perhaps because it was what I wanted to hear. But Colm's killing had frightened and shocked me. My first instinct was to pack it all in and leave the INLA, but after a long and tearful conversation, Pete persuaded me, "You've got to stay and finish the job."

There were to be many more shootings and many more deaths, but none would ever effect me again like Colm's. I still think often about the events of that day, wondering if I could have done anything to save his life.

To the others, Colm's death was just one among many, for the INLA ranks continued to be decimated in gun-fights with the police, the army and the INLA's Republican rivals, the Stickies and the Provies. INLA members were also at risk of being shot by their own side. One of the Derry members, Neil Quinlan, had been out collecting money for an INLA commemoration of Colm, but had kept the money instead of handing it over. Joe Tohill, Chris Bishop, Vincent O'Reilly, Slasher Riley and I went to a meeting to discuss what should be done. Tohill proposed that Quinlan should be knee-capped as punishment. There were no dissenting voices.

The next evening Slasher and I waited in the car park outside the Village Inn, across the street from Quinlan's house. Around five-thirty, Quinlan walked into the Inn but stayed only a couple of minutes before crossing the road to his house. I stayed on watch while Slasher went to phone the Dunlow Bar, where Chris Bishop and Vincent O'Reilly were waiting. They arrived about twenty minutes later, O'Reilly carrying a .38 revolver. They walked over to Quinlan's house and knocked on the door. When he opened it and saw who was there, Quinlan ran back into the house, but O'Reilly and Bishop pursued him and almost immediately we heard two muffled shots.

Shortly afterwards, O'Reilly and Bishop sauntered back over to us.

"Any problems?" ask Slasher.

"No problems," said Bishop. "He ran for it, but we caught him and Vince shot him. He missed his knee-cap though, and shot him through the thigh."

O'Reilly then handed the gun to Slasher before he and Bishop walked off in one direction while Slasher and I set off staggering each other up to Callum Roskell's flat. Slasher handed him the gun and he took it out and hid it in his coal-shed.

Sometime later, Bishop and O'Reilly were to be involved in a much more celebrated incident. Early in March 1979, they sailed for London on a coal boat from the docks at Derry. On the thirtieth of March, the Conservative MP and Northern Ireland Spokesman, Airey Neave, was blown up in his car as he was driving out of the House of Commons car park.

The device used was a mercury-tilt bomb which had been invented less than three months before by an INLA member from Portadown. The actual mercury-tilt switch was advertised legitimately in radio spare-parts catalogues. Mercury and water were stored in separate reservoirs within the device, but became mixed as soon as it was tilted out of the horizontal. That created an electrical current which exploded the bomb.

The INLA man realised that the motion of a car would be enough to trip the switch and detonate a bomb, getting around the problems they were facing with radio-controlled bombs, which could be detected and prematurely exploded by the army's radio scanners.

There was little risk to the bomber in placing the device, but once fixed to the underside of a car with magnets, it would explode within seconds of the car being driven off. The man assembled a prototype bomb for a test. It was taken over the border to a remote area of the Free State and fixed underneath an old scrap car. As the INLA leadership watched from a safe distance, the car was towed at the end of a long rope along a deserted country road. Nothing happened until it began to climb a small hill, when the bomb immediately detonated.

The INLA leadership were highly impressed but demanded a final test in real conditions. The victim of this "field test" was a UDR man, Lance-Corporal Robert McAnally, who was blown up as he drove his Morris Marina out of a car park in Portadown on the 6th March 1979. McAnally had both legs amputated in hospital in a vain attempt to save his life. He died a week later.

The INLA leaders were now convinced of the weapons potential and a unit was immediately despatched to London to kill Airey Neave. He was chosen as the target because of his high-profile as Tory shadow spokesman of Northern Ireland, with an agenda that included the re-introduction of internment, the arrest on sight of known Republicans, irrespective of whether there was any evidence to link them to terrorist activities, and the unrestricted use of the SAS.

Despite the forensic evidence from the McAnally killing, the security forces made no immediate moves to counter the threat of the new mercury-tilt bombs. They were galvanized into action only after the death of Airey Neave.

The INLA unit watched Neave's movements for several days, then went into action. A bomb was attached to the underside of his blue Vauxhall with magnets. As well as a mercury-tilt device, the bomb included a wristwatch primer, set to activate at a time when they knew that Neave would have left the car in the underground car park at the House of Commons. When Neave returned to the car later that day and began driving up the ramp leading out of the car park, the bomb exploded. His legs were blown off and he died thirty minutes later.

Two days after the killing, Vincent O'Reilly and Chris Bishop returned to Derry. Nothing was ever said officially, but the clear understanding among the members of the INLA in Derry was that Bishop and O'Reilly had planted the bomb. When the police released a photofit picture of the one of the suspects, it was an absolute ringer for O'Reilly.

The INLA leaders were ecstatic with their success. One told *Magill magazine*, "We blew Neave to bits inside the impregnable Palace of Westminster… It's time that the Westminster armchair militarists suffer the consequences."

It was the INLA's finest hour, but it was also their last hurrah – at least as far as my Derry unit were concerned. By the end of the year, it had virtually disintegrated, destroyed by the arrests and seizures prompted by my information and by the deaths of its members. I left the INLA on Pete's instructions, although it was also my wish, as I'd just got married.

***

I was one of those guys who fell in love very easily, and Lorraine was my first really steady girlfriend. She was a year younger than me and very beautiful. She had brown hair, usually dyed blonde, and was very kind-hearted, but with a feisty sense of humour. She loved dancing and most nights we would go jiving down at the community centre. On the rare evenings when I had a bit of money in my pocket, we would be off around the bars, finishing up at El Greco's nightclub on the Foyle Road, where there was a guaranteed fight every Friday night.

When I first met Lorraine, she'd been going out with someone else for a few years, a big sporty lad called Coyle. Even when they split up and she started going out with me, she still had a few regrets. She kept seeing him on the odd night, just to see how she still felt about him, I suppose. That drove me mad with jealousy and I would sit at home, deeply depressed and being horrible to everyone within reach, thinking she didn't really love me. Eventually she realised she wasn't being fair to either of us and made her choice. She stopped seeing Coyle and we began making plans to get married.

Those plans had to be abruptly brought forward when she got pregnant. Like good Catholics, we didn't use contraceptives, but like bad Catholics, we still made love, even though we weren't married. The inevitable soon happened. Lorraine wasn't too upset about it, though; she used to get the most awful period pains, being bent double, clutching a hot water-bottle to her belly to try and ease the cramps, and believed an old wives' tale might cure the problem: "To get rid of the pains, have a baby."

We'd being going out for about two years when we got married. I was nineteen, Lorraine, eighteen. At first we were very happy, and our happiness even survived living in her parents' house for the first nine months of our marriage. My relationship with her parents quickly became less blissful, however, simply through the strains of sharing the same roof. Before we were married, I'd always got on well with Lorraine's father, Dinny, but I goaded him so much one night that he flipped and threw a punch at me. I didn't punch him back, because I knew it was my fault that he's lost control, but the incident convinced us we'd have to find a place of our own.

Our son, Raymond, had been born a couple of months before. With a child, we had enough points on the council waiting list to qualify for a house, and we moved into a ground-floor flat in Cromore Gardens, just round the corner from my parents on Balbane Pass.

Pregnancy may have given Lorraine temporary relief from period pains, but Raymond's birth caused her even worse agony. I was in the room with her, but then had to go and wait outside while they may a forceps delivery, though I was still close enough to hear her screams.

Our daughter Denise was born, less painfully, the following year. Unlike my Da, I threw myself into fatherhood with relish, changing nappies, feeding the babies and taking them out for walks. I loved doing it and had a great rapport with my kids, even though I was quite strict with them. From very early on, just like my mother, I tried to teach them right from wrong. If I caught them peeling wallpaper from the walls, for example, as kids sometimes do, I would give them a little tap on the hand and tell them, "No, you don't do that." Their eyes would fill with tears for a moment, almost breaking my heart, but then they would be all smiles again.

For a few months I dropped out of active Republican involvement and even found a proper job for a while, working for DuPont outside Derry. I was still in contact with Pete, however, and if I saw IRA men in cars and thought that something was going on, I would tell him about it. I wasn't getting paid for it, but I still felt that I had a duty to tell him and I stopped or spoiled a few operations that way.

The Derry IRA lost a lot of men, and even though I wasn't a member at that time, I was probably one of the biggest causes of their losses. Eventually they reorganised and were starting to pick up again. At that point, Pete asked me to try to join them. Until then I'd been ready to abandon my double-life for a life of domestic bliss, but that wasn't something the RUC were willing to countenance.

Pete was applying considerable pressure to get me to carry on, and "render even more valuable service to the RUC. You can't just walk away from it, Ray," he said. "It's easy to get de-sensitised by all the killing. The more people the Provies kill, the more people just shrug their shoulders and get on with their lives. Unless they're really atrocious, the murders don't even make headlines any more. But these aren't just traffic accidents, Ray, and you and me are different from most people. We're in a position to do something about it, and we can't just turn our backs and look away.

"Over five hundred policemen and soldiers have been killed by those bastards over the past ten years. If that doesn't persuade you, think of this: for every soldier or policeman that dies, three civilians are killed, people whose only crime was to be in the wrong place, the wrong job, or the wrong religion. Every single week for the last ten years, three innocent people have died somewhere in Northern Ireland. You can't stop the killing in Northern Ireland single-handed, but you can save a hell of a lot of lives in Derry, if you do what we ask."

It was a very hard argument to refute, and as well as the moral pressure there was also a powerful financial incentive. I'd already proved my worth to the RUC, and Pete was now offering a salary of £200 a week plus bonuses for arrests and the seizure of weapons – very good money for those days.

I still took quite a bit of persuading, but despite my initial reluctance, Pete's persistence – and the knowledge of what some extra money could do for my new family – won me over in the end, though I still had one final reservation. "I don't want to be involved in shooting and killing people."

"You won't have to be," said Pete. "If you can get in, you must get a position where you won't be doing a lot of active stuff. Most people in the IRA can't drive. We'd teach you to drive and they'll be glad to use you as a getaway driver."

He actually taught me himself, in his two-litre red Capri, down around the back roads of Shantallow and Culmore. He was a good teacher and I had a talent for it, despite my tendency to pull a few shadowy handbrake turns at the drop of a hat. Although I was a good driver, I didn't take a test, and in all my time driving around Derry for the Provies I never had a full license. It was always a provisional licence, which was quite appropriate the circumstances.

As well as teaching me to drive, Pete also taught me a fair bit of tradecraft, and much of it quickly became instinctive. The longer I was an agent, the more I learned. I began to get a second sense about things. I was aware of everything going on around me and was always on the alert, feeling tension in the air and watching people's mannerisms, constantly looking for anything, however slight, which was out of the ordinary and which could trigger the warning that could save my life.

Pete always told me, "Never let yourself down in a dangerous situation or confrontation, because you're the only person who can do that. Don't show any emotion if you're confronted. Keep your nerve and you'll allay any suspicion. If you panic, you're as good as dead."

Even after years as an agent, however, there were still times when I was petrified with fright. I'd often go to meetings with Pete feeling very insecure and apprehensive, but I'd always come out of them much more confident for having talked to him. In a lot of ways it was like going to see a shrink once or twice a week. I'd get all the stuff that was troubling me off my mind. Not that I looked on Pete as a shrink, for we'd quickly become firm friends and the relationship was more like that of an older brother. There was no one else I could talk to about my double-life, no one at all.

While I'd taken an instant liking to Pete, I'd formed an equally instant dislike for his partner, Stuart. During my first meetings with them, Stuart had remained standing at the back of the room, saying little but making his impatience very clear. Eventually he interrupted. "Why are we wasting time on this tosser, Pete?" "He's just like the rest of his family – scum."

I was on my feet instantly, fists balling. If it had come to a fight, I would have stood no chance, but Pete quelled us both. "Ray, sit down. Stuart, if you've nothing more useful to say, then don't say anything at all."

Stuart flashed Pete a hostile look. "You're wasting your time and mine. This little toe- rag'll be off to hold another Sinn Féin press conference as soon as we let him go."

"I don't think he'll be doing that, will you, Ray?" said Pete.

I shook my head, still glaring at Stuart, who shrugged and went back to his sullen silence. Relations were never anything but strained between us after that, and I never felt that he liked me or appreciated what I was doing. Eventually the RUC realised that they got better value from me if Stuart was not involved, and from then on, Pete became my sole handler.

It was an unusual arrangement, for agents and informers normally had two handlers. It doubled the risk of the informant's cover being compromised, but it ensured that even if a handler was killed, there was still another in place. The two-handler system maintained the flow of information and also made sure that an informer being blackmailed by the police to work for them – as many of them were – couldn't simply give it up or disappear if his handler was killed.

They waived the rules in my case, letting me work with only one handler, simply because the work I was doing was so valuable to them. If ever Pete wasn't around when I had important information to deliver, I would report directly to his boss instead.

Once I'd learned to drive to Pete's satisfaction, he sent me out to try and join the Provies with a few final words of advice. "The most important thing for you to remember is to do whatever you're asked, but at the same time, don't get too pushy. Always listen more than you talk. You aren't expected to be a brilliant tactician. Pretend you haven't got a brain, just loads of balls."

I'd certainly need plenty, for even trying to join the Provies was full of risk. They knew that I'd no reason to love them, for they'd knee-capped two of my brothers, Johnny and Harry. The Provies had little reason to like me either, because I'd been a member of the INLA, who – like the Stickies – were hated rivals of the Provies.

The Provies were contemptuous of the old Stickies, and used to call them "rusty guns" because they never had any weapons worth talking about. The Stickies and Provies had a huge gun battle around the Creggan in the early 1970's. The Provies were a new organisation at the time, but they had more members and volunteers. There were constant running battles until the Provies finally took over completely. Most of the old Stickies went into the IRSP and the INLA, when they broke away from the IRA, furthering the bad blood.

The Provies and the INLA feuded a few times as well, and a lot of people were shot. The Derry OC of the INLA Mickey Montgomery, was haunted by a tragedy from his early days in the Stickies, when he'd accidentally shot dead a young volunteer. He'd never really recovered from it and was prone to depression and bouts of heavy drinking, but the Provies found a new way to remind him of the tragedy during one bitter Republican feud. As he sat in his front room, four men threw the young volunteer's gravestone through the window. Montgomery died of a heart attack not long afterwards.

CHAPTER 5

Although I'd agreed to try and join the Provies, I'd no real idea who to approach. When I was younger, there'd been little secrecy about membership of the IRA, but that had changed rapidly. My only lead into the Provies was Seamus Riever, a guy who lived at the bottom of our street. I'd known him since I was a kid, for we'd gone to Rosemount Junior School together and it was obvious that he was in the Provies. He'd only just come out of gaol after doing time for possession of a gun, and there was always a load of guys going in and out of his house. I went down one day and asked him, "Can you get me into the 'RA?"

He just played dumb and said, "I'm not in it."

"Well, if you know anyone who is, can you ask them for me?"

A couple of weeks passed, then he came back to me and said that he couldn't help me. I might have left it at that, but when I told Pete he said, "Try Paddy McQuirk."

My heart sank. I knew McQuirk slightly and didn't like him at all. He was a Sinn Féin official, often seen attending Republican marches in Derry, at which he appeared to be one of the main men, but he was equally well known locally for beating up kids in the Sinn Féin office.

I later discovered that McQuirk was the Officer Commanding the IRA's Internal Security for the whole of Derry City at the time. He was responsible for passing sentence on people involved in anti-social behaviour, thefts, robberies and sex offences – and behind his back was known as "The Creggan policeman."

The punishment was usually to be shot in the legs or beaten with hurley bats, and McQuirk sometimes took personal charge of the beatings. He gave a man accused of touting a wild hammering one night, and two other members, Jimmy Smith and Jimmy Harkin, got such severe beatings that they were also hospitalised.

I went to McQuirk's house towards the end of the August 1980. Concealing my dislike of him as well as I could, I asked him, "Is there any chance of you getting me into the IRA?"

"Who told you to come to me?"

"Nobody really, I've just seen you about the Creggan, and thought you'd be the right person to ask."

He thought for a moment, then said, "Come back and see me in a few days' time. I may have some news for you then," and closed the door.

When I went back a week later, he took me into his living-room and sat me down. "I have no word as yet about you joining, but tell me now why you want to join and what you can do for the organisation."

"Because I'm fed up with what's going on and I want to do something about it."

He obviously found it hard to believe because he knew about Harry and Johnny being knee-capped. He kept questioning me for half an hour while I stammered my way through some more or less plausible explanations. But they seemed to satisfy him, for he finally said, "All right. Come and see me again in five days' time."

When I returned to his house once more, it was soon obvious that I'd been cleared to be passed to the next link in the chain. McQuirk questioned me for a few minutes about my background and then gave me a warning. "If you're admitted into the Provisional IRA, you have to stay away from marches and keep yourself to yourself. A lot of men have let themselves down by lose talk, or going to marches or running around with well-known IRA men. Right, on your feet, you have to go and see the wee man."

We walked out of his house and around the corner, McQuirk led me to one of the houses where a short man in his early thirties, with his black hair cut in an incongruous page-boy bob, opened the door. When he smiled, which was often, he was all teeth, which jutted out of his mouth in all directions. I knew him well, but the last time I'd seen him was in the Crum.

"This is yer man," said McQuirk, who left without another word. Brendan "Shorty" McNally took me into his front room, a very loud symphony in red and black. There was a garish red carpet and red wallpaper, a black leatherette three-piece-suite and a large Spanish doll sitting on a glass-topped table.

Shorty stepped to the window and gazed out through the net curtains for a momement, then turned to face me. "Why do you want to join the Provisional Irish Republican Army?"

I was getting used to the question by now. "Well, as you know, I have been in the INLA, but in my view the Provies are a much better-organized outfit. It's also to do with my best friend, Colm McNutt, who was shot dead by the British. The INLA have done nothing about it. I want to avenge his death and I think I could do a better job if I was in the Provies."

McNally looked at me appraisingly. "All right, I'll put your name forward at the next meeting, but I'm not promising anything. Come and see me again in a week's time."

A week later, I went back to see Shorty. He asked if I knew any of the history of the 'RA, which I did not.

"Do you fancy learning about it then?"

I expressed great interest in the idea.

"You went to St Peter's School, didn't you, Ray? Then you'll known Padraig Mullane. Go and see him at the school tonight at seven o'clock. He'll give you the Green Book to read and teach you about anti-interrogation techniques, something much more useful than you've ever learned in school."

Mullane had been a supply teacher when I was at school, filling in for teachers when they were ill. He'd taken me for PE a couple of times and I knew he had Republican views, but I'd never thought of him as an IRA member. I walked over to the school that night and found Mullane in the Youth Club, playing pool with a few of the boys. He put down his cue when he saw me, shook my hand and led me out of the room and down the corridor to a store-room between the two science labs. Inside the store, Mullane handed me a soft-backed book with a blue cover.

"This is the Green Book."

"But it's got a blue cover."

"Yes, but it's known as the Green Book. I want you to sit down and read it."

He closed the door and left me alone in the store-room. The Green Book turned out to be a partial history of Ireland since the time of the Vikings and the English conquest, combined with the dry-as-dust statement of the IRA's constitution, objectives rules and disciplinary procedures. Try as I might, I couldn't get particularly inspired by the interminable rules and regulations of the IRA, though part of it, dealing with the punishment for informers, certainly captured my attention.

After interrogation and court martial, the informer would be taken to a place of execution. He would be made to kneel, with a black cloth hood placed over his head and his hands tied behind his back, and would then be shot through the back of the head. The dry phrasing did not do full justice to what would happen, for I knew that interrogation would embrace torture of the most savage kind, and that the place of execution would be a back street in Derry or a ditch at the side of a country road.

I hastily turned the page and sat there for an hour or so, leafing idly through the rest of the book and looking at the pictures. Finally, I went in search of Mullane.

"I've read it," I said, handed it to him.

He looked at me skeptically. "Come back the same time the day after tomorrow and read some more. I want you to read it carefully, because you'll be questioned on it."

In the end I made six visits to the school, always sitting in the same store-room with the Green Book, like a monk cloistered with the Bible. To my relief, on the sixth occasion, in the last week of October 1980, Mullane interrupted my half-hearted study of the Green Book and began to lecture me in what was expected of me in the IRA.

"The first thing I have to tell you is a harsh one, but it must be said. The likelihood is that by joining the Provisional IRA, you are taking a path that may well lead to prison and could even end in your death. That is the level of commitment that you are required to make. If it's too high a price for you to pay, now is the time to say so."

He let the silence grow for a minute, but I raised my eyes and gave him a level stare, saying nothing.

"Good enough," he said, nodding to himself, as if mentally ticking off the points he had to raise.

"Commitment also means other things. You'll have to go on training camps and take part in ambushes of police and soldiers. How do you feel about killing people for the organisation?"

"If I have to do it, I will do it."

"Good man. Now there is a few more things."

I nodded, listlessly turning the pages of the Green Book.

"Pay attention, these are important," Mullane said sharply.

I hastily closed the book and sat upright, like a naughty child caught skiving off in class.

"When you fire a weapon or detonate a bomb, it can take the army as little as two minutes to seal the area. You've got to be away well inside that time. If you've been handling weapons or using them on a job, don't assume that you're safe just because you've got the guns away to the dump and got rid of the getaway car. You've got to change your clothes and give yourself and your clothes a good wash straight away to get rid of the forensics.

"Never talk loosely and be constantly on your guard and on the lookout. Don't assume that you are out of sight of the army or the peelers at any time. Keep a particularly close eye on empty or derelict buildings. The army often use boarded-up shops or bricked-up houses as temporary observation posts. An army unit, or even a single soldier, moves in at night, with enough food to last several days. They take a brick out of the wall or a slate off the roof to give them a view of the area and set up listening devices and cameras. If you're down at the Creggan shops there's every chance that there's more than your mates listening to your conversation, and if you don't watch your tongue, you'll be on their files...always assuming you aren't already."

I shot him a sideways glance, looking for any undertone to his last remark, but he was already off on the next part of the lecture.

"Keep well away from Republican marches and protests, so you don't become known to the security forces. To keep yourself safe, you should also stay away from the Rocking Chair Bar. I go there regularly and you hear lots of volunteers loose-talking about jobs they've done. On many occasions I've had to report them to Brigade staff when I've heard them slabbering away through drink. Be especially careful if ever you've been on a shooting or a bombing job. If you go into a pub after the job, never show any give-away signs. Don't be getting the staff to switch on the TV or the radio so that you can listen to reports about the job, just be cool, discrete and professional.

"The same applies if you get lifted by the RUC. Keep you cool and don't get excited. When you're being interviewed by detectives, think of yourself as being above them. Imagine them walking about in the nude or covered in shit. If you feel like standing on your head, or sitting on the floor, just do it. When you are being interviewed, pick out some object in the room or a spot on the wall and concentrate on it. Say nothing at all, don't even give them your name. Pay careful attention to the questions you're asked, though, because you'll be debriefed by us when you're released and the interrogator may have given things away by the questions he asked."

"What things?"

"He may get cocky and let slip information that can only have come from a tout. We caught one guy who was touting just because of one little slip. He always mispronounced the name of one of the other members of his unit. When one of the other guys was lifted by the peelers, the interrogator mispronounced the guy's name in exactly the same way. When yer man was interrogated, he cracked and confessed. We wouldn't have caught him if it hadn't been for that one little slip."

"All right. That's all I can tell you. Go and see Shorty McNally tomorrow evening about seven. He may want to ask you some questions on the Green Book."

Luckily Shorty had no questions for me when I reached his house, on the Green Book or anything else. He simply sent me to meet a man called Paul Cleary in the grounds of St Mary's Church, where I'd worked as a boy, counting the money from the collection envelopes on Sunday mornings. The chapel stood on a mound beside St Mary's School for girls, giving it a view over the graveyard and right down the Creggan Hill to the Bogside. The chapel grounds had been tarmacked, but outside the blue iron railings was a green with a few trees flagging the path to the Creggan shops. At night it was a very quiet place, with no one around at all.

I stood outside the door of the Chapel for 5 minutes and then a man in a black coat, in his late thirties and running to fat, approached me.

"You Gilmour?"

I nodded.

"Let's go round the side, it's too conspicuous here."

We walked up and down the chapel grounds for half an hour as he questioned me searchingly about my motives for joining the Provies. Finally he stopped pacing and turned to face me, staring into my eyes as he spoke.

"We don't usually let ex-IRSP's [ex-INLA members] into the Provies. I don't trust them myself. I'll be frank with you, if it was up to me, you wouldn't be joining the Provies."

He stared balefully at me for a few moments. I stared back as unemotionally as I could. He shrugged his shoulders, spat and carried on. "You'll be required to attend at least two meetings of your unit each week. If you don't attend regularly you'll be kicked out of the organisation. Meet me at Shorty McNally's house at noon tomorrow to be sworn in."

He turned on his heel and left without even a goodnight.

At noon the next day, I knocked on Shorty's door. He showed me into the living room, where Cleary was already waiting.

"Do you still want to join the Provisional IRA?" Shorty asked.

"I do."

"It will not be easy. A lot will be expected of you and you will have to be prepared to dedicate all your time to the cause."

"I'm prepared to do that."

He nodded and he and Cleary stood up, put on their coats and buttoned them up. Shorty told me to do the same, stand to attention, raise my right hand and repeat after him an oath of loyalty to *Oglaigh na h'Eireann* - the Provisional IRA. When I had done so, he shook my hand and said, "Welcome to the Provisional IRA. Meet me outside McCann's fish and chip shop in the Lecky Road at seven tomorrow night and I'll take you to meet the other members of your unit."

Cleary said nothing and made no attempt to shake my hand, merely scowling at me. The reason I'd been taken in, despite Cleary's obvious objections, was probably that they saw me as a very low security risk. After being deeply penetrated by army and police intelligence they were trying to start off a completely unknown unit, and given my family history, I would be the last person the police or army would expect to be an IRA member. Just the same, I was watched very closely in my first few months as a member. I was careful to keep my nose clean and do nothing to alert anyone's suspicions, using the tradecraft that Pete had taught me to ensure that I wasn't being watched or followed when I went to meet him or even phone him.

Shorty was already standing outside McCann's when I got there the next evening, wearing his customary brown duffel-coat and puffing on his pipe, with his back to the flood of yellow light spilling from the big plate-glass window.

"Don't walk with me," said Shorty, "I'm too well known. Follow about ten yards behind me."

I trailed him along the Lecky Road. After ten minutes of walking, he glanced around him and then went in through a wooden gate and up to the back door of a house in the middle of a terrace. Shorty entered without knocking and, following him in, I found myself in a kitchen, staring at four other people sitting around a table. They looked back at me with some curiosity.

They were obviously to be my comrades-in-arms and I studied them all closely as Shorty made the introductions. He named them only as Eddie, Brendan, Pat and Mary, but I soon got to know their full names.

Eddie McSheffrey, from Donagh Place, was the Cell Leader and an Explosives Officer, responsible for making, placing and detonating bombs. With others, it might have been just a job or a means to an end, but for Eddie it was a passion. He loved bombs and big bangs, but never seemed too bothered about what he blew up or who was injured in the process.

He was balding, with a small moustache, and only about five foot one. He looked even smaller, for he always walked with his head hunched down between his shoulders, as if expecting a crack in the back of the neck at any moment.

Eddie's father was an IRA stalwart who had done a lot of years in prison. He might even have had to do a few more, but his wife went up to the Home Secretary during an official visit to the Brandywell and said, "Would you let my husband out? He's innocent." The Home Secretary asked her name and, astonishingly, a week afterwards Eddie's dad was released.

Brendan McDermott, from Meenan Park, was tall and powerfully built. I recognised him at once, for I'd often seen him down at Andy's Gym, where I used to go to work out. He was into karate and body-building and loved a fight. I often felt that he would rather have taken on the Brits with his bare hands than with guns. He worked as a bouncer at Oscar's night-club and he'd also done a fair bit of time.

Pat McHugh, from Abbots Walk, was a little shorter than Brendan and very thin and wiry. He had dirty fair hair, a big nose and an evil glint in his eye. He later told me that he'd already been involved in several murders, but he'd been drinking heavily when he broke the news, so only McHugh and his God know if it was true.

Mary Cobbe, from Rinmore Drive in the Creggan, was a plump, pretty, blonde-haired sixteen-year-old. She come up through *Cumann na mBann*, the female wing of the Provies. They'd traditionally had been used only as couriers to move guns and bombs around or as cover for IRA men on active service overseas, when a honeymoon couple would arouse far less suspicion than a lone man.

Mary had been an active IRA volunteer since she was just fourteen, joining as the Provies were finally allowing women to take their place in the front-line. Like a few other girls, she'd initially been used as the bate in honey-traps, using the promise of sex to lure off-duty British soldiers to their deaths.

Now she made no use of her sex, never wearing make-up and always dressing in a shapeless camel-haired duffel-coat – perhaps stressing her position as an equal member of the unit and a better shot than all the men. Pete had described her to me as a loose cannon, whose enthusiasm for killing often effected her judgement.

Shorty completed the introductions, then turned to me. "This is your cell – the Brandywell Unit – and you'll be working with these people from now on. We meet once or twice a week in this house. We use first names only, for security reasons, and for the same reason you are unlikely to get to know the members of any other units."

In this he was over-optimistic. The cell structure worked to an extent, but we gradually got to know people from other active service units as they were drafted in for different jobs.

Shorty also warned me and the other members of the cell not to "go around blabbing about yourselves and giving yourselves away as 'RA volunteers," but even if we were as tight-lipped as Trappists on a day-trip, people were not stupid. When they saw you going around with guys like Eddie McSheffrey, they knew exactly what you were involved in.

IRA volunteers would feel confident enough to talk very freely in the local pubs, if they kept their voices low and kept an eye on who was around them, but if a stranger walked in, it would be like a gun slinger walking into the saloon in a Holywood Western. We'd all gone to the same schools and knew all the faces. If anyone strange came in, we knew straight away. All the conversation would stop and every eye in the room would be on him. If he was English, he'd be taken away and interrogated until they found out who he was and what he was doing. After that, unless he had a particularly convincing reason for being there, he'd be killed. Even if the stranger was Irish, if anyone had the least suspicion about him he'd still be taken away and questioned.

As well as the rules and our personal conduct, Shorty also told us to be constantly on the look-out for potential targets and money jobs – banks, security vans and so on. Then he favoured us with a smile and sat down as Eddie took over. He showed me how to drill and fall-in, a ritual that opened and closed every IRA meeting.

After my private tuition, Eddie told us all to button up our coats and fall in. We stood to attention in two rows, with our hands behind our backs and our feet widely spaced. At a command from Eddie – in Irish, which I never understood, but it sounded like "Asuckra" – we hitched our hands a bit higher up our backs. It was always to make me smile to myself, for it was as if we were coming to attention while wearing a pair of handcuffs behind our backs. He then said something else in Irish and we would bring our hands down to our sides, bring our feet together, turn to the right and fall out.

The meeting followed a pattern that was soon to be familiar. There was no rhetoric, no impassioned political speeches, no general discussion at all, just "what's the next job and when's it going to get done?" We might have been the board of small engineering company, discussing pending contracts.

The company rules were strict: no careless talk, not too much drinking, definitely no drugs and no thieving, except on behalf of the IRA. They were not bothered about crime committed in the Protestant areas over in the Waterside, but on their own turf, in areas like the Creggan and the Bogside, they were ruthless.

The first item on the agenda for the meeting was Eddie's plan to plant a bomb to blow up the army sanger – an observation post, fortified with sand bags and half-inch steel-plate - on top of the Rossville Flats. Army observers, using high-powered binoculars and infra-red night-sights, constantly scanned the surrounding streets from the sanger, reporting on suspicious activities in the movements of known IRA activists.

"I need some gelly, Shorty," said Eddie.

"Don't worry, I'll get you some stuff."

At this meeting, as at all the others I would attend, I kept Pete's advice in mind and stayed in the background, listening and being supportive, but without much input. At the same time, I made myself as friendly with the other people in my unit as I possibly could, trying to give them the feeling: Ray's there is you need him. You're safe with him, he'll be beside you, he won't do anything to put you wrong."

Pat McHugh said even less than me at the first meeting, but I discovered afterwards that he didn't trust new members and was weighing me up very carefully.

While Shorty and Eddie were sorting out their gelignite requirements, the last member of the unit, Jimmy Costello, came in. He'd been looking after his children until his wife got in from work. It was one of the many of the jarring incongruities in the Provisional Irish Republican Army. Bombings, assassinations and masked murders would be planned, but only after the baby-sitting had been done, or one of the unit had popped down to the shops for a pound of onions and a packet of fags.

It was agreed to carry out the job as soon as Shorty had procured the gelignite for the bomb and the meeting ended. The next one I attended, the following week, was even more cursory. Shorty, Pat McHugh, Mary Cobbe and I were the only ones present.

"Meet Eddie at the safe house in Chamberlain Street," said Shorty. "The job's on for tonight."

By the time we reached the safe house, the other members of our unit were already there. Gerard Conlow, the owner of the house, opened the door to us and led us down to the hall, past a small cabinet in which his wife kept mass cards for sale to local people. We passed two other IRA volunteers, Louise Halligan and Patsy Duggan, in the hall. They had been to pick up the bell-wire – the command wire for the bomb – from the unit's weapons dump in Lone Moor Gardens and were just about to leave.

Gerard showed us into the front room, where Jimmy Costello and Eddie McSheffrey were lounging on the couch. Vic O'Grady, the Derry Brigade's Explosive Officer, was on his hands and knees on the floor, wearing pink rubber household gloves as he connected wires to an Ever-Ready battery. Alongside him on the floor lay a blue-checked duffel-bag containing a gas cylinder about nine inches in length. It was packed with explosive and sealed with black tape.

"What's the crack?" I asked.

"That's a bomb," said Eddie, superfluously.

His work finished, O'Grady put the bell wire and the battery into the duffel-bag with the bomb and straightened up.

Pat McHugh picked up the bag and carried it out of the house. He and Eddie took it in turns to carry it, while the rest of us stagged them over to the Rosville Flats. We went up to the eighth floor at the top of the flats, underneath the army sanger on the roof.

Eddie told me and Mary, "Keep dick for peelers and Brits."

We stood close together on the balcony by the stairwell, kissing and fooling around like a courting couple as we kept a look-out for army or police and blocked the view down the landing for anyone in the sanger. Eddie went through a window and climbed up onto the roof. Jimmy then passed the duffel-bag up to him.

After a few minutes Eddie reappeared. "It needs to be higher and I can't reach. We need to get something to raise it up a bit."

Eddie and Jimmy went down to the Rocking Chair Bar and came back a few minutes later with a bar stool which they'd either begged or stolen. Eddie climbed back up on to the roof and Jimmy passed the stool up to him. Once he had it in place, Eddie was to prime the bomb and then pass the bell-wire to Jimmy, who would feed it down the refuse chute to Vic, waiting patiently on the fifth floor.

A couple of minutes later, Eddie came back down from the roof and hurried down the stairs, leaving Mary and I as look-outs, making sure there were no passers-by when the bomb was detonated, for we didn't want anyone hurt by falling debris. We waved to Pat on the fifth floor to show him that all was clear and stood back to await the bang.

Nothing happened. After a long pause, we went down to the fifth floor, where I could hear Vic O'Grady's voice. "It's very old wire, there must be a break in it; either that or the battery's dead."

Eddie returned to the roof to try and get the bomb back, but couldn't remove it. Finally he gave up and said he'd go back for it later. We split up and headed for home. The bomb was up there for a few days, during which Pete arranged for it to be made harmless, but about a month later, another bomb did go off at the Rossville sanger. Pat McHugh told me that Eddie had planted it.

It was to be an oft-repeated pattern. No matter how often jobs planned by the unit were abandoned or aborted, they would be resurrected and tried over and over again. Eddie McSheffrey in particular was like a terrier. Some of his planned jobs would keep recurring over weeks, months and in some cases, years, until finally they were successful.

CHAPTER 6

The Derry Provies closed down for Christmas, just like any other business, but the unit quickly got back to work in the New Year. Early in January 1981, Eddie McSheffrey came to see me and told me that there was a meeting at a house in Southend Park, down near the Brandywell Cattle Mart.

At eight o'clock I knocked on the door, and a girl no more than twelve years old opened it. I hesitated, surprised, but the girl ushered me in and led me to the front room, where her parents, Michael and Rose Flynn, were huddled by the coal fire watching a black and white television.

Michael, a short stocky man in his early thirties, with a thatch of curly fair hair, stood up, shook my hand and told me to sit down while I waited for the others. As I did, I practically disappeared through the brown tweed sofa's tangle of broken springs and sprouting stuffing. The sofa smelt musty and felt damp, which was not surprising for the walls of the room were black with mold. Even with the fire burning, the cold chilled me to the bone.

I chatted to the couple for a few minutes as Eddie, Mary, Jimmy, Brendan and Pat appeared one by one, each shown in by the girl. When we were all assembled, Eddie led us down a damp, filthy hallway and into the kitchen, furnished only with a cooker, a sink, a table and two wooden benches. The walls had been lined with polystyrene, but it was a vane attempt to hold back the damp, for strips of yellowing wallpaper hung from the ceiling and trailed down the walls. We sat at the benches around the table, its formica top chipped, scratched and smeared with grease.

After performing the customary ritual of buttoning our coats and falling in, Eddie, as usual, had a plan – a shoot at the security forces from Magee College.

"It'll have to be army though, we've no armour-piercing bullets to get through the armour on the police Land Rovers."

The plan was quickly agreed, and as the meeting ended, Eddie turned to me and said, "We'll take you up to the arms dump now and give you a run over the weapons."

Eddie, Mary and Pat took me over to the dump, hidden in Stephen Fegan's grey, brick bungalow in Lone Moor Gardens. The house was in darkness and the glass in the front door was broken. Pat opened the door and led me through to the kitchen. Eddie and Pat pulled the cooker away from the wall, rolled back the brown oilcloth and lifted some green plastic tiles to expose the concrete floor. I stared at it curiously; there was no sign to show that anything was hidden beneath it.

Mary had meanwhile opened the kitchen cupboard and taken an iron bolt from a yellow plastic cutlery tray. She went to the back door, unlocked it and fetched a rusty iron handle from under a broken bucket in the back yard. She handed the bits of iron to Pat, who slotted the bolt through the handle and then screwed it into a hole in the concrete floor. Grunting with the effort, he pulled out a square block of concrete, revealing a hole about two feet across. I stepped to the edge and looked down on to the barrels of several rifles.

Eddie lifted a couple out of the hole and led me to the bathroom off the kitchen.

"It's safer in here – frosted windows," he said. "If anyone's snooping outside, they'll see nothing. Right. This one is a Armalite."

He handed me a small, surprisingly light rifle with a black plastic stock, and went over the finer points, like a used-car salesman trying to clinch a deal.

"It's Japanese, made as a copy of the American M16, and like most of the stuff the Japs copy, it's better than the original. Feel how light it is? It only weighs seven pounds, and with the stock folded down its less than thirty inches long, so it'll easily fit inside your coat. It's very high velocity, which in layman's terms means it's got a fuck of a lot of killing power."

He let me get the feel of it for a few moments, then took it back and handed me the other rifle, a much bigger and heavier weapon. "This is a Woodmaster rifle, with a telescopic sight. It's very accurate and bloody powerful – it'll blow your head off from half a mile away."

He pointed out the safety catch behind the trigger guard and showed me how to fit the magazine and take it off, and how to cock the rifle by pulling back the cocking handle.

He handed the rifle to me and I pointed it at the window and pulled the trigger. There was a dull, metallic click. Eddie snatched the Woodmaster from me. "Always check the rifle to see if it is unloaded when it's handed to you; never trust anyone who tells you it's unloaded. Always point it in a safe direction and never point it at anyone you are not aiming to kill."

He gave it back to me let me handle it for a few minutes, getting the feel of it, then he wiped off our fingerprints with a piece of soft cloth and put it back in the dump.

While Eddie and Pat closed the dump and replaced the cooker, Mary put the bolt and the iron handle back in their hiding places. Then we all filed out of the door and went for a pint.

I bought the first round and then, to further ingratiate myself, applied a bit of flattery to Eddie. "You certainly know your weapons, Eddie."

He smiled modestly. "Ah, but bombs are my first love."

His eyes took on a far away look. "You know how people always go on about their first fuck? Well, my first bomb was almost as good as that. There was no shortage of gelly then for jobs, and this bomb was a big fucker, a hundred-pounder. We laid it in a drain and ran the bell-wire up the hedge. We'd been there about an hour when an army Land Rover came along. I detonated it right on the money and there was the biggest fucking bang you've ever heard in your life.

"I ducked down instinctively when I hit the switch, and it was just as well, for I could hear bits of shrapnel flying straight over the top of where my head had been. When I stuck my head up again the Land Rover had fucking disappeared. There was just this hole in the ground big enough to bury an elephant."

I began to feel very ill as he went through the corpses, one by one.

"There were bits of Brit all over the place," he said with relish. "I'll swear there was a pair of bollocks hanging on a tree branch just behind me. The engine block had come down square in the chest of one of them, so he wasn't going anywhere. There was this sort of pink froth coming out from his chest, round the edge of the engine block. It looked like strawberry milkshake, though I wouldn't have fancied drinking it."

He laughed and slurped noisily at his pint, making me feel even worse.

"There wasn't enough left of the rest of them to fill a matchbox. The only way you'd have picked them up would've been with a palette knife and a bucket. But do you know the strangest thing of all, Ray?"

He looked up when I didn't reply for a moment, took in my pale green complexion and said, "You all right?"

I nodded my head feebly, wondering how much longer I could keep from throwing up. "Just about. I had a pie for my dinner and I think it was off."

He gave me a sympathetic look and then ploughed on regardless. "Anyway, one of them was spreadeagled on the ground not fifty yards from where I was standing. He was dead as a hammer, but lying there with not a mark on him."

He waited expectantly, but I was unable to take my cue. "Do you know how I knew there wasn't a mark on him?"

I shook my head, swallowing repeatedly, my mouth dry and my forehead drenched in cold sweat.

"He was bollock-naked," he said triumphantly. "The blast had ripped the clothes right off him."

The punchline was innocuous enough after what had gone before, but I was already beyond recall. I ran for the toilet and puked my guts up. When I came out a few minutes later, wiping my mouth, Eddie winked and said, "That'll sort it, Ray. Now, I've got you another pint…"

I gradually recovered and we had a fair skinful before we went home. I waved them off into the night, full of beery bonhomie, then waited in the shadows for a few minutes, taking stock of the evening. If I'd been amused, as usual, by the clumsy *Dad's Army* drill before the meeting, I was impressed by the skill with which the arms dump had been concealed. Eddie's bomb-lust had caught me by surprise, but I was sure he'd taken my story about the pie for the truth and hadn't connected my squeamishness with his stories.

I phoned Pete before I went home and told him about the dump.

"That's great, Ray, I like a nice bit of craftsmanship myself. I'm looking forward to seeing it, when we can find a convenient moment that won't point the finger at you. So… just a moment."

He put his hand over the phone while he spoke to someone else, and when he came back to me, the relaxed tone was gone. "Ray, something's come up, but well done, that was good work. I'll see there's a decent bonus for you."

The bonuses helped to make life a little easier, and despite my being out several nights a week on IRA business, Lorraine and I remained generally very happy. We had our moments, however, particularly when I was working as a roadie for the Diamond Showband a few nights a week, setting up the equipment and moving it from one venue to another.

I enjoyed the work but Lorraine hated me doing it, fearing that groupies would be throwing themselves at me. She'd sometimes chase me down the road, trying to get me to come home.

I told her, "It's a poxy showband, not the bloody Rolling Stones," but she remained deeply suspicious and there'd be furious rows if I came home late, with drink on my breath.

She probably preferred me to be out with the IRA rather than the band, because she knew that if I was out with the Provies, at least I wouldn't be shagging anybody. But the subject of the IRA was never discussed at home. Lorraine must have guessed that the shadowy figures who came to call for me weren't collecting for charity, but she never asked me any questions and I never told her anything.

I couldn't tell her the real reason for my involvement and I didn't want to tell her any lies. It was another added stress in a job that was already stressful enough; I had the first of my four stomach ulcers removed not long after joining the IRA.

If she'd begged me not to go out with the Provies, it would have made things impossible for me, for it was already hard enough to leave Lorraine and the kids to go out on jobs that I knew could end in my death. Every time I shut the front door, I would think, is this the one that's going to get me killed? What would become of my family? But the thought of the £200 pay cheque from the RUC at the end of the week was enough to keep me going. We needed the money desperately, for if I didn't get it, there would be no food in the cupboards and no treats for the kids.

If my work as an agent went wrong, I knew that I'd die and my children would face destitution, but while my luck held, it also enabled me to give them a far better start in life than I'd ever had, or any of my peers could offer their children. If I never got involved with Pete and the Special Branch, I would have become like most of the other guys around the Creggan, eking out a bare existence on the dole until the day I died. I couldn't have moved away, because of my family and without money you can't move.

Apart from pinpointing the IRA's caches of weapons and explosives, my most important function for the Special Branch was giving them advanced warning of planned IRA jobs. Sometimes an ambush would be laid for the IRA Unit, but quite often the information was used simply to keep troops and police away from the danger area on the nights that the jobs were scheduled.

Most jobs were first discussed at meetings and then carried out a few days later, giving me ample time to let Pete know what was planned. I would then share in the general surprise in our unit when the army or police patrols that always went by one route suddenly took a different route on that particular night.

Sometimes jobs would be carried out on the night of the meeting, however, which made it impossible to warn Pete. On those occasions I'd tried to sabotage the job myself, if it was possible to do so without blowing my cover.

There was also a strict rule that if you weren't at the meeting of your unit at which a job was planned, you weren't told anything about it. If you were needed to help with the job, you would only be given details as you set off to carry it out.

I fell foul of that rule after skipping a meeting. Shorty wasn't around, for he was across the border doing something and I assumed that nothing much would be going on. I took the chance for a night out with Lorraine and told Mary, "If anything comes up, you can contact me at Parke's mobile shop in Benevenagh Gardens about eleven tonight."

She turned up there and told me, "There's a job on for tomorrow night, we're meeting at Southend Park at eight-thirty."

"What job's that?" I asked hopefully.

She gave me a withering look. "You know better than that, Ray. You weren't at the meeting, so I can't tell you."

I smiled weakly "Sorry, I forgot."

I arrived a few minutes late the following night. Brendan, Pat and Mary were already there. In my absence the previous night, they'd decided to have a go at Eddie's Magee College job. We were to shoot soldiers from the grounds of the College as they drove along the Strand Road down to Fort George.

Mary had already collected the Colt.38 for the hijack from the arms dump. She handed it to Pat and went back to the dump to get the arms ready for the shoot, while we set off to find a car. It was freezing cold and snowing hard as we headed over to the car park of the Camelot Bar, each clutching our green balaclava masks. We got there at about nine o'clock and stood shivering in the cold, waiting for a four-door car to be driven in.

It had to be four-door, because in the aftermath of the shooting, the extra couple of seconds it takes to get everyone into a two-door car could make a difference between escape and capture ... or death. A succession of two-door cars came and went as we stood there for over an hour without a sniff of a four-door one. Finally, just as we were all getting ready to pack it all in and go home, a red Datsun estate pulled into the car park.

We put on our face masks and walked over, Pat carrying the .38. There were two people in the car. John Devine from Rathlin Drive was in the passenger seat and his brother-in-law was driving.

"Provisional IRA. We want your car," Pat said.

The driver wouldn't hand over the keys at first. "Boys, could you not get another car?"

"No, we're taking yours."

After a bit of an argument, he eventually handed over the keys, without Pat even having to produce the gun.

"Right. Go and sit in the bar and stay there until we get back, and don't report it to the Police – the bar will be watched."

That wasn't true, we had no one spare to watch the bar, but they weren't to know that.

We waited until the two men had gone into the bar before driving off up the Letterkenny Road.

When we got into the dump, Mary and another woman, Clare Bristow, had the Woodmaster and a Armalite loaded and ready on the kitchen floor. Pat picked up the Woodmaster, took off the magazine and checked the breech, while Brendan checked the Armalite. Brendan clipped on two magazines, bound together with blue electrician's tape. The larger held thirty rounds, the smaller ten. They put the guns in the back of the Datsun and we set off, leaving Mary gazing wistfully after us, for she hated to miss a chance of a shoot.

The main roads were clear, but as Brendan navigated me up the Rock Road and through the grounds of the College, we were slipping and sliding on the ice and slush. I turned down a steep hill and Brendan then told me to reverse down a narrow lane that leads out on to the Strand Road. I stopped the car about a hundred yards from the junction at Strand Road and Brendan and Pat got out.

"When you hear the shots," Brendan said, "reverse the car down the hill a bit further so that we can be quicker away."

He and Pat disappeared into the darkness. I turned off the engine and waited. There was total silence, more nerve-wracking than any unexplained sounds, and the thick canopy of trees and heavy cloud cover prevented even the faintest glimmer of light reaching me. It began to rain, at first gently, then building into a downpour.

Having been unable to warn Pete in advance, I was desperate to sabotage the job, fearing that someone would stray into the trap and be killed, but I could think of no convincing reason for recalling Pat and Brendan without alerting their suspicions. I waited in the darkness, straining my ears for the sound of a vehicle on the Strand Road and dreading the gunfire that might follow. Then, above the sound of rain drumming off the roof, I thought I heard the College gates up on Rock Road being closed. It was the only gateway open, for the Northland Road and Strand Road gates were permanently shut.

I started the engine and drove up the hill to see if I could see the gates, but in the darkness and the torrential rain I could see nothing. I didn't dare risk using my lights. As I reversed back down the hill, I decided to make absolutely sure that the job was called off and let the car drift onto the snow, slush and mud on the verge. When it slithered to a halt, I span the wheels furiously, leaving the car well and truly stuck.

I got out and ran down the hill towards the road, calling in a low but urgent voice. Brendan appeared suddenly out of the darkness whispering, "What the fuck's the matter?"

"I think I heard them shutting the gates up on Rock Road and I've got the car stuck in the mud."

"For fuck's sake, Ray."

"I couldn't help it, I couldn't see a fucking thing in this darkness."

Brendan called off the job, and he and Pat came up to help me move the car, angrily throwing the rifles into the boot. I put the two rubber mats from the floor-wells under the back wheels and then Pat and Brendan pushed when I revved it up. They were swearing their heads off as the spinning wheels covered them in mud from head to foot, and were in a foul mood by the time we got it free.

When we got to the gates, they were closed, and we had to reverse back to the door of the College. Brendan got out and fetched the night watchman, a small grey man in an ill-fitting uniform, peering myopically out from behind pebble glasses. He muttered about protecting the College from vandalism before finally unlocking the gates.

When we got back to the dump at Lone Moor Gardens, Mary came running to the door, full of excitement, but went back inside crestfallen when she heard that the job had been called off without even a sight of the army. Pat and Brendan rubbed the rifles down and put them back in the dump while I drove back up towards the Camelot Bar to return the car. Half-way there I saw John Devine and his brother-in-law trudging along at the side of the road. I stopped short of them and put my hand over my face, because I'd left my mask at the dump, then got out and walked away, leaving the door of the car wide open.

We tried three or four more times at Magee College, but each time I was able to inform Pete and they just sent the armour-plated police jeeps through instead. Eventually McDermott and McHugh got so frustrated with the situation that they decided to have a pop at them anyway. One of the policemen got a bloody nose, but that was about it.

McDermott and McHugh never knew how lucky they'd been. Pete later told me that every other time we'd been there, the SAS were lying in wait for us. If anyone had fired a single shot, the SAS would have killed the lot of them.

Sometimes my sabotage of IRA jobs took an even more direct form. At one point Eddie asked me to look after two home-made hand-grenades. They were frighteningly big – about ten inches long and four or five inches in diameter – made of thick galvanized pipe, heavily-scored like the skin of a pineapple. They were sprayed green, and had black plastic caps. I shoved them in the attic and phoned Pete, he told me to bring them down to the Waterside so that he could get them doctored.

I laughed. "If I walk down there with these things I'll be stopped and arrested – if they don't shoot me first."

"Don't worry, I'll sort it out so you aren't stopped."

I got the grenades out of the attic, went down to town and across to the Waterside, and handed them to Pete, who was waiting in his car. Two guys were with him and they took the grenades away.

"What do we do now?" I asked.

"We wait."

"Here? What if I'm spotted?"

"We'll drive around. Lie down on the seat and hide your face."

He was in radio contact with the bomb-disposal guys all the time, but we were driving around for over an hour, with me still lying face down on the seat, before he got word that they'd finished. When they collected the grenades, they looked untouched, but as I examined them closely, I could see that the tops had been tampered with.

On the way back, we were stopped by a police patrol on the bridge. Pete showed them his badge and drove on, while I lay face down on the seat. He dropped me off back at the fountain in the centre of the Diamond and I went home and put the grenades in the attic. About a week later, a couple of members of the unit took the grenades down to Rosemount police station and threw them over the wall, but nothing happened. At the next meeting, I joined in the cursing of the incompetence of the bomb-makers who had put them together.

Although I was privately delighted every time I sabotaged an IRA job, I was well aware that the more successful I was, the quicker I would seal my own fate. My success would both alert the Provies to the fact that they had been penetrated and also indicate the source of the leak.

It was like a game of Russian roulette. However carefully I tried to cover my tracks, each time I sabotaged a job or tipped off the Police, I was holding a gun to my head and pulling the trigger. The longer the game went on, the worse the odds became. Finally I would reach the point where there was only one chamber left – a loaded one which would kill me.

What kept me going, apart from the money, was the knowledge that I was saving lives. If all the operations in which I had been involved had come off, there would have been not just a few, or even tens, but hundreds of people dead. I can't claim all the credit, however. Even without my intervention, many operations were called off because of defective equipment or shortages of explosives and ammunition. Many more failed through bad intelligence, bad timing or sometimes just plain bad luck.

All these factors helped me to operate undetected as an agent for so long, but if there were times when nothing seemed to go right for the Derry Provies, there were others when their luck was in and they proved to be ruthlessly efficient and devastatingly effective. January 1981 was one of those months. It was a very successful time for the Brandywell unit in particular, but that made it a black month for me.

At a meeting at Southend Park a few days after the aborted Magee College job, Eddie proposed another ambush, this time on the Lone Moor Road.

"We've got some armour-piercing bullets now, so police or army, whatever comes down that road – short of a Sherman tank – will be blown away." He give a short, barking laugh.

Mary looked excitedly from one to the other of us; as usual, her eagerness to get started on the killing was only too obvious.

At the end of the meeting, Brendan and Eddie walked over to the dump at Lone Moor Gardens to get the guns ready while Pat, Mary and I went to hijack a car. For once the hijack went like clockwork. Pat and I left Mary at McCann's fish shop in the Lecky Road while we went to a nearby flat on the Bogside to phone Bradley's taxis in Chamberlain Street. We book a cab to come to McCann's then hurried back.

Five minutes later, a taxi – a black Ford Granada - pulled up. Pat and I put on our green balaclavas and walked over to the driver's door. As I opened it, Pat pointed a .38 at the driver. "We want your fucking car."

The driver went white with fright and sat there staring ahead, not speaking.

"Get out of the car," Pat said.

He shot a terrified look at Pat, fearing he was about to be shot, then scrambled out of the car and stood trembling at the side of the road. We marched him to the narrow laneway beside McCann's. It was as black as your hat in there, but I put a balaclava over the taxi-driver's head anyway, back to front, to be sure he couldn't see anything.

Pat gave Mary the gun. "Watch him. If he gives you any trouble, shoot him. When you hear us firing that'll be the signal to let him go."

Pat and I peeled off our masks and walked back up to the taxi. I drove us down to Lone Moor Gardens, turning it around in the cramped cul-de-sac and parking it outside the house.

Eddie and Brendan already had the guns out of the dump ready for the shoot. The original plan had been for just Eddie and Brendan to do the firing, but Pat kept pestering Eddie to let him shoot too. In the end Eddie relented. "All right, for Christ's sake. You can have the smaller Woodmaster, if you can get it to work. Last time I used it, the fucker jammed on me."

Eddie handed him one of the Woodmasters and kept the other himself. Brendan had the Armalite. The three of them masked up and then padded off in single file, down the cul-de-sac and into a little laneway leading on to the Lone Moor Road.

I reversed the car down to the end and sat there waiting in the darkness. After ten minutes or so a pair of headlights stabbed through the night as a car turned into the Gardens. I hunched down instinctively behind the wheel, but the car stopped at the end and after a moment a woman got out, blew a kiss to the driver and disappeared into one of the houses. The car reversed out and drove off.

The minutes ticked by agonisingly slowly. I was alert to every sound and every flicker of movement, but the only things on the street were two tom cats, circling each other warily before launching into a spitting, snarling fight.

I sat there for another three-quarters of an hour before there was a sudden burst of gunfire – at least seven and maybe as many as ten shots. As the last echoes died away, Eddie, Brendan and Pat came sprinting past me. I started the engine and drove along side them. As they reached the gateway of number 15, Eddie and Brendan dumped their weapons on the ground and leapt into the car. As Pat scooped the guns up and ran into the house to hide them in the dump, I could hear him grumbling about his rifle, "Useless piece of shit." As Eddie had predicted, it had jammed.

I shot off up Southway, screeching the tyres as I pulled a right-hander into Rathlin Drive.

"For fuck's sake, Ray, slow down!" Eddie barked. "You'll have every fucking Brit in Derry on our tail."

There were no headlights following us and I whipped into Kildrum Gardens and pulled up.

"What happened to your gun?" Brendan asked Eddie as he got out of the car.

"It bloody jammed as well. I only got one round off. Those Woodmasters are shite."

"Did you hit them?" I asked.

Eddie gave a grim nod of satisfaction. "Aye."

My heart sank, but I forced a smile and said, "Great."

We split up at the corner and I hurried back up the hill past the cemetery towards home. Later that night I heard on the news that two police Landrovers had been hit on the Lone Moor Road. There was no word yet of any casualties.

We had the debrief of the job the following day. As usual after a successful hit, Shorty was at his most ebullient, his manic grins giving us all a close-up of years of indifferent dentistry.

"Good job, boys, good job," he beamed, rubbing his hands together. "It's a shame the Woodmasters jammed, but we still got a couple of RUC men."

"Stiffs?" asked Pat hopefully.

"No, only wounded, but that doesn't alter the fact that it was a bloody good job. You went in, did the job and got away clean – no traces, no witnesses"

"There's one witness."

We all turned to look at Mary.

She blushed at the sudden attention. "The taxi driver."

Shorty shrugged, "But he was blindfolded, wasn't he?"

"Aye, but he could've got a sight of me. I was waiting outside McCann's as he pulled up. If anyone spotted the car after the job, we could be in trouble. He was shitting himself that much, I don't know what he'd do if the RUC lifted him."

Shorty flicked out a hand in a dismissive gesture, waving aside her concerns as if he was wafting away a fly. "If the worst comes to the worst, Dermott McCormick can cover it. He works as a driver for Bradley's. If the RUC start asking questions, he can go in and say he was hijacked. Dermott'll stand up to anything they can throw at him."

The others all left the meeting in great good humour, heading for the pub to celebrate. I said I'd an errand to run and would join them later, for I wanted to phone Pete. I was furious that two RUC men had been shot after my tip-off had apparently been ignored. I walked down into the town and called him from a pay-phone.

When he answered, I pitched straight into him without even bothering to say hello. "What the fuck is the point of me risking my life to get you information if you don't even act on it?" I warned you about the ambush and you let two police cars drive straight into it."

"Hold on, Ray, you warned us, yes, and the warning was passed on, but unfortunately the most important bit of information got lost in translation. We told the uniformed branch that your unit had acquired some armour-piercing rounds, but that message wasn't relayed down the line. The uniforms drove along there believing they'd only be facing conventional bullets. As a result they were hit, but they were lucky. Two lads were injured but no one was killed."

We talked for quite a while, with Pete soothing me down, as he always did. Then I hung up and went to join my comrades in their celebrations. They had even greater cause for rejoicing shortly afterwards, for the security forces were to be less lucky in the Brandywell unit's next operation.

I was powerless to stop the death of a soldier, shot by the Castle Gate on 20 January 1981. It was the only successful kill in all the operations in which I was involved, but it haunts me to this day.

The job had been planned for ages, but so many attempts had been unsuccessful that they tried to change their luck by catching it on the off-night, a night when we would not normally have been going out. Brendan McDermott just turned up at my door early one evening. "Will you come on a job with me?"

We had so many jobs on at the time, I didn't know which one he was talking about. "Aye, no problem, which job?"

"The shoot on the soldiers at Castle Gate."

The time that the gates were closed varied from day to day as a security measure, but we knew that the soldiers usually shut them sometime between six and eight-thirty.

I got into Brendan's car and we drove down to the town and parked outside the Stardust Ballroom. Eddie McSheffrey's mother-in-law lived just opposite and Eddie had been raided by the police and army at his own home so often that he'd taken up virtually permanent residence at his mother-in-law's. Brendan wanted Eddie's help with the shooting, but as cell leader at the time he also had to be consulted before going ahead with the job.

When Eddie came to the door, Brendan told him, "The shoot's on for the soldiers at the Castle Gate. Have we your permission and will you come with us and give us a hand?"

"Of course you've got my permission lads, it's a good job, but I can't come with you. I wish I could, but me and the wife are fighting and she is giving me too many problems as it is. Go and get Pat McHugh or Mary Cobbe to give you a hand, and if they refuse, tell them that I order them to go on it. Good luck, lads."

He went back inside looking rather sheepish, while Brendan and I set off to Mary Cobbe's house. Mary needed little persuasion and came with us to the arms dump in Lone Moor Gardens for a short – a handgun – to carry out a hijacking. We opened the hide and Mary reached in and took a plastic bag from one of the clips fixed to the side. It held the Colt.45 we often used on hijackings.

We needed a big fast car for this job. People in the Creggan were well aware of the risks involved in being a car owner. If they were not linked in any way to the IRA, their cars could be hijacked for use in jobs or taken and burned during riots. If the owners were being held during a hijacking, then the car might be brought back to them, but otherwise it would either be dumped or torched. A little bit of joy-riding went on as well from time to time, but any joy-riders caught were knee-capped, so not many took the risk.

Mary knew a bloke at the bottom of Rathowen, with an Audi. He wasn't a private owner, but a taxi man. Since they paid off the Provies, taxis were normally exempt from hijackings, but sometimes, in desperation we would take one. We left Mary to prepare the rifles for the shoot while Brendan and I, masked, gloved and armed with a Colt.45, paid a call on the taxi man. He came to the door himself and we pushed our way in. His wife and children were sitting at the kitchen table eating their tea and I closed the door on them, leaving us alone in the hall.

For a change, I did most of the talking. "Provisional IRA, we want your car."

"I can't give it to you – it's not mine, it's a taxi."

"I don't care, we're taking it and we want the keys."

"But I pay my money every week."

"You'll get it back and it won't be damaged," Brendan chipped in.

"I don't care, you're not getting the keys."

I had the Colt stuffed in my wasteband and eventually I got it out and waved it around, not with any intention of using it, but just to scare him enough to make him give us the keys. It did the trick, for he went white and handed them over right away. As we left, we gave the customary warning about not informing the police because someone would be watching his house. As usual, nobody would be watching, but no sensible Creggan resident was likely to take a chance on that.

The car was a dream - a very fast, dark green Audi with power steering – and we blasted off up the road, both whooping like kids at the acceleration. Sometimes, it just seemed like a game, a bunch of school boys joy- riding around in a hot car, but I could never forget for long that it was a deadly game. I'd only to hear the cold finality of a round being slipped into the breech of a gun to be brought back to reality, the smile wiped from my face. It was total freedom, but one slip and I was dead. That's what kept me awake at nights, staring into the darkness, but it was also what gave it the edge.

We picked up Mary and the rifles – an Armalite and a Woodmaster. Brendan got into his car and we followed him over to the Lone Moor Road, where he wanted to leave his car so he could go straight home after the shooting. He stopped about a hundred yards from Westland Street on the Brandywell side of the new road, and walked over to us carrying a blue boiler suit which he'd nicked from the bakery in Pennyburn where he worked.

While he struggled into it in the passenger seat, I drove down to Harvey Street, close to the Castle Gate. Mary got out and walked up the hill to wait for the soldiers coming to shut the gates. After about ten minutes, she came running down to say that the soldiers were on their way. Brendan grabbed the Armalite and gave me the Woodmaster. I left the car engine running and we ran up to the top of Harvey Street. Brendan crouched down beside a van while I stood behind it, resting my rifle along its roof. We were almost invisible in the darkness, well away from the pools of light cast by the street lights.

The soldiers were already shutting the gates and Brendan, who could see their feet in the gap between the bottom of the gates and the ground, told me to hold my fire for a minute until they'd closed them completely. He needn't have worried, I'd no intention of firing under any circumstances. The Woodmaster was so powerful that it would have blown holes everywhere. I kept the safety catch on and aimed the rifle at the wall, well away from the gate, as an extra precaution.

Suddenly Brendan began firing, single shots, six or seven in all. The acrid smell of cordite filled my nostrils. As the echo of the last shot faded away, he was on his feet, shouting to me, "Come on. Come on. We're leaving."

As we ran back down the street, he said, "Run to the car, I'll cover you," and fired a volley of shots in the air to keep the soldiers' heads down.

I sprinted to the car and threw the rifle into the back seat, where Mary was sitting. Brendan ran past the car, saying he'd give us cover until we got out of the street. He ran to the corner and crouched down by a bookies, pointing his rifle back up the street.

I started the car and drove it flat out around the corner into Chamberlain Street. I pulled up for a moment at the taxi stand while Brendan jumped in, still holding his rifle. Dermott McCormick was standing at the taxi stand and certainly saw us, but he was staunch IRA and we weren't worried about him turning us in.

As I started to drive off again, a white van came over the narrow bridge from William Street. Seeing us coming at him, he stopped and sat motionless in the middle of the bridge, completely blocking the way. I recognised the driver, Daniel Brody, who had his wife sitting along side him. I waved at him to get out of the way, but he wouldn't budge, stubbornly waiting for us to reverse and let him through. I started to panic, imagining soldiers appearing at any moment.

There was no time to argue – Brendan just got out of the car and pointed the Armalite at Brody. As he did so, I put the car in first and pushed the van up onto the footpath out of the way. Brendan leapt back in we laid a trail of rubber all the way up William Street.

As we started to breath easier, sure that we were now safe from pursuit, Brendan asked, "Why didn't you fire your weapon?"

"I don't know, I think it's either broken or jammed." As I stammered out my explanation, I couldn't stop a nervous catch in my voice. There was a long silence while I sat there tensed and holding my breath, staring ahead through the windscreen, not daring to risk a glance at Brendan. Fortunately, the inquest didn't continue, because Mary could stand the suspense no longer. "Did you get them? Did you get them?"

"I shot the soldier with the flash lamp and the one locking the gate," Brendan said proudly.

"Did you kill them?"

"I think I killed the one with the lamp."

Mary almost had an orgasm on the spot and Brendan was not far behind; it was unbelievable how much it got to them.

We dropped Brendan off at his car and went back to Lone Moor Gardens. Mary put the guns back in the dump while I waited in the car. As we were driving off, two army jeeps came haring round the corner and flashed past us. We dumped the car hastily in Rathkeele Way, Mary saying that she would post the keys through the taxi man's letter box on the way home. One of the headlights had been smashed when I'd shoved the car past Brody's van, but the owner was getting off lightly compared to most people whose cars had been hijacked; at least he was getting his back.

Later that night I took Lorraine to a Prisoner Dependents' Fund dance at Oscar's in Waterloo Place. One of the locals came up to me and told me that a soldier had been shot dead and another seriously injured at the Castle Gate. I felt sick, for despite Brendan's confidence I'd still had been hoping that no one had been killed. It wasn't the ideal way to celebrate my twentieth birthday. I still think of that night often.

The next day, Eddie McSheffrey was arrested by the police under Section Eleven of the Prevention of Terrorism (Temporary Provisions) Act. While he was being held at Strand Road, the police raided the house at 15 Lone Moor Gardens and seized the weapons hidden in our dump there.

Even though they they'd known about the dump for some time, they'd left it alone after fitting bugs in the weapons, in the hope that they'd be moved to other dumps. After the death of the soldier, however, they decided to take the guns out of circulation.

At the meeting of our unit a few nights later, Shorty McNally was as pleased as punch with the killing, but concerned about our sloppiness on the getaway. "You did a very good job, but you were very foolish not to wear masks. You were recognised by Daniel Brody and Dermott McCormick. They won't talk to the police, but you were lucky that no one else spotted you...as far as we know. Now, Ray, why did you not fire your weapon?"

By now I had my story rather better rehearsed. "I don't know, Shorty. I think it was either broken or jammed. I've not been trained properly with it though, so I could have done something wrong. I'm not sure."

I let my voice trail away, gave a weak smile and shrugged my shoulders helplessly. To my relief, Shorty grunted and let it go; he had something much more pressing on his mind.

"I have to tell you that the army raided Lone Moor Gardens and found the arms dump. Mary, you put the weapons away, didn't you?"

She nodded, wearily.

"Are you sure that you put all the weapons in the dump?"

"Yes."

"Absolutely certain?"

"Shorty, why you asking all this?" Brendan asked.

"Because I've heard that the army found a revolver on the settee. That gave them the excuse to tear the place apart and that's how they found the dump."

"And who told you this? It sounds like a typical cover story from the peelers, to disguise a tip from an informer."

"Stephen Fegan was lifted when they found the gun. He told his lawyer it was on the sofa. That's what gave the dump away. Mary, I'll ask you again. Did you put all the weapons in the dump?"

Mary reddened and there was a long pause. "I may have put the pistol on the sofa, but it wasn't just lying there, I put it under the cushions."

Shorty silently raised his eyes to heaven. Mine were already there, thanking God that Mary's monumental stupidity had distracted Shorty from wondering about the reason for the army's raid on Lone More Gardens.

In any event, if I needed a scapegoat other than Mary, one had already been provided. The RUC had used Eddie McSheffrey's arrest as good cover for the raid on the Lone Moor dump, deliberately timing it to implicate him.

I rarely discussed with Pete how he would act on the information I gave him, but we'd talk about how I could cover myself. The Special Branch would always try and time arrests or seizures based on my information to throw false scents to the IRA. On this occasion, as the Branch intended, suspicion did indeed fall on Eddie.

When he was released a few days later, he was suspended from the unit and taken away by the boys from Internal Affairs. He was given a savage battering by Robert Dooley and Tom McGinley, who were Intelligence Officers at the time, as they tried to make him confess to giving the police information while he was being held.

Shorty broke the news at our next meeting. He was full of himself, for he'd been promoted and was now Officer Commanding of the whole Provisional IRA in Derry, taking over from Paddy McQuirk. Shorty introduced us to Tom McGinley at the meeting, telling us proudly, "Tom is now my assistant and second-in-command to me for the 'RA. There's also another change in your Unit, for the moment at least. Brendan will be unit leader until further notice. Eddie McSheffrey is temporarily suspended because he's suspected of touting."

There were a few gasps of surprise from the others and I hastily joined in the chorus. "Surely Eddie's no tout!"

"I'm not saying he is yet, but it's to be investigated. We lost the Lone Moor dump while he was in Strand Road, so he's suspended until I find out who gave the information to the peelers."

Pat McHugh was certainly convinced of Eddie's guilt, for he disappeared straight after the meeting and went on the run to Buncrana. He didn't reappear for a few weeks.

I felt a few pangs of guilt about the battering Eddie had taken, until I reminded myself of his murderous love of planting bombs, so strong that it would jeopardise the lives of innocent bystanders without a second thought. He was eventually cleared of touting and allowed to re-join the unit as Explosives Officer, and his enthusiasm for the IRA – and for bombs – remained undaunted by his experience. It was later to cost him his life, for he and Paddy Deery blew themselves up while planting a bomb several years later – crisps they were, at the end.

It wasn't too long before the problem caused by my lack of weapons training was remedied. Shorty appeared at a routine meeting of my unit one night. "Ray, you need to learn how to use the weapons. You've never been to a training camp, have you?"

"No, but I'm happy to go on one any time."

"Good, you're going on one tomorrow night. Tell your missus you'll be away for a couple of days. You'll need some heavy clothes and a pair of boots. Do you know the Ballysea Bar, about a mile over the border from Cosquin?"

I nodded.

"Be there at eight tomorrow night. Somebody in the bar will contact you."

The next evening I put on my work boots, a dirty pair of trousers, a pullover and a thick green jacket, and walked down to the rank to get a taxi over the border. I got to the Ballysea Bar just before eight, walked in and bought a pint of Harp, then sat watching *The Eagle Has Landed* on the television over the bar for almost an hour, waiting for my contact.

Finally, Dermott McCormick appeared and walked over to me. "You ready?"

"Aye."

He took me outside where three people were standing by his blue Saab car. James Barr and Tommy Walsh from Shantallow got in the back seat with me; the other passenger was a woman, Mairead Scully.

Dermott took us out past Letterkenny, deep into the Donegal countryside, before finally turning off into a narrow track and parking by a decrepit-looking bungalow. It was an absolutely pitch-black night, with no lights visible anywhere, but as we got out of the car, two southerners, one from Dublin, the other from Cork, materialised out of the darkness and greeted us. Dermott drove off back to Derry, while we were led into the bungalow and told to make ourselves comfortable for the night in sleeping bags on the floor. The two southerners mounted guard.

The next morning we began our lessons in a room which was even equipped with a blackboard and chalk. The two of them produced an Armalite, a mini Ruger, a Remington, a Mauser and a Colt.38 pistol, and we were shown how to strip down, load and unload each of the weapons in turn.

We weren't allowed to fire them on the first day. "That comes tomorrow," said the man from Cork, who, like his colleague from Dublin, never revealed his name throughout our time there.

In the afternoon the Dubliner took over and showed us how to construct a bomb. It was the same technique that I'd learned from my INLA instructors in County Wicklow, using a cheap watch, a battery and some wire, but it definitely wasn't the place to mention my INLA experiences, so I played dumb and pretended I'd never seen it done before.

That evening our lecturers gave us some tinned stew and some cans of Guinness and left us to chat about jobs we'd done, while they kept themselves slightly aloof at the other end of the room. I wasn't looking forward to another uncomfortable night on the floor, but as it turned out I needn't have worried. We were told to turn in early because we were to be up at dawn.

As I made for my sleeping bag, the Dubliner called me and Tommy Walsh back and told us it was our turn to mount guard. We were each given a hammer to defend ourselves and left to patrol the dark lane for the night while the others slept.

At five-thirty in the morning, red-eyed from lack of sleep, I and the others stumbled down to the bottom of the lane, where we were told that we would be picked up. The two southerners followed on, carrying the guns in green canvas bags. A few minutes later, a red Ford Cortina drove up. All six of us climbed in and were driven even deeper into the country, coming to a stop at the end of a rough track at the foot of a mountain.

Before we got out of the car, the man from Cork swivelled in his seat and lectured the four of us wedged in the back.

"I am sure you keep a copy of the Green Book by your bedsides," he said sarcastically. "So you'll just all know it be heart, but just in case one of youse has forgotten, I'm going to read you General Order Number Eight. Keep it in mind we're up in the mountain. Any deviation from it will be punished by court martial, if I don't shoot you for it myself first."

He paused dramatically to let the message sink in and then began reading from a crumpled sheet of paper, spoiling the drama a little by stumbling over the longer words. "One. Volunteers are strictly forbidden to take any military action against Twenty-six County forces under any circumstances whatsoever. The importance of this order in present circumstances, especially in the border areas, cannot be over-emphasised."

Again he paused, giving us all a meaningful look before continuing.

"Two. Minimum arms shall be used in training in the Twenty-six County area. In the event of a raid, every effort shall be made to get the arms away safely. If this fails, the arms shall be rendered useless and abandoned.

"Three. Maximum security precautions must be taken when training. Scouts must always be posted to warn of emergency. Volunteers arrested during the training or in possession of arms will point out that the arms were for use against the British forces of occupation only. This statement should be repeated at all subsequent court proceedings. "Four. At all times volunteers must make it clear that the policy of the army is to drive the British forces of occupation out of Ireland."

He folded the sheet of paper carefully and put it back in his breast pocket. "Right. Any questions?" We all shook our heads. The principle, if not the exact wording, of the order was familiar to all of us. It dated back to the foundation of the Provisionals in the early 1970's, when the Fianna Fáil government in Dublin had given them covert support – including money and weapons – in return for the Provisionals' agreement to refrain from military operations within the Republic.

As far back as the 1930's, the previous Fianna Fáil governments of De Valera and Lemass had hounded the old IRA, for the Stickies' ideology called for the overthrow of the Dublin government and the establishment of a Marxist United Ireland. It was a battle fought with all the ferocity of the conflict with Britain. Indeed, internment and hungry strike – the notorious weapon and counter-weapon of the Brits' modern war with the Provies — were both first used in the South years before.

The Provisionals were different, rooted purely in nationalism and Catholicism, and unencumbered by the Stickies' Marxist and socialist baggage. Their self-proclaimed role as patriotic defenders of the Northern Catholics appealed to Dublin politicians as much as it did to young IRA men, fed up with the timid, rusty-guns leadership of the Stickies.

Provided the Provies kept their side of the bargain, Fianna Fáil would not only turn a blind eye to their activities, it would even arm and subsidise them. That historic deal with Fianna Fáil had been of incalculable value to the Provies over the following decade, and nothing, least of all careless or trigger-happy IRA volunteers, was to be allowed to sour it.

The Cortina drove back the way it had come while we started to climb the flank of the mountain , following a faint path. After plodding upwards for half an hour, we breasted a ridge and looked down into a hidden valley, surrounded on all sides by steep slopes of bracken and heather, pierced by sheer walls of rock. Apart from ourselves, there was no living thing to be seen — no people, no sheep, not even a bird.

The Dubliner remained on guard on the ridge, carrying a rifle, while we walked down into the valley towards a series of battered wooden targets, shot full of holes. The man from Cork handed out paper targets which we tacked to the boards. We then paced out twenty-five yards and practised firing the pistol. Ammunition for the .38 was in short supply, and each of us was only allowed to fire three rounds at the target. He then examined our handiwork. He showed me mine. One bullet had clipped the edge, the other two had missed altogether.

He raised a quizzical eyebrow. "What do you usually do in your unit?"

"Driver."

"Just as well."

As a punishment he sent me up to the Dubliner on the ridge with the .38, which I swapped for his rifle. When I got back to the group, we moved further away from the targets, about one hundred yards, to practice with the rifles. They had more ammunition for those, so we had ten rounds with the Mauser and the Remington and fifteen with the Armalite and the Mini Ruger.

We spent the whole day up in the valley, getting the feel of the weapons and firing at the targets. In the later afternoon, they led us back down to the track where the red Cortina was again waiting. Back at the bungalow, they sat us down and talked to us about the IRA, asking us what our feelings were about the organisation and what jobs we were currently planning.

Tommy Walsh entertained them with a plan that his unit in Derry – the Shantallow unit – had hatched to kill a policeman. He drew them a street plan on the blackboard and marked with crosses the positions that the members of his unit would all adopt. "We've got a tape-recording of a child crying. When he comes home from work, we'll set it going outside his back gate. When he comes outside to see what's happening, we'll shoot him dead."

Everyone was mightily impressed with the ingenuity of this plan, but I never discovered whether it was successful.

Later that night Dermot McCormick reappeared in his Saab and drove us back to the Ballysea Bar. Dermot drove off with Mairead Scully, while Tommy Walsh and James Barr stopped off for a drink. I walked straight back over the border and down into Derry.

I hoped that there would be no more jobs in which I'd have to hold a rifle. I could no longer use the excuse that I was untrained and didn't know what I was doing. Next time I would have to fire my weapon, or risk a bullet myself. It was an ominous, terrifying thought.

CHAPTER 7

With our weapons in the hands of the RUC and no secure dump available to store replacements, the unit's operations had to be scaled down for a while, but I soon found myself roped in on a job for another unit.

Tom McGinley, who was leader of another cell in Derry, had taken to attending a few meetings of my unit. After one meeting that winter he asked Jimmy Costello and me to stay behind. He waited until the others had left and then told us, "Be at 12 Beechwood Street at three o'clock tomorrow afternoon. There's a job on."

He didn't explain what the job was and we didn't ask; it was one of the rules to preserve secrecy.

When I went to the house the next day, the door was opened by Robert Dooley. I'd seen him a couple of times at dances around Derry. He was short and wore gold-rimmed glasses, but fancied himself as a bit of a ladies' man. He was constantly smoothing down his dark, wavy hair and stroking his moustache like a stage villain.

I followed him down the hallway and into the living room. Tom McGinley and Dermot Caulkin were already waiting. Caulkin was a tall, black-haired man who worked as a driver for Ulsterbus. I knew him slightly, for I used to go to his father's shop in the New Road in Derry, but this was the first time I'd been involved with him on IRA business.

We sat around chatting idly for a couple of minutes until there was another knock at the door and Jimmy Costello was ushered into the room. McGinley didn't waste any time on the usual formalities. As we shambled to our feet to fall in, he snapped, "Never mind all that, let's get down to business. Jimmy, Ray, you'll be helping out our unit with a shoot on a UDR man."

It took McGinley fifteen minutes to talk us through the plan. The UDR man worked at the back of Key's timber yard in Strand Road, facing on to Derry Docks. Jimmy and I were to help Caulkin hijack a car. While Jimmy and I guarded the car owner, Caulkin would pick up Dooley and McGinley and drive them to the docks. They would go to the back of Key's yard, shoot the UDR man and then escape in the hijacked car.

After the meeting Dooley drove the three of us across the Lone Moor Road and along the back of St Eugene's Cathedral. He stopped the car down a side-street at the back gate of the cathedral and handed a loaded .45 pistol to Jimmy, who stuffed it into the waistband of his trousers. We got out of the car and walked along the street to a small garage by the church hall, just below the library. There was a wee Datsun parked in front of it.

Only Jimmy had a balaclava mask with him. He pulled it over his face, while I wrapped a brown scarf around mine and Caulkin raised the hood of his duffel-coat and held his hands in front of his face. Then we went into the garage. There were two mechanics working on a car. Jimmy went over to one of them, took out the .45 to show them we meant business and said, "Provisional IRA. We want that car outside."

The man looked past him at the Datsun and then shook his head nervously. "Sorry, lads, but it isn't ours. I don't know whose it is."

"Well, do you have any other cars?" Jimmy asked helplessly.

"No, just this one we're working on and you wouldn't want this one, believe me, the head gasket's blown." He shrugged his shoulders and gestured around the empty garage.

Jimmy swore, shoved the gun back in his waistband and covered it with his coat. We turned our backs, uncovered our faces and walked out, going back to the side-street where Dooley was waiting. We decided to drive around the area on the off-chance that we would spot a car that we could take.

As we were driving along Creggan Street, I noticed a red Alpine parked outside the fish and chip shop. I knew that it belonged to the owner. Dooley dropped us off at the end of the street and waited there to make sure we got the Alpine. This time Caulkin handed me the gun. As we walked towards the chip shop, I pulled the scarf up around my face and Jimmy put his mask on.

The door of the shop was locked. I banged on it and after a minute I heard the bolts were drawn back. The owner half-opened the door, saw the gun and the masks and tried to bang it shut again, but the three of us pushed our way in. He stood there shaking with fright, and when I asked him for the keys of his car, he handed them over right away.

An old man standing behind the counter began to curse us, spit flecking his lips as he banged his bony fists down, emphasising his words. "You murderous, thieving bastards . You bleed us white and then come back for more."

The owner cast a terrified look at us. "Please don't hurt him, he's my father, he's an old man, he doesn't know what he's saying."

"He knows right enough," said Jimmy. "Tell the old fool to shut up or I'll give my fist to chew on."

As his son pleaded with him, the old man gave him a contemptuous look but fell silent as we hustled them through to the back of the shop.

Jimmy peered out of the window. "There's a wee shed in the back yard, we can put them in there."

I turned the key and opened the door. There was a blood-curdling growl and I looked up to see a huge Doberman standing just to the side of the door. I froze in panic for a moment then slammed the door shut again, just as the dog launched itself. I heard its claws scraping the door and there was a ferocious burst of barking.

I turned to Jimmy, whose face was as white as mine. "Fuck that for a game of soldiers, we'll put them upstairs."

The old man had a smirk on his face and Jimmy seized him roughly and propelled him up the stairs. I waved the .45 in a vaguely threatening way and his son followed them up, taking the stairs two at a time. We shut them in a small bathroom at the end of the corridor.

Jimmy shouted at them through the door. "Stay there and don't move. We'll be checking you, and if either of you so much as puts the end of your nose outside this door, I'll fucking blow it off."

We went back downstairs and I gave Caulkin the car-keys and the gun. After he left, I looked the door behind him. Jimmy looked at the clock. "Ten past four, Ray. Fancy a fry?"

We nosed about behind the counter, but couldn't work out how to turn on the fish friers. There was some bread and cheese in the kitchen at the back and we made ourselves a cheese sandwich instead, ignoring another paroxysm of barking from the Doberman outside.

I went up and checked the two men every few minutes, but they hadn't moved. I could make out their outlines through the frosted glass in the bathroom door and hear their voices, the old man's irritable mutterings answered by his son's soothing replies.

When I went back down, Jimmy was rummaging through the coats and jackets hanging on the hooks by the back door. He turned to me in triumph, brandishing a wad of notes that he'd pulled from the pocket of an overcoat. He stuff the cash in the pocket of his jeans and put the coat on.

Just before six o'clock, we slipped out of the shop. We didn't tell the men they were free, we just left them sitting up in the bathroom and closed the shop door quietly behind us. Jimmy was still wearing his new overcoat.

As we walked off down the road I asked him, "What do you want with that poxy coat, Jimmy?"

Jimmy gave me a pitying look, like a teacher questioned by a particularly backward pupil. "If those two complain that we've nicked their money and Brendan or Shorty finds out, we'll be fucking knee-capped. I'm taking the coat as cover. If we're pulled about it, we'll just say that we took the coat and threw it away and didn't even know there was any money in it. All right?"

I nodded. We walked along Lone Moor Road and up the steps at the bottom of Beechwood Avenue. We stopped in the little laneway while Jimmy turned out the other pockets of the coat. There was a driver's licence and a few other personal documents, but he tore those up and scattered them to the winds. A few hundred yards further on, he took off the coat and threw it away behind a wall.

He took out the money and counted it. "Fifty punts, Ray. Better than a kick in the balls."

He handed me half of it and I tucked it away in my wallet. We walked up Beechwood Avenue and met up with McGinley and Caulkin. "How did the job go, boys? Did you get your man?"

McGinley spat. "No, the fucker wasn't there, but I'll get him soon enough."

He was true to his word. Ten days after the first attempt, I heard on the television news that a UDR man had been shot dead in Key's timber yard. *McGinley's got his man*, I thought to myself.

Jimmy and I left McGinley and Caulkin standing at the roadside and went up to the Beechwood Bar at the shops, where we drank our hearts out with the money we'd taken from the coat. The fish shop owner duly complained to the IRA about the stolen money and Shorty raised it with us during our next unit meeting. On the surface he was happy with Jimmy's explanation, but I caught a thoughtful look in Shorty's eye as he turned away.

I decided that from then on I'd have no part in any more of Jimmy's extramural activities. It wasn't so much a matter of morality as self-preservation. I'd no wish at all to have my knee-caps perforated, but there was also my role as an agent to consider. My usefulness to the RUC rested on me being an accepted and respected member of my unit. I couldn't afford to be disgraced and expelled because of some petty theft. Jimmy had no such compunctions and kept thieving, but inevitably the Provies found out about it. After he'd done a couple of break-ins down in the centre of Derry, he was suspended from the unit.

At the next meeting Shorty told us, "Jimmy will have to be done. We can't have any hoods in the Provisional IRA. Jimmy'll have to be disciplined, and the only way to do it is to shoot him in the leg. The problem is there is only a .45 pistol in the whole town at the moment, so I want this unit to do it. If I let any of the others loose with a .45, they'll only blow the fucking leg off him. I've more faith in you to do the shooting because I know you'll handle a short better. Now," he said brightly. Looking from face to face like a teacher deciding who'd get the gold star for good conduct, "Who's going to do it?"

There was a brief silence, then Eddie McSheffrey said, "I'll do it. He's my mate, it's only right that I should do it."

Shorty nodded and turned away for a private word with Brendan McDermott.

I was puzzled why Eddie would want to do the job himself and whispered to him, "Why don't you let one of the others do it?"

He looked round to make sure Shorty wasn't listening. "Because if I do it, I know I'll not blow his fucking leg off or shoot him through the artery or leave him to bleed to death. I'll just shoot him in the calf muscle and it'll be in and out as clean as a whistle."

I nodded sagely, but I was remembering that my brother Harry was shot in the same part of the leg. "As clean as a whistle" wasn't the phrase I'd have used to describe the exit wound from his leg, and he wasn't shot with as heavier caliber weapon as the .45 Eddie was going to use.

Shorty called us to order. "I've just one more item for you. Bob Dooley's been lifted, and from what we hear, he's singing like a fucking canary."

I stole a glance at Eddie. He had a grim smile fixed to his face, like a dead man's rictus. Dooley was one of the interrogators who'd tried to beat a confession to touting out of Eddie a few weeks before. It was a savage irony that Dooley himself should have broken under his first taste of RUC interrogation.

"I'll have more to say about Mr fucking Dooley at the next meeting." said Shorty, sending us out into the night.

Dooley was item one on the next agenda. "I've an important announcement to make," said Shorty, drawing himself up to his full height – which still left him inches shorter than everybody else – and puffing out his chest like a bullfrog. "The next meeting is Thursday night, usual time and place." No excuses for this one lads, I want you all there."

He paused dramatically for a moment and looked around the room, as excited as the president of a Women's Institute on unveiling the guest speaker for a cake decoration class. "Martin McGuinness will be giving us a lecture on why Bobby Dooley broke under interrogation at Castlereagh."

I tried hard to look impressed.

We all dutifully turned up on Thursday night, but when Shorty arrived, he had a hunted look. "I think I was followed by army men," he said peeping out from behind the blinds. "I'm calling the meeting off. Leave one at a time. I'll go first to try and draw them off. Brendan, you go next and phone McGuinness straight away. You know the number. Tell him it's off."

I watched from the window as Shorty left. There was no sign of a tail. Either the Army guys were very good or Shorty's paranoia was getting the better of him. Just the same, the rest of us sat there tense and not speaking gradually reducing in numbers as people slipped away at five minute intervals. I was the last to leave but if anyone was on my tail, I never saw them. They wouldn't have had much of interest to report on my case. I just went and picked up Lorraine from bingo and then we went home to bed.

Still without an arms dump, our cell was badly hampered in trying to carry out operations. We were forced to try and borrow guns from other units, but they were understandably reluctant to lend their precious weapons to anyone.

For a while that didn't matter, because when the H-block protests started, all units were under orders to keep things cool and not carry out any attack that would cost the protesters on the blanket to loose support within the Catholic community. Hunger strikes, had been going on intermittently in Long Kesh – the Maze Prison – since the autumn of 1979 but they'd been called off in December 1980.

Bobby Sands then began another on the first of March. He was to die sixty-five days later, one of ten men to starve themselves to death before the hunger strike was finally called off in August. Patsy O'Hara, one of the men I'd delivered ammunition to on my first job for the INLA, was another to die.

The National Census was being taken as Sands began to protest, and Shorty told us that we were to hassle the census-collectors "Take the forms from them and burn them."

Brendan McDermott obviously found the idea a bit beneath his dignity, muttering, "That's work for fucking kids, not men."

"It's an essential part of the protest the hunger strikers are waging against conditions in the Kesh," Shorty said pompously.

I couldn't see the slightest connection, and anyway had no intention of bothering any census-collectors. Others obviously had different ideas, however. At the beginning of April a 27-year-old woman, Joanna Mathers, collecting census forms to earn pin money was shot dead in the Gobnascale area of Derry. The Provie gunmen took the census forms from her and then shot her in the neck at point-blank range. She was married, with an infant son.

It was hard to imagine an act more likely to cost the IRA support within the Catholic community. At our next meeting all the unit members vented our anger about the incident. Even Mary Cobbe put her normally insatiable blood-lust to one side as she berated Shorty. "It wasn't right and it shouldn't have been done," she said.

To my astonishment, Shorty contemptuously shrugged off the criticism. "So what? She's dead now, isn't she? Bleating about it is just wasting breath."

He stood there, hands on hips, facing each of us down in turn, then nodded briskly to himself and said, "Right, next business. I've information that uniform police are using Breen's café in John Street all the time. I think we should pay them a visit there."

He smiled, showing everyone of his gobful of teeth. There was stirring of interest and the argument was soon forgotten as he explained his plans. Mary's eyes were glowing as she contemplated the carnage to come. Her conversion to pacifism had lasted all of five minutes.

Shorty's plan required us to hijack a van with side doors. We still had no guns of our own, but Shorty assured us he could get some from another unit. We were to wait in a side-street near the café until a few police went inside. Then I was to drive the van up to the café and park it directly outside. The shooters would either pull the sliding doors back and rake the place with gunfire from the van, or, if the café was full of people, they'd walk inside and shoot the policemen dead at close range. Mary Cobbe spent a couple of weeks doing surveillance of Breen's ready for the shoot, but the police had already stopped using the café after I warned Pete of the danger.

There was always a risk involved in phoning Pete, even to set up one of our routine meetings. Very few people around the Creggan had phones anyway, and volunteers were discouraged from calling IRA contacts in case they were being bugged by the security forces. To be spotted slipping into a phone-box at any time was to invite the unanswerable question, "Who were you calling?" The risk was doubled if I had to phone Pete in a hurry to alert him to a short-notice job or a major risk like the Breen's café shoot. If I was seen hurrying to a pay-phone straight after a meeting of my unit, questions would certainly be asked, and without a convincing answer – which could easily be checked by asking the person I claimed to have been calling – I'd be doomed.

There was also a risk that the abrupt disappearance of the police from one of their regular haunts would cause suspicion in the unit about an informer. But it was a risk that had to be taken; the consequences of not alerting the uniformed police could have been horrendous. In any event, nothing was said. The security forces changed their haunts from time to time anyway, and Shorty and the others just assumed that the timing of this switch had been a coincidence.

CHAPTER 8

As we got further into spring and the weather improved, the rioting in support of the H-Block protest redoubled. There was a riot in the Bogside every night. We were out almost every night as well, freelancing – with carte blanche to do what ever we wanted – and were hijacking cars left, right and centre.

After the failure to get a few carefully planned operations off the ground, Eddie decided to improvise instead, using the Bogside riots as a cover. "Tomorrow night we're just going on a mad tare through the Bogside and we'll shoot any security forces, either peelers or Brits, you're out with the rioters."

"Where are we going to get the weapons, Eddie?"

"Don't worry. I've fixed to borrow some from another unit."

I went down to Southend Park at about half-past seven the following night. The weapons were already there. As usual it was a random assortment: an Armalite AR15, an M16 and a Woodmaster with a telescopic sight where all propped against the kitchen wall.

The lack of a standard range of weapons was always one of the IRA's biggest problems. As well as AR15's, M16's and Woodmasters, we might find ourselves using grease guns – Second World War American submachine guns; Thompson guns – the traditional IRA weapon, but heavy, inaccurate and hard to operate, or a motley range of rifles and pistols from a dozen different countries.

While British soldiers trained on one weapon to high standards of accuracy, IRA men were constantly chopping and changing weapons which affected their accuracy and also caused constant problems in matching ammunition to the weapons.

As well as the three rifles laid out for the shoot, there was also two blast bombs on the kitchen table. They were made from sodium chlorate and brown sugar, packed in Harp lager cans with cortex fuses sticking out of the top.

As usual we needed a car to do the shooting, but for once we didn't have to go and find one. Brendan McDermott already had the keys for an Escort van parked over in the Bogside that had been hijacked earlier in the day. Eddie divided the weapons. "I'll take the AR15; Brendan, you have the M16; and Pat can use a Woodmaster. Ray, when we've finished the shoot, you and Mary can take the blast bombs and do what ever you want with them."

Brendan left to get the hijacked Escort and was back a quarter of an hour later. He handed me the keys and I went outside to have a look at the van. It was light blue and split new. When I looked in the back, I saw a box of electrical tools. I went back into the house again and told Eddie about them.

"Great. We'll drive up to Sinn Féin centre and drop them off on our way." He went back to preparing his rifle. Eddie, Brendan and Pat all cleaned their weapons and put the magazines back on again. Eddie put a round up the breech and we then filed out to the van, Mary carrying the blast bombs like a kid taking fireworks to a Bonfire Night party.

I drove out to the Lecky Road and stopped the van outside the Sinn Féin centre. Eddie lifted the tool-box out of the back and took it inside. He was back straight away and we headed on up the Lecky Road towards Rossville Street. I drove up Westland Street and turned into Westland Avenue, a cul-de-sac just behind the Bull Park, where the worst rioting was going on. I turned the van around at the top and parked it facing down towards the bottom of the street. Eddie told Mary and me, "You can take the blast bombs if you want and chuck them at the police from in among the rioters."

I wasn't at all keen on that idea. "No, I'll stay with the van, you might need a quick getaway."

He shrugged and they turned away, walking abreast up the street as if they were heading for the shoot-out at the OK Corral. They disappeared into the darkness and I settled down to wait. Mary fidgeted around outside the van and fingered the blast bombs in the back. She obviously didn't fancy taking them on her own, and in the end she closed the doors and leaned against them, staring into the night up towards the Bull Park. As we waited, I could hear the rioting spilling over the Lone Moor Road at the front of the park. A couple of blast bombs exploded and there was a hollow rattle of plastic bullets being fired, but I didn't hear the sharp crack of any shots from the rifles.

About fifteen minutes after the guys had left with the rifles, a yellow Escort car came up Westland Avenue and pulled up in front of the van. I could see four men silhouetted in the car and froze for a moment in absolute terror. My mind racing, I began to look around frantically, searching for a way out. There was none. If the men were army or SAS and a shoot-out started, Mary and I would be pigs in the middle between the soldiers and Eddie, Brendan and Pat. Mary whipped the back doors open, ready to dump the bombs into a garden, but I relaxed as a recognised the occupants of the car, four men of another unit, Paddy Lawler, George McBrearty, Charlie "Pop" Maguire and Donal Tiernan.

As the Escort stopped along side us, Eddie, Brendan and Pat appeared out of the darkness and tossed the rifles into the back of the van.

"It's no fucking good," Eddie said. "We can't get a clear shot for the fucking rioters."

He went over to talk to Paddy Lawler. After a couple of minutes, Lawler and Maguire got out of the car. Brendan opened the van doors and handed them the rifles, though he left the blast bombs in the back of the van. Lawler and his boys then drove off.

Eddie and the others got back in the van and he told me to drive up the Lone Moor Road to the Bull Park. As I drove slowly along, we could see the crowds rioting up ahead and the flash as a couple of blast bombs were thrown. I pulled in to the side of the road just short of the crowds, but Eddie urged me forward again. "Come on Ray, let's burn the fucker. Drive it up to the front."

The police lines were at the Middlelet Stores above St Eugene's Cathedral. I drove the van up through the rioters and then we all leapt out of the van, Pat McHugh grabbing the blast bombs. The rioters immediately gathered round the van and gave us a hand overturning it. As it crashed onto its side, petrol began spilling from the tank. Some of the rioters threw matches on to the spilled petrol and the van was instantly engulfed in flames.

The heat drove the crowd back a little. I looked around me at the wild excited faces of the kids, some as young as nine or ten. The next generation of Eddie McSheffreys and Brendan McDermotts were already learning their trade. There was a cheer from them as the petrol tank of the van exploded. Debris flew in all directions, but the rioters barely flinched before resuming the taunting, stoning and petrol bombing of the police.

As the crowd kept up a chant of "RUC – SS! RUC – SS! RUC – SS!", police snatch squads made a couple of brief forays trying to arrest rioters, but each time they were met by a fresh volley of rocks and bottles and dropped back empty-handed. In the end the police seemed content to simply hold the line behind their shields and let the riot, like the van, burn itself out.

Pat showed no inclination to expose himself as a target by throwing the blast bombs, and in the end Eddie told me to stag him down to Southend Park with them.

When we got there, we went out the back yard, which was concreted and had a high brick wall around it. There was a battered old gas cooker and a wooden cabinet at the far side of the yard. Pat left one of the bombs in the old cooker and the other in the cabinet. As I walked home, I could still see sparks rising into the sky from over towards the Bull Park, and I could hear the faint sound of yells, screams and explosions answered by the rattle of plastic bullets.

The next day was an expensive one for the IRA. Kieran McAllister, who'd been rioting on the Lone Moor Road, lost an eye after he was hit in the face by a plastic bullet that ricocheted off the surface of the road. Two other IRA men were even less lucky. George McBrearty and Pop Maguire were shot dead, still carrying the rifles they'd picked up from us in Westland Avenue. The details came from Paddy Lawler, for McBrearty and Maguire were past talking to anyone and Donal Tiernan was in hospital, badly wounded and under police guard.

They'd already hijacked one car, but were looking for a second one for the job they had on. Like Colm McNutt, however, they made the mistake of stopping an undercover SAS man, at the junction of Southway with the Lone Moor Road. He said he was unarmed and put his hands above his head to show that he was harmless, but he had a gun hidden on the sun visa. He pulled it out and shot McBrearty, whose M16 was on fully automatic. As McBrearty fell to the ground, mortally wounded, his gun went off, raking Maguire and Tiernan on the way down.

Paddy Lawler was still sitting in the get away car. The SAS man pointed his gun towards him and Lawler dived down behind the wheel. By the time he poked his head back up a minute later, the soldier had gone and the road was empty. Lawler rushed over to the bodies lying in the road. McBrearty was already dead as a hammer, for the bullet had gone in through the bridge of his nose and blown off the back of his head. Maguire was also dead, cut to ribbons by the fire from the M16. Tiernan was still breathing, but only just, and blood was pouring from him.

Lawler had to drag the bodies into the car then drove off up Southway to the Creggan. He got a couple of guys out of the Telstar Bar to give him a hand pulling the dead bodies out of the car. They drove Tiernan over to tame doctor's house.

The doctor was often woken in the middle of the night to extract bullets, patch up gun shot wounds and administer a shot to ease the pain, but this time he took one look at Tiernan and told them the only chance of saving his life was to get him to hospital immediately. They had to shove him in a black taxi because they couldn't risk taking him in the stolen car. While a cab took Tiernan to hospital, they drove the car round to Fanad Drive and torched it.

Lawler headed for home and wasn't lifted for his part in the day's work, but his unit had been wiped out: two dead, and another badly wounded and lying in a hospital bed under heavy police guard.

The deaths fuelled fresh riots that night. I'd gone to the wakes for McBrearty and Maguire with Brendan, but we didn't stay long at either and finished up just driving aimlessly around Derry in his blue Cortina. It was the early hours of the morning and the rioting was dying down for the night, there were still a few isolated shouts and bangs. The familiar smell of the night air in Derry – smoke and soot, hung on the breeze and fat grey ashes drifted down like snowflakes as we cruised along the Lone Moor Road and turned back up the hill towards the Creggan.

As we drove past the shops on Central Drive, Brendan saw another IRA man, Denis Wolfe, standing at the side of the road. He pulled over and Wolfe climbed into the back seat.

As we drove off again, Brendan turned to Wolfe. "Where can we get some petrol bombs, Denis?"

"There are some at the back of the shops in Arran Court. What do you want them for?"

Brendan starting going on about bombing the Argyle Arms. He claimed it was because the landlord was touting, but it could just have easily been a personal grudge. It was a job he'd raised several times in unit meetings, but had never got the backing to do it. Now he'd obviously decided to do it first and ask questions afterwards.

Wolfe asked no questions at all as Brendan drove us straight round to Arran Court. He parked at the front of the shops and we all walked round to the yard at the back. Dawn was just beginning to break and in the faint light, Wolfe pointed to a red plastic milk crate behind some dustbins. There were a dozen bottles filled with petrol, with cloth fuses trailing down the sides. There were a score of such petrol bomb stashes around the Creggan and Bogside ready for the local kids and IRA men to use in the daily riot.

We picked up a couple of bottles each and walked back to the car. Wolfe and I nursed them as Brendan drove fast towards the Rosemount. He parked in a side street off Argyle Terrace and we walked down towards the pub, each of us carrying two bottles.

We walked along the side of the pub on Argyle Street and Wolfe then lit the fuses. Brendan went first, hurling his bottles through the big glass windows. As Wolfe threw his in, flames were already sneaking up the curtains. I could feel the heat in my face as I tossed my bottles against the wall alongside a window, close enough that it would look like a bad throw. I shrugged apologetically at Brendan, but he didn't care, the building was well alight as we turned and ran for the car.

As we drove off I could see black smoke billowing upwards into the dawn sky. Brendan was still grinning when he dropped me off ten minutes later. I never did discover the real reason why he wanted to burn it so badly.

Pat McHugh and Eddie McSheffrey had also been out that night with another Woodmaster that Shorty had conjured up from somewhere. I met Pat in the pub the following day, and he was already drunk and full of himself. He bought me a pint, a rarity in itself, and steered me to a corner table.

After a careful look around the room, he leaned confidentially over the table and muttered. "I shot one of the bastards last night."

"Army?"

"Police." He sat back with a smug smile on his face for a moment, then leaned forward again to fill in the details. "A couple of the lads were firing at them from the cemetery. Eddie and me got at the back of them in the Brandywell and let them have it from there. I'm sure I hit one because I saw his helmet flying off and then he hit the deck like a sack of spuds."

"There was nothing on the news."

"No, but if I hit him he's dead alright. I was firing armour-piercing rounds. I reckon they're going to bury him without saying anything. The dickhead stood under a street light. It must be the only one working in the whole of Derry. He had a flak jacket on but I must have blown a hole straight through the front of it. I swear I was 150 yards away if it was an inch, Ray, and I put a single shot straight through him. He must have been dead before he hit the ground."

Pat McHugh was such a bullshitter when drunk, it was impossible to tell if he'd really killed a man or not, but I must have let the mask slip for a moment, staring at him with revulsion as he gloried in the kill. He suddenly looked sharply at me and said, "What the fuck's up with you?"

"What? Er ... nothing."

"So what's the sour fucking look for?"

I cursed myself inwardly, though I tried to keep an expression of puzzled innocence on my face. Right from the start, Pat had always seemed the most mistrustful of me, and I'd worked hard to win him round. Now I'd put myself right back under suspicion.

"Nothing," I said hastily. "I am just jealous because I wasn't there, that's all. Right, this calls for a pint."

My palms damp with sweat and my heart still beating wildly, I headed for the bar, leaving him savoring his triumph.

Despite these occasional successes, Shorty was growing desperate for us to find someone willing to house a new arms dump, so that the unit could get back on a fully-operational footing. He raised it again at the next meeting, held at my flat, while Lorraine was out at bingo. When I suggested Dympna McGrail, who I'd known for a few years and who had a maisonette in Rathlin Drive, he sent Brendan McDermott and me straight round to see her.

We got there at half-past eight that evening. Dympna answered the door. Without introducing Brendan, I told her I wanted to see her about something. She led us through to the kitchen, separated by a glass partition from the living-room, where her kids were still milling about. Dympna had a few kids and they must have been pissing and shitting everywhere, because the place was filthy and the stench was appalling. There was a very tattered and torn three-piece-suit, a badly stained dark brown carpet, a coin-slot TV that took fifty-pence pieces and virtually nothing else in the place, apart from a pile of empty bottles in the corner. When we got into the kitchen, I asked her straight out. "Would you hold a dump for the 'RA in your house? We'd be putting guns in it."

"What if I get caught?"

"You won't get caught. No one will know it's there but the members of the unit, and they're hardly likely to tell the police, are they?"

In fact one of them would be doing precisely that at the first opportunity, but this was scarcely the moment to say so.

She was very nervous about the idea at first, but when she asked "Where will it be?" I knew we'd won her over.

"We'd make a hole in the floor under the washing machine and put it there."

"Okay."

It was as simple as that. We were back outside in under five minutes. When we let Shorty know, he borrowed a Hilti gun – a jack-hammer - for us from Charlie Clohessy in Cromore Gardens and I went round to Dympna's to start work the next day. She was out, but the back door was open and I let myself in. Ignoring the stench, I dragged the washing machine out of the corner of the kitchen and prised off a few of the green plastic floor tiles with a kitchen knife.

I'd used a Hilti gun when I was working as a laborer, and started breaking out a hole in the concrete about eighteen inches square. We carried on working on it over the next few weeks, and by mid-August 1981 we had a hole about four and a half feet deep. The bottom was concreted and the hole lined with plastic bags.

Shorty then told us to take a piece of drainage pipe from the Water Board depot on the Culmore Road, down a Shantallow – the 'RA doesn't steel things in Derry, it just takes them. We went down there about half-past six one evening, and shinned over the back fence. Brendan McDermott and I took turns with the hacksaw as we cut a four-foot section from the thick, brown plastic pipe.

We took it back to Dympna McGrail's and put it in the hole in the floor, sealing it around with plastic to keep it absolutely water tight. We fixed hooks around the inside of the pipe, to hold pistols, magazines and bags of ammunition, and the rifles went straight down the middle. There was a thick sheet of lead – also stolen – on the top, so that the weapons couldn't be found by anyone using a metal detector. On top of that was a concrete cap, which was fitted out using a key that screwed into it.

Soon after it was completed, we moved the .45 pistol, an M16 rifle and two Armalite AR15s, all with magazines and ammunition, into it. A couple of weeks later, an SKS rifle and some armour-piercing ammunition were added to the weapons in the dump. We also left a black guitar case in the kitchen cupboard, used to carry the guns on jobs.

Whenever we needed guns it was a five-minute task to move the washer, lift the plastic tiles, pull out the concrete cap, lift off the lead and get out the weapons. Dympna showed as much interest in the dump as any of us, peering over our shoulders as we put the guns into it and smiling proudly, as if it was a badge of respect to have these weapons under her washing machine.

When we tidied up afterwards, brushing dust into the joints and replacing the tiles and the washer, there was nothing to show her or anyone else that anything had been disturbed. It was a fine piece of work, and I also felt sorry that Special Branch already knew it was there.

With the new dump in place, the unit could resume normal service. Top priority, as far as Eddie was concerned, was one of his own pet projects – planting a bomb in the grounds of St Columb's College and then firing at the army sanger on the city walls from the site. When the police or army came to do the follow-up search, Eddie would be hiding in one of the derelict houses in Folly Lane to detonate the bomb by bell-wire.

We were on with the same job for months, but it never came off. First we didn't have the explosives, then we didn't have the bell-wire, or the bell-push, or the detonator, or the switch. In desperation, on a Friday night towards the end of June 1981, Eddie announced that even though we still had no bell-wire or detonator, we'd plant the bomb that night and activate the plan as soon as we received the rest of the equipment.

We met down at the safe house in Southend Park, down the Brandywell, and Eddie produced his bomb – a pub gas cylinder, packed with explosive and re-sealed with black tape. Eddie carried the bomb in a duffel-bag, while Mary Cobbe, Pat McHugh, Sean Ahearne and myself stagged him down to the college.

It was only just past the longest day and still light as we set off, crossing the Lecky Road and scrambling up a grassy bank behind the new houses on Bishop Street, before taking a narrow path that runs down the hill along the edge of the college grounds. We went in through a hole in the wire fence at the side of the college and walked over to the far side. Pat and I scraped a rough hole for the bomb and Eddie buried it in loose grass next to a low wall overlooking the flyover. We split up and went home, though I paused on the way long enough to phone Pete from a call-box and tip him off.

As usual, I hung back until the others had disappeared before I made the call. I normally tried to phone Pete from out of town, where I was less likely to be seen, but it meant a longer walk. Through carelessness or sheer laziness, I sometimes used the phones by the Creggan shops instead, even though I knew it was asking for trouble. Eyes were always watching and ears always listening around the Creggan.

A chance remark or an overhead snatch of conversation could have been enough to seal my fate. Even an innocuous comment like "Ray Gilmour makes a lot of phone calls" might have brought down a visit from the IRA's Internal Affairs men – the same ones who had given Eddie McSheffrey such a fearful battering. I wasn't a coward, but I was far from certain that I could handle that sort of treatment without cracking.

A few days later, Eddie sent Brendan McDermott and me down to check that the bomb was still undisturbed. I scraped the grass off it, showed it to Brendan and we then covered it up again. It appeared to be untouched, but I suspected that the army's bomb- disposal squad had already been down undercover of darkness.

It was another two weeks before Eddie announced that Shorty had managed to get the bell-wire, bell-push, switch and detonator from the Shantallow unit, and everything was at last ready… except for one small detail. The plan was now to be made even complicated.

"We can't be sure that anyone in the sanger will actually see where the shooting is coming from," said Eddie. "So we need to get the hijacked car that's been lying in Iona Court, crash that into the flyover and then shoot at the police or army when they come to investigate. When they do the follow up search for that, I'll detonate the bomb."

He looked triumphantly around the room. The glazed expressions on our faces were not what he had expected to see. "What the fuck is up with youse lot?"

We all harrumphed and muttered, "Nothing," but in truth there was quite a lot to worry about, not least the hijacked car. Unrest over the IRA hunger strikers was still building up and there were riots almost every night in Derry. Every night there was also casualties and fatalities, one of the saddest an eleven-year-old boy, Stephen Conway, killed by a plastic bullet fired at the rioters.

The hijacked car Eddie was so keen for us to use had been taken by rioters a week before. Brendan McDermott had the keys to it, but we were afraid that the army knew about it and were watching it. We argued about it for some time, but Eddie lost patience, calling us "gutless wankers," we agreed to take a chance on the car. Eddie sent Pat McHugh and me to get it and pick up the rifle for the shoot, while the rest of them went up to the college to get the bomb ready. Brendan would crash the car into the bridge and Pat would do the firing at the army or police.

As we were all leaving, Eddie bumped into Jimmy Costello and a mate of his, Ciaran McQuillan, and invited them along, as if we were going to a party. Neither of them should have been brought into the operation; Jimmy was still suspended from the unit for thieving and McQuillan was not even a member of the IRA at the time. But nobody was in the mood to spark another argument with Eddie.

Pat and I found the car, a beige Cortina estate, and picked up the rifle without any problems. When we got to the college, the light was fading fast into the dusk. The impatient Eddie and Jimmy were already unrolling the bell-wire, while Mary, Sean and Ciaran made half-hearted attempts to kick grass, dust and leaves over it. There seemed like a mile of the wire, snaking down from the bomb towards the derelict houses in Folly Lane, and Eddie was laying it straight down the road, passing a number of occupied houses on the way.

As Eddie continued to unroll the bell-wire, shouts and angry voices started coming from the Folly. People were coming out of their houses and screaming, "What the hell do you think you're doing?"

"Get the fuck out of here!"

"You're setting no bombs around here!"

I could hear Eddie shouting back at them, but then fearing that one of them had already called the police, he yelled to Pat to pull the wire out of the bomb.

Pat didn't move an inch at first, too scared to go near the bomb in case it went off, but Eddie's voice rose louder and louder above the competing shouts, until he was screaming, "Pat, pull the wire out of the bomb! Pull the fucking wire out!"

Pat moved very tentatively towards it. As he did so, I was moving rather less tentatively in the opposite direction, just in case. He made a few ineffectual attempts to pull out the wire, but couldn't do it. He shrugged his shoulders helplessly at me and then shouted down to Eddie: "I can't get it out. It's stuck."

That was the signal for a thermo-nuclear explosion of rage from Eddie, who drowned out every other voice for a mile around screaming, "Cut the wire! Cut the wire! *Cut the fucking wire!*"

None of us had a knife, and we just stood there looking helplessly at each other. I thought Eddie might blow even more gaskets and expire on the spot, but as Pat cast desperately around, he saw a piece of broken glass lying in the grass. He fell on it, whimpering with gratitude as if it was a fifty-pound note, and sawed frantically at the wire until it at last frayed and snapped.

By this time everyone in the area was shouting and roaring to be heard, and it was a wonder that the entire Derry police force hadn't already descended on us. Eddie re-appeared up the hill, rolling up the bell-wire as fast as he could, puce-faced and still pursued by a few irate residents. When he reached us, he gazed around us all in fury, then tossed the bell-wire in a heap against the wall and left it there.

We walked down to the laneway off the Lecky Road to wait for Ciaran McQuillan to bring the car up, and stood there is silence, no one wanting to fuel Eddie's rage still further by talking about the job. When Ciaran appeared, I threw the gun into the boot. His foul mood somewhat abated, Eddie went back for the bell-wire, realizing that Shorty's even more volatile temper would be stretched to breaking point if he found that Eddie had simply left it there.

Brendan tried to salvage something from the wreckage of Eddie's master-plan. "There's rioting going on in William Street. While we've got the guns anyway, why don't we go and have a shoot at the peelers trying to control it?"

Eddie clutched at the idea like a drowning man, and most of the others were keen enough too, but I'd had enough for one day.

"I can't go," I said. "I fixed to meet the wife down the town." It wasn't true, but they weren't to know that.

Pat McHugh chimed in as well, saying he'd also arranged to meet someone. Eddie wasn't bothered because there were too many of us to fit in the car anyway, so he gave us the bell-wire and told us to leave it back at Southend Park.

While the other six jammed into the Cortina and drove to William Street, Pat and I set off with the bell-wire. He put it up inside his duffel-coat and held it there by pressing his arm against his side. I went ahead, stagging him, and we walked to Southend Park from the laneway on the Lecky Road, not far from the Brandywell Bar.

A woman opened the door. When she saw us, she just grunted and went back into the living room without saying a word. We went through to the back yard and Pat took the bell-wire from underneath his coat and put it in the old cooker. Then we split up and went home.

About one o'clock the next day Ciaran McQuillan came to my flat and asked if I could give him a hand to move the Woodmaster.

"Can we not wait for dark?" I asked. "It's a bit risky in broad daylight."

"No, it's down in my granny's back yard and I daren't leave it there. If she finds it, she'll go light.

"What's it doing there anyway?"

"We had a shoot in William Street last night and I had to get rid of it in a hurry."

"Did you get any?"

"Brendan got three or four shots off at a Land Rover. He thought he hit one the peelers."

I got my coat, thinking I could hide the rifle under it, and we were walking down to his granny's house in Westland Street when I saw Paul Cleary and Dermott McCormick standing beside McCormick's Saab in Butcher Street. They looked as if they were waiting for us, for they straightened up and started walking towards us.

Cleary nodded to us and said, "Where is it?"

"My granny's yard."

Ciaran and I were about to go and pick it up when Tom McGinley and Clare Bristow came up Westland Street and joined the four of us. Clare was wearing a three-quarter length pink duffel-coat.

"Here's the woman that will go round for it," Cleary said showing a few bad teeth as he smiled at her. "You can put it up inside your coat."

"Put what up my coat? What's the crack?" she asked.

Ciaran told her and she went off happily enough. Tom and Ciaran went along to stag her on the way back, while the rest of us stood around chatting. They were back inside five minutes. McCormick opened the boot of his car and we crowded together, like flies around shit, while Clare pulled the Woodmaster down from under her coat and handed it to Cleary. He put it in the boot of the car and he and McCormick drove off.

That night we had a debrief on the St Columb's College job. Eddie would probably have preferred it never to be mentioned again, but Shorty had plenty to say about it. He launched straight into Eddie, without even waiting for us to fall in. "Where the fuck were you going with the bell-wire down the Folly?"

Eddie bridled. 'The job would have been all right if all those daft old fuckers round there had minded their own business. They were all on to me, "You're putting no fucking bombs here," "You're putting no fucking bombs here."'

Shorty rubbed a hand over his face, restraining himself with a visible effort. "There's another thing, Eddie, quite apart from the way you tried to do the job. You had two people, Ciaran McQuillan and Jimmy Costello, on that bombing job who were not members of the Provisional IRA."

Eddie started to say something, but Shorty held up his hand magisterially. "You know the rules as well as anyone. Membership of the Republican Army is only possible through being an active member of a unit. Much as he'd like to be a member, Ciaran McQuillan has not yet been admitted to the RA and Jimmy Costello was expelled for anti-social activities. The rules in the Green Book are clear on that as well, only the Army Council or delegated authority have the power to sanction reinstatement of a dismissed member. I don't care how short-handed you are on a job or how good friends you are with anyone. Those rules are for your own protection, because untrained or undisciplined men could put you all at risk."

No matter how many reverses or slap-downs he suffered, however, Eddie was an incurable optimist and an indefatigable hatcher of plans. He, Mary and I were walking along the path outside the Derry wall, just above Butcher Gate, the next day when Eddie's eye was caught by a movement on the roof of the Rossville flats.

He pointed upwards. "Jesus, would you look at that. The things you see when you haven't got your gun."

A couple of soldiers were on their hunkers, crawling out of the sanger on top of the flats, towards a breeze-block shack nearby. We stood and waited. A couple of minutes later they came out of the breeze-block building and crawled back to the sanger. They were in full view of us all the way: if we'd had guns with us we could have shot both of them.

"Got it," Eddie said triumphantly. "That's their shit-house. We can lie up with a couple of rifles, wait for them to go to the toilet and shoot them as they're coming back."

He looked around, marking the place carefully. We were facing towards the Lecky flyover, about twenty yards above Butcher Street.

"Right, let's get out of here before we're spotted."

At the next unit meeting at Southend Park, Eddie told Shorty what we'd seen. It was agreed that we'd hijack a car and I'd park it in Water Street, near Butcher Gate. Eddie and Brendan would stay in the car while Mary went to the path and watched for the soldiers going to the toilet. She'd then signal down to us and the gunmen would go up and shoot the soldiers dead as they came out again.

The job was agreed but never carried out, because by the next day Eddie was off an another tangent. "I've watched the Brits close the Bishop Street gates most nights this week. The time varies between eight and nine. When they get out of the Pig outside the gate to give cover to the soldiers closing the gate, they usually go to the small bushes a few feet away on the Long Tower side, for cover. That gives us our chance. If we put a bomb in those bushes, we can lead a bell-wire from it to the houses they're building just opposite the Fountain Estate, and I'll detonate it from there."

"How big's the bomb going to be?" Brendan asked.

There was a pause while Eddie thought about it, screwing up his face as he wrestled with some complex mental arithmetic. "A twenty-pounder should be plenty big enough."

"What about the bell-wire?" Brendan asked doubtfully. "What if the Brits spot it?"

"No chance," McSheffrey said eagerly. "We can cover the wire with bits of soil and grass. I'll get the bomb ready and all you've got to do is help me plant it and keep look-out for the Brits."

He looked round expectantly, but there were no other questions. "I've also got another plan, but we'll need a shit-load of explosive. This one's going to be massive, a three-hundred, maybe four-hundred pounder."

This plan sounded like the wildest yet. I glanced to my right and caught Pat rolling his eyes at Mary, but as usual, Eddie's childlike enthusiasm for blowing things to pieces had got the better of him. He carried on breathlessly, oblivious of any fidgeting from his audience. "I can get a landmine into a drain under the Buncrana Road between the Whitehouse Filing Station and the checkpoint near the border. I've watched the peelers and Brits going in and out of the checkpoint. They usually move along the Buncrana Road at a fair lick, so we'd need something to slow them down a bit and give me good enough time to detonate the bomb when they're right on top of the drain."

"We can fire a couple of shots at them," Brendan said helpfully. "That'll slow the fuckers down right enough."

"What if they stop altogether before they get to the drain?" Eddie asked suspiciously.

"Then what's the difference? We'll just shoot them instead."

After an interminable discussion they finally got the plan sorted out. The command wire would run from the drain underneath the road to the top of a field near the checkpoint, where Eddie McSheffrey would be the switch man. A couple of our unit would fire the shots from behind the hedge just by him, and we'd escape in the getaway car I'd have waiting on the road at the top of the field.

Eddie and Brendan thought it was a great idea, but the rest of us weren't so keen. Even Mary's normal enthusiasm for killing Brits was tempered by the possibility of innocent people getting caught up in the blast. To keep the peace with Eddie, we all agreed to the plan, but it went the same way as the Butcher Gate bomb and the shoot at the sanger.

We had quite a few other planned jobs that also went out the window at this time. With the H-Block protest still in full swing, you couldn't get anything organised for the havoc that was being created. There were so many freelance jobs being done off-the-cuff that there were never the guns, ammunition or explosives available for Eddie's grandiose schemes.

CHAPTER 9

Ciaran McQuillan's experiences on the St Columb's College job had obviously not put him off the IRA, and Shorty introduced him as a new member of the cell soon afterwards. He replaced Eddie McSheffrey, who had taken over a full-time bombing unit as Explosives Officer. I wasn't sorry to see him go.

The SKS rifle stored in the dump at Dympna McGrail's was a new weapon to us, and Shorty gave Ciaran permission to carry out a test-firing. I stagged him over to the fields at the back of High Park, the south-western edge of the Creggan. He fired off seven or eight rounds straight up into the air, which must have disturbed the contemplative atmosphere of the St Joseph's Carmelite Retreat just across the field.

It didn't do much for my composure either, "Christ, Ciaran, let's get out of here. Those bullets will be going just as fast by the time they get down again."

He gave me a patronising smile. "Don't be ridiculous, Ray. Do you know what the odds are against them coming back down in exactly the same place?"

"No I don't, and I bet you don't either. What I do know is that what goes up must come down somewhere, so let's make sure it's not through the top of our fucking heads."

I set off back towards the dump at top speed, with Ciaran labouring in my wake.

It wasn't long before Ciaran got the chance to fire a rifle in earnest, and one of his first official jobs almost ended in the death of a policeman. The plan had been discussed at several meetings. We were to hijack a car, pick up the weapons from the dump and then drive past Strand Road Police Station a few times, hoping to spot a car pulling out. We would then follow it, pull alongside it and shoot the driver.

One September evening, I was slumped in a chair watching television when there was a knock at the door. Mary and Ciaran were standing on the step. "The job's on tonight, Ray, we need you to do driver."

We drove down to the dump in Ciaran's car. He and Mary went off with the .45 to hijack a car while I was left behind to get an Armalite ready. I loaded one up and put it in the black guitar case we kept for the purpose, then covered up the dump again and waited for about half an hour before they returned. It was a familiar story.

"We can't get a car," Ciaran said. "We tried to stop a boy in an Escort but he just put his foot down and drove straight at us. I had to jump for it or he'd have gone right over the fucking top of me."

"So what's happening? Is the job off?" I asked hopefully.

"No, we'll go and try again," Mary said firmly, steering Ciaran out of the door.

This time they were back inside twenty minutes with smiles of triumph on their faces. It was a wine-coloured Cortina estate, with Free State plates. They'd dropped the owner at a house in Rinmore Drive, where he was being held captive until our return from the job.

I took the car for a quick spin to make sure it was all right, then Ciaran got into the back seat with the Armalite, so that he could shoot from either side, depending on the situation. Mary sat in the passenger seat with the .45 tucked in the waistband of her trousers.

We drove along Strand Road, and as we approached the police station, I saw the front of a car coming out of the gates. It was a beige Ford Escort with alloy wheels.

"We'll get that one," Ciaran shouted.

I slowed down and flashed my lights to let the driver out into the stream of traffic, which was still heavy even in mid-evening. I knew from the angle of his car that he was going to drive up Strand Road towards the town centre, as most police did when they came out of the station. He waved his hand to acknowledge my courtesy and pulled out in front of us. He was in plain clothes, with short black hair and a neatly-trimmed moustache.

We followed him down the Strand Road as Ciaran fumbled with the Armalite. He finally got it out of the guitar case, unfolded the stock, released the safety catch and cocked it. Mary, in the passenger seat, had pulled the .45 out of her waistband and was waving it about in her excitement, screaming, "Shoot the bastard! Shoot the bastard!"

The Escort drove along the expressway, still with us right behind him, but at the back of the Guildhall he pulled out into the overtaking lane and sped away from us.

"Don't lose the bastard, Ray," shouted Ciaran.

I pulled out and accelerated after him. The Escort stopped at the John Street traffic lights and I pulled up to the left and slightly behind it. Ciaran would down his window, pointed the snub snout of the Armalite at the Escort and began t fire.

I was holding the car on the clutch and kept jerking it forward a few inches, trying to prevent Ciaran getting a good aim at the guy. Ciaran was cursing me as he fired, yelling, "Keep the fucking car steady, I can't get a good shot!"

The Escort driver tried to mount the pavement to get away, but was stuck. I caught a glimpse of his white, terrified face as he sat paralysed, unable to escape. Ciaran fired five or six shots and Mary stuck her .45 behind the back of my head, trying to get a shot at him herself. I said, "You'd better not, I don't want you blowing my fucking head off," and she gave up on the idea.

As the lights turned to green, I stomped on the accelerator and we screeched off over the Foyle Road, the car fishtailing under the acceleration. As we roared past the Escort, Ciaran shouted, "I'll get you, you fucking bastard," out of the window.

I knew then for sure that he'd missed the driver. We blasted up the Letterkenny Road at eighty miles an hour, holding a ferocious argument. Mary was spitting feathers because we hadn't killed the man and Ciaran and I were blaming each other.

"If it hadn't been for your lousy driving, he'd have been dead meat."

"It's not my lousy driving that's at fault, it's your lousy shooting."

We dropped off Ciaran, still grumbling, with the weapons at the dump, and Mary and I went on to get rid of the car and release the driver. We left the car in a laneway at the back of the steps, and walked round to Rinmore Drive. Mary knocked on the door of a house and Morag Fraser, a good-looking woman in her early twenties, with dark hair cascading around her shoulders, opened the door. I knew her, for I had dated her before I got married, taking her to the pictures a couple of times. She smiled in recognition, but said nothing and went back into the house, while Mary and I went straight upstairs to the front bedroom.

A man in a green cardigan was sitting on the bed with a mask over his face and his hands tied behind his back. Mary untied his hands and we let him downstairs, out of the back door and through the houses on to Rinmore Drive. We walked him up the road for a few yards, then turned in at the side of one of the houses. We stood him face to the wall and Mary told him, "Turn your head away."

He twitched nervously, perhaps wondering if this was a prelude to being shot in the head, but then his shoulders relaxed as Mary lifted off his mask. There was a glint of light from the frames of his gold-rimmed glasses.

Mary jabbed him in the ribs. "Don't look round and don't move from this spot for five minutes. Your car's off Rinmore Drive, behind the steps." He didn't move or speak. Mary and I then walked away.

I listened to the news the next morning just be sure that the policeman was alright. There was an item about a Derry policeman being shot at from a hijacked car, but he'd escaped unhurt. I breathed a sigh of relief.

Every IRA man tuned in to the BBC's early morning Northern Ireland bulletin, but I'd certainly have been the only one with a smile on my face that morning. The bulletin always gave a catalogue of all the previous night's bombings, shootings, hijackings, knee-cappings, riots, arrests and arms finds. It was like the football results on a Saturday afternoon.

Every IRA volunteer and sympathiser listened to find out what had happened the previous night and how many had been killed. Then they'd be away down to the Creggan shops to discuss it, crowing over the British and RUC deaths, or commiserating with the hollow-eyed relatives of dead Provies.

Two days later, Mary, Ciaran and I had to explain our failure to Shorty at our unit meeting. I wasn't looking forward to it, but as Ciaran began to try and explain about the car jerking as he was shooting, Shorty cut him short. "You stupid wee bastard. Why did you not get out at the lights, then go over to the car and shoot him dead from point-blank range?"

Ciaran said nothing, squirming with embarrassment and hanging his head in shame.

"It was a good job wasted," said Shorty. "The policeman should have been dead that night."

Sadly, it proved to be only a temporary reprieve. A month or two later Pete told me that the guy I'd saved had shot himself. He'd become deeply depressed after the shooting and, when his wife then left him, he'd killed himself, unable to bear the stress any longer. I was sickened. The IRA had murdered him as surely as if Ciaran McQuillan's bullets had found their target.

Ciaran wasn't the newest unit member for long. At our next meeting, at the house in the Brandywell, Shorty brought in another new member, fussing around him like a mother hen.

"This young man's Niall," Shorty said proudly. "He's a volunteer joining this unit."

As usual Shorty didn't mention the boy's surname, but as usual we found it out within minutes. He was called Niall Blakely. We stared at him, weighing him up. He was still in his teens, tall and thin, with straggling blonde hair and skin as pale as the head on a Guinness.

Brendan McDermott looked him over and snorted dismissively. "Christ, we'll be getting them from the cradle next."

"Sorry, Brendan?" Shorty said. "I didn't catch that."

"I said he looks a handy man in a fight," said McDermott, squaring his own powerful shoulders to point the contrast with Blakely's feeble frame.

Shorty stared balefully at Brendan. "The important thing is he's now a member of this unit."

Blakely gave a nervous giggle. Brendan started to say something, but then changed his mind and shrugged.

Shorty cleared his throat. "Now unless anybody else has anything to say…" He paused, glancing round at the rest of us. "No? Let's get on with the meeting then."

Shorty had complained at the last few meetings that the IRA was short of money, and he again raised the subject at the start of this one. "Lads, can we not get a few jobs lined up to help the funds of the RA?"

Why the Provies were perpetually short of cash was a mystery, for they certainly had plenty of sources of income, and apart from paying for guns, explosives and ammunition, their outgoings were not large.

Even the full-time active volunteers, who were supposed to be ready to go on a job at a moment's notice, twenty-four hours a day, seven days a week, were only paid about £20 a week, though that was supplemented by food, drink and shelter provided by IRA sympathisers. The IRA claimed around five hundred full-time volunteers, of which a third were in Belfast and another seventy in South Armagh.

Full-timers were never supposed to sleep in their own homes, to protect them from army or police snatch squads. In return for their modest weekly wages, full-timers were also expected to do without social security payments, since the IRA believed that the weekly trips to sign on at the dole office made them vulnerable to police or army surveillance.

The IRA could certainly have increased their wages, for quite apart from the robberies and cash jobs, they had many other sources of funds. From the moment the barricades went up in 1969, the Provies began raking off money from a host of different scams. The barricades themselves provided a ready source of profit, for they were created by ramming hijacked lorries into each other. The goods on the back of those lorries quickly disappeared, either looted by the mob or removed by the IRA for re-sale.

Brewers drays proved particularly popular targets, for the hijacked beer and spirits could quickly be turned into hard cash. Many pubs and bars had been torched in the rioting and the IRA quickly filled the gap, setting up shebeens and drinking clubs in the areas under their control; the booze was cheap, the profit high and most of it went into the Provisionals' war chest. Inevitably some of it also stuck to the hands of a few leading lights in the Provisionals, who were living it up like Mafia godfathers.

Before long, the Provies didn't even have to bother hijacking the booze. Instead the alcohol for their shebeens was often donated by legitimate breweries in return for safe passage for deliveries to their own outlets in IRA-controlled areas. The Provies even had appointees on the boards of some breweries, overseeing their dealings with them.

By the time the barricades came down, the Provisionals had an unshakeable hold on whole areas of the city. No business activity of any sort took place without their consent and without a tithe being paid to them. Collections were made for the poor and homeless, but everybody knew the true destination of the cash.

Smugglers crossing the ramshackle border between County Derry and the Free State rarely had to worry about the excise men, for the Provies had intimidated the customs officers on both sides of the border. Instead smugglers paid the Provisionals duty on the cargoes of alcohol, cars, cattle and every other kind of farm produce, all of which were far more expensive in the South than in the North.

Provie protection rackets thrived as well, with everyone from prostitutes to bankers and captains of industry paying off the IRA for the right to operate. Several banks even had Provie minders, who pursued bank-robbers, knee-capping them and return stolen money – less a handling charge – to the bank.

In that atmosphere of intimidation, gullible businessmen even found themselves paying protection money to two or three different organisations. Some were the genuine article, others were con-men posing as paramilitaries, but only a very brave or very foolish businessman would turn them down. If he guessed wrong, he'd be dead.

One guy with a business in Derry complained to the Provies that someone else was extorting money from him. It did him little good. He never saw the other man again, but on top of their own weekly bribe, the Provies made him pay them the money he'd been giving to the other guy as well.

The Provisionals also began setting up or taking over legitimate and semi-legitimate businesses. They set up security firms as a respectable cover for their protection rackets, for example, but they were not averse to taking over any profitable business. Anyone who was too successful, despite the pay-offs, was liable to find himself in receipt of an IRA takeover bid at a non-negotiable price. Those foolish enough to turn down the offer would have their legs broken or see their businesses burned to the ground.

The IRA also ran a string of pubs, though their ownership was indirect to avoid problems with the licensing authorities. Most of the bars up around Castle Street were Provie-controlled in one way or another. The Telstar Bar, the Rocking Chair Bar and the Bogside Inn were all Provie bars, while the Dunloe Bar – originally an INLA bar – had also been taken over.

As well as the pubs and shebeens, they also had what was called an "ex-servicemen's hut" at the bottom of my street, and despite the name, all the money from that - like the bars, shebeens and slot machines – went to the IRA. The overheads must have been pretty low, for even the electricity was free. They simply tapped into the street lamp outside and ran a cable into the hut.

The ex-servicemen's hut was genuine in one sense. Danny Gillespie, who ran it, really was an ex-serviceman, but he was also up to his neck in the IRA. The RUC knew that those places were IRA fronts but couldn't do much about them. As fast as they closed one down, another would open.

The Provies took money from adults and children alike. Card schools in the pubs raised money for the IRA, and there were sheds fitted out with slot machines and pool tables at the back of the houses and blocks of flats, which raked in money from the kids.

Taxis were another lucrative source of revenue. There were taxi ranks in the Creggan and the Bogside and the drivers had to pay the IRA £30 a week to stay on the ranks. In Belfast it was a bigger operation, with black taxis, but in Derry the taxis were just normal cars. The taxi-drivers also knew that if we wanted a ride, they had to take us where we wanted to go and not charge a fare. We would give them an IOU, but no one would have been foolish enough to try and cash it.

The IRA in turn prevented buses going on to the estates. They burned a few and told the drivers of the others, "This is a no-go area, don't be coming up here again. If you do, we'll burn your bus and shoot you." That way everyone had to use the taxis, which gave the Provies even more money to skim off.

Most normal businesses suffered under the Provies, but a few grew fat on their largesse. Builders, glaziers, plumbers, joiners and electricians must have been down on their hands and knees every night, thanking God for the blessed Troubles, for every bomb that went off meant more work for them, rebuilding the shattered shops and houses. Scrap metal men were just as grateful, for the endless stream of hijacked and burned-out card soon found their way into their yards. Proof of ownership was not required; the army wanted them off the streets and the scrap men were only too happy to oblige.

Even government money poured into the Provies' coffers. Cash from Irish government agencies, intended for the support of Catholics in the North, was plundered by the Provies for their own particular brand of Catholic aid. The British government was also systematically ripped off, as the IRA used fictitious companies and forged tax-exemption certificates to skim hundreds of thousands of pounds from building contracts.

The Provies would remove uncompliant contractors from building sites at gunpoint and even took a slice of the workers' wages. They would either deduct "voluntary contributions to good causes" or employ the workers through a sub-contractor. It invoiced the main contractor at say £200 a week for each man, but only passed half of that on. The scale of the rackets even led the rival paramilitaries to make deals amongst themselves, giving each group their own exclusive territory. IRA, INLA, UDA and UVF leaders sat down together to carve up the city between them.

The IRA's tolerance of crime only extended to organised crime, however, unless you were lucky enough to be one of the high-ups. A lowly IRA member or a teenage hood who stepped out of line could expect little mercy. There was one set of rules for the lower ranks and quite another for the hierarchy.

I had ample proof of that when I went on the annual trip to Ballina, where an IRA hero, Joseph O'Loughlin, is buried. It was supposed to be a fishing trip, but it was really just an excuse for a piss-up. We had a keg of Smithwicks, a keg of Harp and a crate of spirits in the front of the bus, and after a few miles the guys were already so pissed that they were mooning at passing traffic. They then ripped the underpants off everyone on the trip, whatever the state of them, and used them as bunting on each side of the bus.

Paddy Lawler, Sean McArdle, Tam 'Stud' McGinty, 'Tapper' McFadden, Con 'Dixie' Bingham and a lot of the other big IRA men in Derry were on the trip, and Mickey McFarlane was there as well, though I was careful to keep out of his way, for we never got on after that first meeting in the Crum.

Martin McGuinness also came down for the night with a few of his cronies, and they just about wrecked the hotel we were staying in. They sprayed water all over every bedroom and smashed the floorboards on the landing and stairs. There was about £5,000 worth of damage altogether, which was quietly paid out of IRA funds.

The boys also nicked thousands of pounds of gear from a fishing-tackle shop. We all piled in there, and while I and a few of the others were buying hooks and bait, Stud McGinty, Sean McArdle and Paddy Lawler sneaked out of the door with four or five fishing rods each. I couldn't believe my eyes. If any kid had tried it, he'd have been knee-capped, but here were the top Derry IRA men, claiming to be the upholders of the law, hooding with impunity. The owner sensed something was going on, but was probably too scared to say anything.

When he heard Shorty's plea for cash jobs, Blakely immediately put his hand in the air like a schoolboy in class. As we sniggered to each other, he stammered out, "I used to work in Scott's shirt factory in Patrick Street. We got paid on Thursdays."

"Cash or cheques?" snapped Shorty.

"Cash. The boss went to the bank in his own car and got the money every Thursday afternoon."

"What's his car?" asked Brendan.

"A green Renault."

Shorty asked Blakely to describe the office where the money was kept and then hatched his plan. "We'll do it this Thursday. Brendan and Pat, you'll go into the factory with a short and get the money and the keys for the boss's car. Ray, you'll be waiting outside the factory to do driver."

"Just one problem, Shorty," said Brendan. "We haven't got a fucking short. We lent it to the Shantallow unit, remember, and it never came back."

"Boys, have I ever let you down? I'll get you a short. Pat, you and Ray meet me at Mailey's Bar on the Lecky Road about half-seven tomorrow. I'll have it for you then."

I met Pat by the Creggan shops the following night and we walked down to the Brandywell. Mailey's is a tiny place and I saw Shorty as soon as we went in. He was standing warming the seat of his pants by the coal fire as he drank a pint of Harp and chatted to James Barr, who'd been on the training camp in Donegal with me the previous month.

It obviously wasn't Shorty's first pint, for he was in an expansive mood, showing his full set of teeth every time he spoke. He told Pat and me to go down to a house in Shantallow. "A fellow called Barton'll by there, he'll give you the short."

Pat grimaced. "Christ, Shorty, that's miles away and I'm skint."

"So am I," I added hastily.

Shorty produced a fiver with a flourish, handed it to me and told us to get a taxi. "When you've go the short, leave it in the dump and then pick up some ammo from Joseph McCluskey. He'll be waiting at John Parke's mobile shop in Benevenagh Gardens around eleven o'clock."

Pat and I headed over to the taxi stand on William Street and got a cab up to Shantallow. The fare cost us £1.20. Pat smiled as I paid it. "There's a couple of pints for us on the way back then."

We sauntered up to Shantallow and knocked on the front door of the house. A man answered it and showed no surprise at seeing us there.

"Is there a man called Barton here?" Pat asked.

"Boys, you've just missed him, but he's just gone out the back. If you're sharp, you might catch him."

We walked through the house and into the back yard. The only light was that spilling from the doorway, but we could just make out a gold Datsun, parked at the back. I'd seen Shorty in the car a couple of times before. Pat shouted, "Barton," and a few seconds later two men got out of the car and strolled over to us.

"You Barton?" Pat asked. The shorter of the two men stepped forward and nodded. He was short, chubby and obviously balding, despite the flat cap pulled down over his head.

"Have you the short for us?"

"It's in the dump. Stay there and I'll got and get it for you."

We waited about fifteen minutes at the back of the house, stamping our feet in the cold, our breath fogging in the frosty air. Finally Barton reappeared. He pulled a gun, a revolver, from underneath his duffel-coat and handed it to Pat, who stuffed it into the waistband of his trousers underneath his coat.

"Are there any black taxis about that could take us back to the Creggan?"

"You can get a taxi at the Shantallow shops."

Barton nodded to us and the two men disappeared into the darkness.

Pat and I walked over to the taxi stand and got a cab back to the Creggan shops on Central Drive. We walked up to Rathlin Drive, planning to leave the short in the dump at Dympna McGrails's house.

Pat had the key and we let ourselves in through the back door of the house. As I turned on the lights in the kitchen, I heard voices upstairs. Before we even had time to pull out the washing machine ready to put the revolver in the dump, a man ran down the stairs and burst in the kitchen. I knew him right away – he was Dympna's boyfriend, but it was obvious that he hadn't come down to say hello and make us a cup of tea.

The veins were standing out on his forehead as he roared at Pat and me, "Get that fucking thing out of here!"

"What thing?" I said, playing for time, because I didn't know if Dympna had told him about the weapons dump.

By now he was too angry to speak and he just stood there, red-faced and mute, pointing with a shaking finger at the kitchen cupboard beside the washing machine. Pat and I looked blankly at each other, not having the faintest idea what he was talking about. We knew there were guns in the dump but we didn't know anything about the cupboard.

Pat finally walked across the room and opened the cupboard door. As we peered inside, we saw a big black rifle, like an SLR, but smaller and heavier looking. Neither of us touched it, we just stood there paralysed, staring at each other, trying to work out how it had got there and who had left it.

"Well?" demanded the boyfriend, still furious.

"I don't know anything about the gun. It must belong to another unit."

"Well, get it out of here now, and you can shift all those guns from the fucking dump as well. If you don't, I'll do it myself. When you've done that, you can come back tomorrow and fill the fucking dump in. You'll not be using it again."

By this time Pat was almost as angry as he was, and started shouting back at him, "Don't you fucking tell me what to do, gobshite. You touch anything at all, the rifle or anything in the dump, and you'll get fucking nutted."

He pulled the revolver out of his waistband and waved it at him to emphasise his words. The boyfriend's colour went from bright red to deathly white in the space of five seconds. We left him standing open-mouthed in the middle of the kitchen and walked out.

"What now?" I asked Pat.

"He glanced at his watch. "Eleven o'clock. We'd better go and pick up the ammo."

He kept the gun and I stagged him up Lislane Drive and along Benevenagh Gardens to John Parke's shop. Joseph McCluskey wasn't there. We stood around for a while, but he didn't turn up. Finally Pat had had enough. "Fuck this. Let's find a car to move that gun. I wouldn't trust that bastard not to just pitch it out into the street."

As we walked up from Benevenagh Gardens, we saw Niall "Tapper" McFadden, an IRA man not long released from the Maze Prison. He was six foot tall but walked a lot smaller, his shoulders stooped and his arms swinging low. He had a big lantern jaw but it contrasted oddly with his small mouth, the lips pursed like a rosebud. He was standing on the corner, talking to Charlie Maguire's twin sisters, Pinky and Porky, as some Provie wit had christened them.

Pat called Tapper over. "We've a wee problem, Tapper. There's a big black gun in the kitchen cupboard at Dympna McGrail's. Her man found it and is cutting up rough about it. He knows about the dump there as well. Do you know anyone with a car that could move the rifle for us?"

Tapper thought for a moment and then pointed to a yellow Toyota van parked down Lislane Drive. "Go and take that."

Pat and I walked over to the van. The driver, pale, dirty and overweight, was sitting in the front seat.

Pat yanked the door open. "Provisional IRA. We want your van, give us the keys."

The man shook his head. "No way are you getting my van."

Pat pulled out the revolver. We didn't have any ammunition for it but the man wasn't to know that. He was now showing every sign of co-operation, struggling to prise his beer gut off the steering wheel so he could get out of the van, but just then, a woman came running out of the house shouting, "Tommy Yates, Tommy Yates, they're taking the van!" She shouted for him several times and then ran over to his house nearby. I knew Yates, for I'd taken drink with him and spoken to him in the Dunloe Bar. He was a well-known member of the Provies.

The driver had stopped half-in and half-out of the van while he awaited developments. He looked expectantly at me. I looked at Pat. "Oh fuck it, let's get out of here."

Tapper had disappeared by now, so we dandered back across to Benevenagh Gardens and stood in a dark entry between two houses, not knowing what to do. A moment later, Tommy Yates came striding over towards us, his hands thrust deep into the pockets of the duffel-coat he always wore. He peering into the alley. "Ray is it? And Pat?"

We shuffled our feet awkwardly and took a couple of steps forward.

He shrugged his shoulders and spread his arms wide in a "what can I do?" gesture. "Boys, you can't take that van. There's a very sick man in that house. He's just come of the Royal Victoria Hospital. I'm asking you boys, as a favour to me, go take a car somewhere else."

"Fair enough. We weren't to know."

"That you weren't. Goodnight boys, and good luck with the job, whatever it is."

As Yates walked away, he kept his eyes fixed on the ground and his shoulders hunched, as if trying to make himself invisible. Pat and I exchanged self-conscious grins and then walked back down the street towards John Parke's shop. There was still no sign of McCluskey. We were standing by the electric power box, trying to decide what to do next, when a guy named Conor Whitcomb came along in a dark Ford Escort. When he saw us, he pulled in to the kerb and Pat went over to him.

"Conor, we're in a spot. Can you help us move a rifle from Dympna McGrail's?"

"Your wish is my command," Whitcomb said. His clothes and his way of speaking were oddly old-fashioned, an impression strengthened by the centre-parting in his mousey brown hair.

Pat came back over to me. "Take this." He handed me the revolver. It had a brown wooden handle and a big, long, rusty-looking barrel.

"What am I supposed to do with it?"

"Well, you could stick it up your arse," he said testily, "but maybe it'd be better if you took it back to your place and hid it somewhere till tomorrow."

"Of course I could stick it up your arse instead, but then we'd never be able to hear what you were saying."

"You could try," said Pat, both amused and nettled.

"Girls, girls," said Whitcomb. "I hate to interrupt, but I'm hoping to get to bed sometime before dawn. Could you scratch each other's eyes out later?"

Pat laughed and got in the car. As they drove off, I put the revolver down the waistband of my trousers then walked home to Cromore Gardens. The flat was in darkness. Lorraine wasn't a night-owl and would have been in bed hours ago. I went into the living-room and took out the gun.

The safety catch wasn't even on, which didn't worry me until I opened it up and saw a live round in the chamber. I cursed Barton and Pat McHugh black and blue. If the trigger had snagged on my belt as I put the gun into my waistband, I could have blown my balls off. I took the round out of the chamber, then went out to the coal-shed and stashed the gun and the bullet under a bit of old carpet.

CHAPTER 10

I was still asleep the next morning when there was a knock at the door of the flat. Lorraine answered it and then came into the bedroom. "There's a fellow at the door asking for you."

"Who is it?"

"I don't know. He didn't say."

I was always apprehensive when a stranger turned up on the doorstep, for if the IRA ever got wise to me, the first I would know about it might be an unexpected visitor with an unrefusable offer of a trip over the border. I thought of getting the pistol from the shed before I went to the door, but told myself not to be so paranoid. I struggled into my clothes and opened the front door.

Joseph McCluskey was standing on the step. His shoulders were hunched and he talked out of the side of his mouth, trying to be unobtrusive, but he looked as obvious as a stage villain in a bad pantomime. He didn't explain where he'd been the night before, but said, "This is what you were looking for." He dug in his pocket and produced a red plastic clip holding fifteen or sixteen rounds of ammunition."

As he turned to go away, I called him back. "Have you seen Tapper McFadden anywhere about this morning?"

"Aye. He was over at the shops in Central Drive ten minutes ago."

As soon as he'd gone, I put the ammunition out in the coal-shed with the revolver and then hurried over to the shops. Tapper was still standing outside one of them, shooting the breeze with a couple of guys.

I took him to one side. "We got the rifle from the cupboard at Dympna's away last night, but there's still the stuff in the dump. Her boyfriend was cracking up and threatening to throw it all out himself. Can you give us a hand to shift it?"

"What's in there?"

"Just the grease gun and some ammunition."

"Right you are, Ray, no time like the present. It'll cost you a pint, mind."

"You're on."

We went down to Dympna McGrail's. I opened the kitchen door rather nervously, but there was nobody in the house. I pulled back the washing machine and Tapper produced two screws from his pocket to lift the cement lid off the dump. He saw my surprise that he had his own set, winked and tapped his nose. "Yours isn't the only dump around here, Ray."

I looked down into the hole, half-expecting it to be empty, but the stubby black snout of the grease gun – a sub-machine gun that looks like the grease guns mechanics use – was still there. I lifted it gingerly out of the hole, holding it by the magazine. There were about a hundred rounds of ammunition in the dump as well. I scooped them out and then looked around for something to put everything in.

There was a brown sack, like a spud sack, in the corner, overflowing with used nappies and rubbish. Tapper picked it up, looked round vaguely for a dustbin, then muttered, "Fuck it. This place is such a shit-tip anyway, a bit more won't make any difference," and dumped the whole lot on the floor.

Tapper held the bag while I slid the grease gun into it and dropped in the spare ammunition. I put the cement lid back on top of the hole, brushed a bit of dust over it with my hand, then replaced the plastic tiles and dragged the washing machine back on top. We left the house by the back door, Tapper carrying the sack.

I was desperate to see where the other arms dump was, but Tapper didn't say where he was going to leave the gun and I couldn't ask him; company rules were very strict on that. I volunteered to stag him over to the dump, but Tapper just said, "No need, Ray, it isn't far. Go and get the pints in. I'll join you in a couple of minutes."

I watched him head off towards Kildrum Gardens, just below Dympna McGrail's house, but didn't dare follow him. I walked over to the pub and by the time I'd bought a couple of pints and sat down at a table, Tapper was coming in through the door, licking his lips. He downed his pint in a couple of gulps, smacked his lips and said, "I've a taste for it today, Ray, are you on for a session?"

"I can't, we've a job on this afternoon."

I bought him another pint and then headed back home. Lorraine and the kids were out somewhere. I fetched the gun from the coal-shed, went into the kitchen and broke open the revolver, loading it with ammunition from the clip. I had to prise out the rounds with a knife.

I put the gun down the waistband of my trousers, having made triply sure this time that the safety catch was on. I put he spare rounds back underneath the bit of carpet in the coal-shed and then got a taxi from the Creggan shop down to the Bogside Inn. I was last to arrive. Brendan, Pat, Mary, Ciaran and Niall Blakely were already there, standing around outside.

Brendan looked pointedly at his watch and then said, "Right. Now we're all here, let's get started. There's one small change of plan. Ciaran and Mary will be in a house in Princess Street with the rifle. They'll have a shoot at the peelers or the Brits if they come when the robbery's over."

I was worried. It was the first mention of a shoot at the security forces, and it was now too late to warn Pete. Lost in thought, I didn't hear Brendan's next words. I looked up to find them all staring at me. My first guilty reaction was to imagine that somehow I'd given myself away. Fear flooded into me and my brain was momentarily paralysed with fright. Come on, Ray, I thought to myself, say something – anything.

"Well?" Brendan demanded.

I smiled like a simpleton and said, "Sorry, what did you say?"

Brendan shook his head in disbelief. "For fuck's sake, Ray, get a grip. I said, have you the revolver?"

"Aye."

"Is it loaded?"

"Aye."

"Good. We'll take my car and leave it in Great James Street. Let's do it."

Brendan's car, a blue Ford Cortina, was parked in Lisfannon Park. We all piled in and he drove over to Great James Street and parked above the health centre in the wee street beside the Derby Bar. Before getting out of the car, I put the revolver underneath the front seat. We left the other gun – a bolt-action rifle – in the boot as well, while we had a scout around Patrick Street to see what police or army were about.

We split up, Mary and Ciaran walking with me, while Brendan, Pat and Blakely kept a bit behind us. As usual the thought of impending bloodshed had turned Ciaran and Mary on. They were walking close together and Ciaran kept leaning over to her and whispering in her ear. Mary flushed and squeezed his hand. Just as we turned into Patrick Street, however, Ciaran nudged me in the ribs. "Those two cars we just passed. I think they're Special Branch."

We walked another hundred yards and then stopped to allow the others to catch up.

"Ciaran thinks he saw some Special Branch men," I told Brendan, eager to get the job abandoned.

To my relief, he nodded. "I know. I saw them too. It's too risky, I'm calling the job off."

We headed back to the car. "I'll get rid of the rifle in a dump in the Bogside," Brendan said. "Mary and Ciaran can stag you down to the taxi stand in William Street, Ray." I nodded, got the pistol from under the seat and shoved it back in my waistband.

Mary and Ciaran saw me safely to the taxi stand and then took off towards the Bogside, no doubt hoping that sex would compensate for the absence of bloodshed.

I got in a taxi and said, "Creggan shop."

The driver nodded but made no attempt to start the engine.

"What are we waiting for, Christmas?"

"No, another two or three people, unless you've the money for a solo ride."

I pulled out the gun. "Provisional IRA. Now will you fucking get going?"

He was already in second gear before I'd finished speaking. I got out at the Creggan shops without even bothering to offer the customary charade of an IOU and went home. Lorraine was in the kitchen making tea.

"I'll get some coal," I volunteered.

"You're too late, I've just got some in."

"I'll top up the bucket then."

She gave me a curious look, but said nothing else as I disappeared into the coal-shed and hid the revolver under the carpet. I re-emerged, clutching a few pieces of coal as an alibi, which only earned me another, even more curious look from Lorraine.

As soon as I'd had my tea, I got up from the table and headed for the door.

Up to her elbows in washing-up, Lorraine gazed at me disbelievingly. "You're never off out again?"

"Afraid so. I've got to meet a couple of the lads."

She shook her head wearily, too used to the ways of Creggan men to complain. "Stick your head round the kids' door before you go then, just so they'll recognize you next time you're home."

I slipped my arms around her waist and nuzzled the back of her neck. "Should I give you something to remember me by as well?"

She flicked a handful of soap bubbles over her shoulder at me. "Why, it's not Friday already is it?"

We both laughed and I held her in my arms for a long moment, crushing her to me. If I were killed, what would happen to her and kids? She spotted the tear in my eye as we pulled apart and gave me a gentle smile. She kissed me again, then pushed me away. "I've got work to do, away out with you, you big soft lump."

I was on my way to meet Pete in our usual place up in town, by the fountain. I checked carefully behind me as I walked down the hill, watching for any sign that I was being followed. I checked discreetly, using the reflections in windows and shiny cars to avoid showing signs of unease to a watcher. I listened as well, ears pricked for dawdling footsteps or idling car engines, but as far as I could tell, I was safe.

As I was walking past the Telstar Bar, however, Sean Dennehy called out to me.

"Ray, I need the short."

I didn't ask how he knew I had the gun. I just said, "Give me ten minutes," and turned to go back up home.

Lorraine was still in the kitchen as I tiptoed in through the back yard and started rummaging in the dark coal-shed for the gun and ammunition. As I left, I tripped over a shovel, bringing Lorraine running to the back door, still clutching the dishcloth and shouting, "Who's that?"

"It's only me. I forgot something."

"If you'd rather live in the shed, I can move your stuff out there."

"It might not be a bad idea. It's probably cleaner than the house."

I ducked as she threw the dishcloth at me and blew her a kiss as I slipped out the back gate. I went back to the Telstar Bar and handed

Dennehy the short, then caught a taxi down into the town and went for my weekly meeting with Pete.

At my next unit meeting the following night, the shirt factory job was rescheduled, as I expected, for the next pay day. To my relief, Brendan had now decided that it was a bad idea to try and combine the robbery with a shoot at the police or army after the robbery was done. Nobody disagreed with him. We arranged to meet the next Thursday afternoon in Brendan's father's flat, across the street from the Bogside Inn.

"Before you all disappear," Shorty said, "tell me what happened to the G3 gun?"

We all looked blank.

"Christ alive. The big, black gun that was in Dympna McGrail's house. Where the fuck is it?"

"It's safe," Pat said. "Conor Whitcomb took it down to his unit's dump."

"Thank fuck for that," said Shorty. "I lifted it from a unit in Donegal. If it had been lost somebody would have been court-martialled for it. Now what about Dympna McGrail? Ray, I hear she's fallen out with her boyfriend. Is there any chance she'd agree to us using the dump again?"

"I don't know. We can ask."

"Why don't you and Brendan slip up there after the meeting and see if you can persuade her? You can always give her one if you think it would help?"

Shorty gazed expectantly around, waiting for us to fall about laughing at his wit. Ciaran obligingly sniggered.

The thought of making love to Dympna McGrail surrounded by piles of dirt and stinking nappies didn't exactly set my pulses racing. "I think she's got a bit of a thing for Ciaran," I lied. "Could we not borrow him tonight, Mary?"

She shot me a furious look. "Ciaran's not my property, he can do what he wants."

We all turned to stare at Ciaran. He was a bit slow to deny any interest in the idea and was rewarded with an even more furious look from Mary.

Brendan and I went to see Dympna straight after the meeting. She answered the door wearing only a tee shirt and a pair of knickers, and sat cross-legged on the sofa, painting her toenails, while we talked to her. Her knickers were grubby and had a hole in them, through which a few errant strands of pubic hair were poking. She was no Sharon Stone, but it was still quite difficult to keep our minds on the conversation.

Brendan was trying to give her the full spiel about her duty to her people, to the IRA and to Ireland, but every few seconds he'd lose track of his place in the script and flounder around for a few moments, red-faced as he tried to look everywhere except the one place he wanted to. Dympna knew full well what she was doing and kept winding him up, while acting the innocent. "Go on, Brendan," she said, uncrossing and re-crossing her legs. "What were you saying?"

Brendan just kept stammering as he stared ahead, like a rabbit caught in the headlights.

Dympna was very reluctant to allow us to use the dump again at first, but eventually she was either won over, or grew bored of her game. She yawned, shrugged her shoulders and said, "Ah, what the fuck, put them back in there."

As we walked back down the road, Brendan was mopping his brow.

"Something wrong, Brendan?" I asked innocently.

"Christ, Ray, I swear it was winking at me."

We moved the guns back in the following night. I noticed that Brendan had combed his hair and was wearing after-shave, but if he was planning a further conversation with Dympna about her patriotic duty, he was out of luck. We could hear noises from the bedroom, but no one came downstairs and shortly afterwards there was the unmistakable sound of an orgasm.

"Dirty bitch," said Brendan enviously as we closed the dump and slipped out of the back door.

As arranged, we met at his father's flat the following Thursday, ready for the job at the shirt factory. His father let us in, but then Brendan gave him a few quid and said, "Here's a couple of bob, get yourself a pint while me and the boys have a chat."

His old man winked at us and was out of the door and over the road to the Bogside Inn in ten seconds flat. "Right, lads," said Brendan. "the new plan. Ciaran, Pat and myself will go into the factory when yer man gets back with the money. Ray, you wait outside for the keys to his car. Mary and Niall, you stand at the bookies down at Patrick Street and keep dick for peelers and Brits."

Mary handed out green woolen balaclava masks to everyone, then pulled the revolver out of her waistband and handed it to Ciaran. We went in pairs down to Patrick Street, walking a few yards apart. I went with Brendan, Mary was with Ciaran, and Pat walked with Blakely. We turned into a wee lane at the side of Duffy's bookmakers and stood peering up towards Scott's factory.

We waited there for almost an hour before an old man with a few greying strands of hair plastered across his bald head came out of the front door of the factory and got into the green Renault parked outside. He drove off up Patrick Street towards Queen Street.

"That's him," Blakely said. "Yer man's away for the money."

About half an hour later the Renault turned in from the Strand Road and pulled up outside the factory. We watched as the old man got out of his car and disappeared inside.

Brendan looked at his watch. "We'll give him a few minutes."

We waited about five more minutes outside the bookies, then Brendan told Mary and Blakely to keep dick. Ciaran, Pat and Brendan put their balaclavas on top of their heads and then stepped out of the laneway and walked up Patrick Street towards the factory. I tagged along, a few paces behind. When they reached the front door, they pulled their masks down over their faces and stepped inside. I tried the doors of the Renault, but they were locked, so I stood waiting to the side of the factory door, level with the car.

Two minutes after they'd gone into the factory, I heard a muffled shot. Before the echoes had died away, Brendan came running out. He tore his mask off and said, "Run like fuck?", then sprinted down the street to the bookies where Mary and Blakely were standing.

I didn't need a second invitation. I sprinted up the street and didn't slow down until I was in the Lower Road. I leaned on the wall, coughing my guts up until I got my breath back and then dandered over to the Bogside Inn.

Brendan was already there. As soon as Mary, Ciaran and Pat joined us, he demanded, "What the fuck happened in there?"

Ciaran shrugged. "The old bastard wouldn't give us the money."

"So?" said Brendan, rounding on Pat, who flushed nervously.

"I went into the office and asked him for the money and the car keys. He gave me the keys all right, but then he suddenly lifted this big stick and started hitting me with it."

He pulled back the sleeves of his pullover to show off some angry red welts on his arms. "I told Ciaran to shoot him, but he missed and the bullet went through a glass door. The old man was still pasting me and people were screaming and hollering all over the place, so we gave up and ran for it."

There was a long silence. "What did you do with the keys, Brendan?" I asked, more to break the silence than out of genuine curiosity.

"I threw them in the cistern above the toilet in the Derby Bar." He stood lost in thought for a few moments.

"What a fuck-up." He said bitterly, though he seemed to be reserving most of his anger for the old man at the factory rather than Pat and Ciaran. "I'll phone the old bastard one night and tell him to leave the money somewhere. If he doesn't we'll fucking nut him."

We all harrumphed and nodded vigorously, even though we knew it was just a way of saving face.

"We could do it just to scare the fuck out of him," Pat said with feeling, still fingering his bruises.

Brendan nodded absently, his mind perhaps already running over the explosion from Shorty when he told him we'd screwed up the job. "Anyway, where's Blakely?" he asked abruptly.

We all shrugged our shoulders. Blakely's first taste of IRA active service was also his last for the moment, for he didn't turn up at the Bogside Inn and vanished into thin air for the next couple of weeks until he got back his nerve. We all split up and I headed home.

At our meeting that night, Shorty was incandescent that we hadn't got any money from the robbery, giving us all a bollocking and complaining, "You should have shot the old bastard."

"I tried to," Ciaran said plaintively, which only earned him another mouthful from Shorty.

Ciaran had evidently had more success with his pursuit of Mary than he had with shooting the owner of the factory, for they were locked into an intense affair. The mutual attraction can only have been fired by a shared interest in murder and death, because Ciaran was a singularly unattractive character. He was tall and dark, but definitely not handsome, with a pock-marked face covered in blackheads. He also had the musty, sweaty smell that people get when they don't wash. Despite it all, he and Mary were clearly in lust, if not love, hard though they tried to hide it from the rest of us.

Most people settle for a drink or a cigarette after making love, but Ciaran and Mary seemed to prefer trying to kill people. They came up to my flat one evening, still flushed from their exertions, again wanting to try shooting a policeman as he came out of the Strand Road barracks. We picked up Brendan and Pat and collected a short from the dump at Dympna McGrail's, then drove out to the Camelot Bar on the Letterkenny Road.

As usual, there wasn't a four-door car to be seen, and we had to sit in the car chatting for almost an hour before a blue Mazda 323 pulled into the car park. Ciaran and I masked up and walked over to the guy just as he was getting out fo the car. We didn't even have to produce the gun. I just said, "Provisional IRA. We want your car," and he handed over the keys as good as gold.

"Boys, I work as a barman here, is it alright if I go to work?"

"Work away," I said, "but don't leave the bar or try to contact the police. You'll be watched."

"I wouldn't do that, you can count on me."

The guy disappeared into the bar and Brendan sent Pat in to keep an eye on him while the rest of us drove back to the dump to pick up the guns for the shoot – an M16 for Brendan, an Armalite for Ciaran and the revolver for Mary.

Brendan told me to drive down to Tinney's Bar on Patrick Street. I parked the car opposite the bar and waited while the other three walked to the end of the street and kept a look-out for policemen coming out of the barracks. After about ten minutes they came sprinting back to the car.

Brendan leapt in the front seat, yelling, "Quick, there's a peeler driving up Strand Road. Drive round to the lights at Great James Street."

"We're facing the wrong way."

"Then fucking turn it round!"

I did so, but I didn't break my neck about it and halfway to the lights, Brendan said, "Don't fucking bother, he'll be away by now. That's it, fuck it, the shoot's off."

I started to head back towards the dump. We drove along Lone Moor Road and I turned off by the playground beside the cathedral chapel. There's a blind-spot there, preventing you from seeing to the left until you've made the turn. There were two army checkpoints blocking the road, no more than twenty feet away from me.

I froze for what felt like minutes, but was probably only about two seconds, while the others were all shouting at me, "Fucking reverse! Get the fuck out of here!"

I banged it into reverse. I hit some iron railings then threw it into first and began to spin it around. As I did so, I heard the army commander shout in impeccable Oxbridge tones, "Do not fire."

I thought, thank fuck for that, for I had my head sunk as low as it would go between my shoulders, like a fully-retracted tortoise, waiting for the first bullet to hit me. I have no idea why he told his men not to shoot, but he saved my life, for they could hardly have missed if they'd opened up from that range.

I threw the car into a handbrake turn. When I glanced in the mirror, I discovered that I was alone. Mary, Ciaran and Brendan had all jumped out and run for it, Mary throwing the revolver down at her feet as she ran, and Brendan tossing the M16 intoh te grounds of the Parochial House. Only Ciaran hung on to his weapon as he ran off down towards the Bogside.

I didn't stop to remonstrate with them, but went flying off as fast as I could go. A brown Escort was partially blocking the road, but I drove straight at it, giving it a glancing blow as I forced it out of the way. I stopped for a split second round the corner but the others had all disappeared, so I blasted off again into the Rosemount, hurtling up Creggan Road and into Marlborough Road.

Heart still pounding, I turned into the first side-street in Marlborough Road and dumped the car immediately, because I knew that every army patrol would be looking for it. I threw the keys into a garden and then walked back down the hill. There was an unbelievable commotion, with army jeeps and Land Rovers flying around and soldiers and police everywhere.

Two army jeeps came slowly past me as I was crossing the road and I heard a soldier shout, "There's one of them. There's one of them," but I just kept walking slowly and they didn't stop.

I had to phone Pete and tell him what was going on. I slipped into McCann's fish and chip shop, put ten pence in the phone-box and dialed the number I knew better than my own name. Just as Pete answered, I heard someone behind me go, "Pssst. Pssst."

I turned round and saw Brendan standing behind the counter alongside the serving girl. He'd run in, jumped over the counter, put on a white coat and started serving fish and chips with a face as white as his coat.

I slammed the phone down. "Where's Ciaran?"

"He's run down the Bogside with his gun."

"Where's Mary?"

"I dunno. Who were you trying to ring, Shorty?"

"Yeah. I was going to."

"Don't do it. They could be bugging his phone."

I was shaking like a leaf, but so was Brendan. I hoped he would put my nerves down to the close call with the army, but in truth it was not as close as the one that I'd just had in the fish shop. I was no more than two seconds from signing my own death warrant. Had Brendan not whispered to me, I would have started speaking to Pete and Brendan couldn't have failed to hear me.

I stayed a few minutes chatting to him and then left in search of a safer phone. There was no need to worry about Brendan overhearing the next call, for he was too scared to leave the shop, wanting to stay close to the girl who was going to give him an alibi if the police arrived. In the end he stayed there all night.

I couldn't get through to Pete again that night and had to ring him first thing the next morning from someone's living room in the flats.

Pete still wasn't there and his boss took the call.

"Is this Ray?"

"Yeah."

"Was that you last night?"

"Yeah." I couldn't speak too freely, for I didn't want to raise the suspicions of the people who lived in the flat, but speaking in a sort of code, I managed to let him know that the gun was in the grounds of the Parochial House. I needn't have bothered, for he told me that the army had found it anyway during the follow-up search.

When I got back to my flat, Ciaran was waiting for me. "Shorty wants to see us all right now, over at the shops." We walked over to the Creggan shops, where we could see Shorty pacing up and down, his face working as he muttered to himself. Even from two hundred yards away it was obvious he was not in a pleasant mood.

"Let's just wait here a wee while, Ray," Ciaran said nervously. "No point in going over there and getting a bollocking now and then another one when the others arrive."

We hung around the corner till we saw Brendan and Mary roll up, then dandered over ourselves, putting on suitably funereal expressions as we got within range of Shorty.

He stared at us, speechless, with rage for a moment, then demanded, "Right, where's the fucking M16?"

Brendan coloured and said, "I chucked it into the chapel grounds when we legged it."

"If it's lost, heads will fucking roll."

He rounded on Ciaran. "Where's the rifle?"

"I ran down to the Bog with it and hid it round the back of the Dove Gardens flats, just up the road from my house."

Mary was next in line. "And the short?" Shorty said, scowling at her.

"I...I dropped it when I ran for it, but ..."

Mary got no further for Shorty held his hand up to silence her. "I'll have more to say to you all tonight when we debrief the job. For the moment, I want that rifle shifted to the dump as soon as possible, but before that, I want you all down the chapel grounds searching till you find that M16. Do I make myself clear?"

We nodded.

"Right. Now get out of my sight, the lot of youse."

We went down to the chapel grounds and rummaged around without finding a trace of it. I was ready to give up almost at once, but then I already knew it wasn't there. Brendan kept obsessively searching the grounds over and over, scared shitless that he'd be court-martialled if he turned up at the unit meeting without it.

Eventually I lost patience. "For fuck's sake, Brendan, we've already searched every blade of grass twice. It isn't there. We're going to go and shift the rifle."

"You go where you like, I'm staying here till I find it," muttered Brendan, beginning another sweep through the grounds.

We shrugged and left him to it. Ciaran and I walked down to Blucher Street and borrowed Gerry McCracken's Transit van. We didn't tell him what we wanted it for, but he was happy to let us use it. We drove round to the Dove Gardens flats and Ciaran scurried into the enclosure where they dumped their rubbish and pulled the rifle out of a mound of black plastic bags. We dropped it off at the dump without any problems and had the van back at McCrakcn's house within the hour.

Shorty's temper had not abated during the day, and the formal inquest into the previous night's shambles was far from friendly. Ciaran and I were spared the worst of his temper, for Shorty praised me for getting away with the car and Ciaran had at least kept hold of his gun. The normally urbane Shorty gave Mary and Brendan a ferocious savaging for throwing their weapons away, however, nearly biting through the stem of his pipe in anger.

"I can't understand why you all got out of the car and ran while Ray was still fit to turn it round and get away. Mary, I thought you had more about you than to throw your gun at your backside and run off like that, and Brendan, that M16 was a good weapon. We've probably lost it now, thanks to your stupidity. Someone is going to be court-martialled for this cock-up."

"I've searched and searched down there," Brendan began, but Shorty was unrelenting.

"You wouldn't have had to if you hadn't thrown it in there in the first place you dozy bastard."

Brendan stiffened at the insult, but though he towered over Shorty's diminutive frame, the wee man faced him down. "We've lost the short and we've probably lost the M16 too, but there's just one faint hope. Pat and Ray, I want you to go down to the Parochial House after the meeting and ask the priests if they found the gun. If they did, they may have hidden it."

We nodded our agreement. I already knew that it too would be a fruitless errand, but I could hardly tell Shorty that.

CHAPTER 11

After those two near-misses – one with the army roadblock, the other with Brendan McDermott in the fish shop – I desperately needed time to think. I'd been lucky so far, but I was well aware that the clock was ticking towards midnight. I had already survived much longer than many police and army agents, but every IRA job I got through merely made the odds worse on the next one.

Arrest and imprisonment were the least of my worries, for every time I went on a job I was risking my life twice over. My death might come in an ambush or shoot-out with the security forces, for only two or three people in the whole of Northern Ireland knew me to be an agent. Every day that passed also increased the risk of detection by the IRA, and if that happened, there could be only one outcome.

I'd missed arrest – or worse – at the army roadblock by seconds, but the next time I was not to be so lucky. One of the advantages of being know as an RUC agent only to Pete and a couple of his colleagues was that the chances of my cover being blown to the IRA were substantially reduced. While that greatly improved my prospects of staying alive, the disadvantage was that since virtually no one in the RUC knew that I was an informant, I was as liable to arrest as any other IRA member. In November 1981, I was duly lifted, along with Mary Cobbe, Ciaran McQuillan and Pat McHugh.

The job was to have been a shoot at the army from the window of a flat at the back of Kells Walk, overlooking the Pilot's Row Community Centre. We'd been to survey it a couple of weeks before, and had fixed on a small window on the top floor of the flats which looked along a pathway straight into the Community Centre, less than two hundred yards away.

The plan was to arrange a disturbance outside the centre and then shoot the police when they arrived to deal with it. Mary, the best shot in the unit, according to Shorty, had been complaining that she was not getting enough chances to shoot, and Brendan had agreed that she should use the rifle on this job but no date was set for when we would carry it out.

I was on my way out of my house to fetch a bag of coal when Ciaran appeared on the doorstep and said, "are you coming on this job?"

"Which one?"

"Pilot's Row."

"All right, but I have to get a bag of coal on the way back."

Such was life in the unpaid ranks of the Republican Army: kill a few soldiers, but don't forget the shopping on the way home.

I could see Mary, Pat and the new guy, Niall Blakely – who'd obviously now recovered from his fright at Scott's shirt factory – already sitting in Ciaran's yellow Cavalier over the road. I grabbed my coat and the leather gloves that, like the others, I wore on every job to avoid leaving fingerprints. Ciaran wore the same gloves: we bought them at the House of Value down Strand Road, next door to the police station, which made us both laugh.

We drove down to Dympna McGrail's. There were only two weapons in the dump at the time, a bolt-action Japanese sniper's rifle and a revolver. Mary and Ciaran went in to get them and re-emerged a few minutes later, Ciaran clutching the rifle,, while Mary had the revolver and a handful of balaclavas.

Ciaran stuck the rifle in the boot and Mary distributed the balaclavas, as excited as if she was handing out paper hats at a kid's party. She'd also brought a small orange bath sponge to act as a rest for the rifle barrel, stopping it from sliding around on the window ledge of the flat as she was shooting. As usual, the mere thought of killing was enough to have Mary wetting herself with excitement.

"Look at her," I said to Pat. "Sure it's dripping from her mouth."

Ciaran and I were to hijack a car from the Bogside for the job and, as usual, getting the car was the main problem. He parked his car in Cable Street, facing down the road towards Stanley's Walk, and we left the other three sitting in it, with the rifle still in the boot, while we went in search of a car. Ciaran carried the revolver in his waistband in case persuasion was needed.

We went up Stanley's Walk, looking without success for a four-door car, and then continued towards the Lone Moor Road, where we saw a woman getting into a lime-green Renault. Ciaran and I took the masks out of our pockets, put them on and crossed over the road to the car. The woman, a blonde in her early thirties, had already started the engine, but Ciaran yanked open the driver's door, pointed the gun at her and said, "Provisional IRA. We want your car. Get out."

Politely but firmly, she said, "I'm sorry, you're not getting this car."

We were soon both down on our hunkers, arguing with the woman, with Ciaran threatening to blow her head off if she did not get out and the woman calmly insisting that she was not going to do so, when I saw a red Escort drive past us, heading towards the gas works. There were two men in plain clothes in the car, but I had seen it before and knew it was a police car.

I said to Ciaran, "That's two CID men."

As we hesitated, the woman slammed her door and drove off. The red Escort was still going away up the road, but I could see the passenger staring back at us. We both stood up, turned our backs and pulled off our masks, and Ciaran stuffed the revolver back in his waistband before we hurried off up the street. The Escort did not return.

We went back to Cable Street. Mary, Pat and Niall Blakely were standing in a group just up the street from the car, too paranoid to sit inside it with a rifle in the boot. They were hopping from foot to foot trying to keep warm.

"What's the crack, lads?" Pat asked.

"We can't get a fucking car."

There were groans from the three of them.

"We'll go try over by the Credit Union," Ciaran said.

"Well make it quick then. It's fucking freezing standing here."

Ciaran and I hurried over to the Credit Union office, beside the Stardust Ballroom, but there were no four-door cars to be seen when we go there. We wandered on to the Glenfadda car park, where there was an old white van parked outside the little office, next to a derelict block of flats. Ciaran tugged my arm. "Come on, that'll do.

We masked up and Ciaran pulled out the handgun as we burst into the office. An old man, short, bald and bespectacled looked up.

"Hello, boys," he mildly. "What can I be doing for you?"

"We want the keys of that van," said Ciaran, brandishing the gun.

The man's old-fashioned courtesy did not fade for an instant, even at the sight of a revolver trained on his Adam's apple.

"Of course, but I'm afraid it hasn't been working too well."

He took the keys out of his pocket and pushed them across the desk. I took the van for a test drive while Ciaran kept the man covered. He hadn't been kidding about the van. It had a column gear change and was a terrible thing to drive. The engine misfired like mad and it wouldn't pick up in second gear. A supermarket trolley would have been a better getaway vehicle.

I drove it back into the car park, put my mask back on and gave the double-knock on the office door to let Ciaran know it was me. I walked in, dumping the keys back on the desk. After two hours of traipsing around the Bogside in the freezing cold, I was dying to go to the toilet, so I used the one in the office, while Ciaran kept the old man covered.

"We're leaving, but don't report this to the police," I said, as I came out again.

"What, you using the toilet?" said the old man, who was clearly beginning to enjoy the situation.

We turned our backs on him, took off our masks and walked out, heading back over to the Credit Union office in the desperate hope that there might be a car there by now. There was. A man was getting into a beige Ford Capri, parked right outside the office. It was only a two-door car, but by then I would have hijacked a car with no doors at all, just as long as it had a heater.

We walked over to the car, pulling on our masks yet again.

"Provisional IRA. We're taking your car," said Ciaran. "Get out."

I kept getting the strangest sense of *déjà vu*. Mercifully this man had rather less spunk than the woman in the Renault. He didn't say a word, but got out looking frightened to death.

Ciaran told him, "Now get in the back seat and lie face down."

We got in, pulled off our masks and drove away.

As we were heading up William Street, the man was obviously feeling a little braver, for he piped up from the back, "Can you drop me off at home on the way?" We dropped him off up the Creggan, warning him not to contact the police for half an hour, and then drove down to Cable Street, where the other three, almost blue with cold, were still standing in a huddle, down the street from Ciaran's car. I parked right in front of it. Blakely then sat in Ciaran's car, while Mary and Pat joined me and Ciaran in the Capri to get warm and have a discussion about what to do next.

We were all agreed that we had to have a four-door car for the getaway after the shoot, and decided to go and have a look at a Volvo I remembered seeing in a street off the Lone Moor Road. Ciaran left the revolver with Blakely while we went to look the Volvo over, and had just got back into the car when suddenly Mary spotted a police Land Rover coming up the street from Stanley's Walk. We were all absolutely shitting ourselves as it came towards us, crawling along at about twenty-five miles an hour.

Mary said, "Just sit where you are," but Ciaran and I got out, hoping to walk off without the police paying us any attention.

Instead they stopped right alongside us. I threw the car keys over the hedge, hoping to stop them opening the boot, and dropped my mask kicking it under the car.

Three policemen leaped out and pointed guns at us, shouting, "Put your hands on the bonnet."

Ciaran was already halfway across the road, but was dragged back and spread-eagled on the bonnet alongside me. The police ordered Mary and Pat out of the car and one barked at us, "Who owns this car?"

No one said anything.

"Right. I'm arresting you under Section Eleven of the Prevention of Terrorism Act."

They hustled us into the back of the Land Rover. By this time people were beginning to spill out of the houses and a crowd started to gather round the Land Rover, making the police very agitated. They drove off with us with us in a hurry, leaving Niall Blakely still sitting in Ciaran's car and both cars unexamined. Being arrested was bad enough, but had they searched the cars, they couldn't have failed to find the rifle and the short. As it was, the worst they could now charge us with was hijacking.

At the police station, we were all put in separate rooms. After a few minutes alone, a big policeman came in and starting shouting at me, emphasizing his words with a few slaps to the back of the head. I ignored him and said nothing. After a while, he gave up and left. The next policeman to appear was Sergeant Ivor Semple, who had interrogated me after my first arrest, for the robbery with Noel Kavanagh several years before. He stared intently at me for a moment, and gave me a big smile and said, "Hello, Ray."

Semple always sucked his teeth and smacked his lips in between phrases, and his greeting became, "Hello, Ray," suck, smack; "How are you doing?" suck, smack.

I had a lot of respect for Semple and admired his courage. He would often drive through the Creggan on his own, which for a known policeman was virtual suicide. In the end he pushed his luck too far and the IRA shot him by the Craigavon Bridge on day. He's still alive, but has never recovered. Pete had also been inches from the same fate, for Pop Maguire and George McBrearty spotted him driving round the Creggan one day and fired, just missing him.

Despite my respect for Semple, I continued to say nothing. Only Pete's partner and his boss knew that I was an agent, and I wasn't going to blow my cover by speaking to anyone other than Pete himself. Ivor's Mr Nice treatment got him no further than the previous Mr Nasty, and he too gave up and left.

Eventually to my great relief, Pete appeared, but the message he brought was not a comforting one.

"Don't say anything to any of these guys, Ray, keep your cover."

"So what's going to happen?"

"You'll probably be sent up the river for a few months, but don't worry, I'll sort something out."

He winked and slipped out. Whatever Pete was going to sort out didn't save me from almost six months in prison. After three days under interrogation in Strand Road and a brief appearance at Bishop Street Court, we were sent to the Crum at the end of November 1981, the grimy old Victorian prison on the Crumlin Road in Belfast.

The prison was so damp that the bricks smelled as if it was dissolving, and so filthy that the half-hearted sweeping and mopping by the prisoners merely re-arranged the dirt into fresh patterns. We were crammed in three to a cell, pissing and shitting into a bucket which we slopped out every morning. To ease the stench in the cell, we used to shit in newspapers instead and post our newspaper parcels out of the window.

The conditions were bad enough, but there were other worries about going there. As soon as I arrived I was debriefed by Provies from Belfast, who were always paranoid about British military intelligence slipping informers into the prison. I was told there was a spokesman for each floor of A-Wing, and no one else was allowed to speak to the prison officials for fear that they might pass on information out of earshot of the other prisoners. I was to be in A1, and the spokesman for the floor would voice any complaints I had to the officials.

I soon had a complaint to raise. The first morning I was there, a warder who didn't realise I was a Provie prisoner punched and slapped me around. I mentioned it to the Provie OC of the wing, and a few minutes later he actually hauled the warder into my cell and made him apologise to me. It was a vivid demonstration of the balance of power inside the Crum.

I got safely through my debriefing, but still had Liam Hanrahan to face. He'd been convicted of possession of firearms and was the leader of the

Provisionals in the Crum at the time, along with all the other really hard IRA men. I wasn't looking forward to renewing my acquaintance with him after the beating he'd given me on our previous meeting, but this time, being an IRA volunteer rather than a teenage hood, I avoided a pasting.

Others were not so lucky. A couple of months after we arrived there, the IRA men rioted and broke into the protection area which was caged off on the top floor of A-Wing. All the hoods in there were dragged out and given a good kicking by Liam and his boys. The rest of us staying in the canteen area, having sing-songs while the boys were out prowling around.

The A-Wing of the Crum was completely wrecked in the riot, but the Governor reached a compromise with Hanrahan and the other Provie leaders, guaranteeing that there would be no reprisals and no one hurt if they gave themselves up. The next day we were all put into different cells with different people. I kept saying to myself, *you must remember these guys*, because they were all from Armagh and were real hard IRA men.

With A-Wing a write-off, we were quickly sent up to the H-Blocks of Long Kesh – the Maze. It was cleaner than the Crum because it was newer, but it was a terrible place. Ciaran McQuillan and I were on the same wing. Liam Hanrahan, inevitably, was there again, along with Marty Gilligan, Hugh O'Donnell and his brother Frankie, a friend of Mairead Farrell, who was later shot dead by the SAS in Gibraltar with Sean Savage and Danny McCann.

The IRA were offering temporary immunity to informers, and Marty Gilligan went round everybody on the wing to remind us of our duty and ask each of us to our face, "You been informing?"

I said, "No," and obviously didn't betray any signs of guilt, for he passed on to the next prisoner.

Later on he came up to me again. "We're thinking about having another blanket protest. Would you go on it, if you were asked?"

I knew the right answer to that one and immediately said, "Yes, of course," though I was praying I would be out of there before they started it. They'd had 300 prisoners on the dirty protest at one stage, and I wasn't too keen to be number 301 when they started smearing shit all over the cell walls again.

I also met Donal Tiernan in Long Kesh, who'd been with Pop Maguire and George McBrearty when they were killed trying to hijack a car driven by an SAS man. Like Maguire, Tiernan had been hit by fire from McBrearty's M16 as he fell dying to the ground. Unlike Maguire he survived, but he had been badly wounded and still had some impressive scars. He pulled up his shirt and dropped his trousers to reveal a chain of bullet holes running up his buttock and back. "Would you fucking believe it, Ray? Shot in the arse by McBrearty."

We drilled every Sunday while we were in prison. The UDA had their military parade and the Provies had theirs, while the authorities tolerated the situation and even played along with it. If the Provie command were dissatisfied with anything, they would go and see the head of the wing or the governor and try to get it sorted out. They were usually successful, because there was always a threat hovering over the prison officers' heads; if they messed around with the IRA or UDA men, there were people on the outside who could get to them very easily.

The Deputy Governor of the Maze, Albert Miles, had been shot dead by the Ardoyne IRA in November 1978, and eighteen prison warders had been killed between 1976 and 1980. One of the dead, Michael Cassidy, had been one of the few friendly faces in the Crum when I'd been banged up there with Noel Kavanagh.

Cassidy was a Catholic, but that didn't stop the Provies from blowing him away in the most hideous manner possible. They murdered him at the church where his sister was getting married. He was walking out of the church porch after the service, holding his three-year-old daughter's hand, when masked Provie gunmen confronted him and shot him with Armalites at point-blank range. As he lay dying on the ground in a pool of blood, surrounded by his screaming relatives, the gunmen shot him again in the head.

Women prison officers were just as vulnerable. One was killed and three wounded after a car full of Provie gunmen pulled up alongside them in the street. They raked them with automatic fire and then threw a handgrenade into the middle of them. As the killers drove off they fired a few more bursts into the heap of bodies on the pavement. It was a miracle that only one of the women died.

Prison Officers were left in no doubt that if they crossed IRA prisoners, the threat to their lives was genuine. They just did their job and didn't give anyone a hard time.

Lorraine came up to see me once or twice a week, a long journey on the Long Kesh special, the bus packed with wives and mothers making the pilgrimage for a half-hour visit with their men. I cried when I saw her, for she was looking terrible. She'd dark circles around her eyes and had lost a lot of weight, worrying both about me and about our finances.

I'd been bringing in plenty of money and had filled the cupboards with food every week. Now, suddenly, all she had to feed and clothe herself and the children was a few quid a week, the standard payment the IRA made to the wives of political prisoners. It was Lorraine's first proof that I was involved with the IRA. I'd still never discussed it with her, though she must have had her suspicions from the number of times I would disappear with a car-load of strangers, not returning until late at night.

The knowledge wouldn't have upset her. Her father was staunch IRA, an old Stickie with guns under his sofa, but though she liked to think she supported the IRA herself, I suspect it was just because she was supporting her husband and family. Deep down, I don't think she thought about it at all; she'd no strong views on anything.

A few of the other guys were full-time IRA volunteers. They were paid – though not much – and could be called upon at any time. Tapper McFadden was full-time, and one of his jobs was to collect the weekly brown envelopes from Paul Cleary for the other Derry full-timers. I was with him one time when he handed them out to Ruari Spears, Tam McGinty, Paddy Lawler and Pat McHugh.

"We each get around £15 to £20 a week," Tapper told me. "It's not a fortune, but it's better than a kick in the bollocks. Right," he said happily, shredding his own brown envelope, "my round."

I was never asked to become full-time and was never paid – except by the RUC. While I was in prison I obviously couldn't collect my usual cash from Pete. The IRA money wasn't enough to pay the bills and I was frantic with worry about Lorraine. I kept looking at her as I chewed the insides of my cheeks, and I couldn't stand the thought of her going home and starving herself to save enough money to keep the kids clothed and fed. I took an enormous risk – what was one more, after all, among the risks I already took – and got her to give Pete a ring, so that he could send her some money every week.

She accepted the idea without question, even though she had no idea who Pete was or where the money was coming from, but there was a desperately close thing when her father found the envelope on the table and asked, "Who send this money?"

She just said, "Some friend of Ray's," and luckily he didn't push it any further. When she told me that her father had been asking questions about the money, it nearly gave me heart failure.

I couldn't really do much with the cash I got from Pete. If I'd put it in the building society or bought a new car or some flash clothes, it would just have drawn attention to me. All I could do was buy groceries with it or spend it on drink and the horses.

Ever since I'd become a full-time agent for the RUC, I'd done a lot of gambling in various bookmakers to hide the real source of my money. If anyone queried my affluence, my excuse was either that I'd had a good win on the horses, or that I'd got it from my sister. It was well known that she'd received a big lump sum in compensation after a very bad accident a few years previously. Neither excuse would have covered the arrival of an anonymous envelope full of cash through my letterbox, but my father-in-law was apparently satisfied with Lorraine's explanation.

I was frantic to get out of Long Kesh and get home to Lorraine and the kids, and the RUC were desperate to get me out too, for they were definitely missing me. There had been a big upsurge in successful IRA operations in Derry while I had been in prison, and several bombs had gone off in the city centre, devastating the commercial area. The RUC had other informants, but they weren't doing as good a job, and the Special Branch were very keen to get me back on the streets. After much pressure from them, we were released without charge on April Fools' Day, 1982. My release came too late to save the lives of two plain-clothes soldiers, however, who were shot dead in a machine gun attack in the city on the day we came out of the Maze.

I got a lift back to Derry from Lisburn. As we drove into the familiar streets, I knew my holiday was over; it was time to go back to work.

CHAPTER 12

Our unit had been disbanded after our arrest, and before we could be assigned to a new cell after our release, we were all required to go through a debriefing by a senior IRA man. I wasn't unduly worried, because it was standard practice for all volunteers who'd been arrested or imprisoned. Ciaran came around to my place a few days after we got back to Derry and told me we had to go and see Shorty at Barnie Whelan's flat in Stanley Walk, down the Bogside. Ciaran was on foot, for his yellow Cavalier, his pride and joy, had been repossessed by the hire-purchase crowd while he was on remand.

I arrived a few minutes before Ciaran and Shorty, and sat waiting in Whelan's living room. Barnie used to be in charge of the old gasworks nearby, and there was a really strong stench of gas around the place. He was also a very well-known Sinn Féin man, and the walls of his living-room were covered with pictures drawn on hankies by guys in Long Kesh. People often framed them and put them on their walls, but Barnie had loads of them; I'd never seen as many. He also had harps and crosses carved out of wood by guys in the Kesh, and there was a bronze statue of Cuchullain the Brave, complete with the crow which pecked out his eyes.

It was like being inside an IRA church, with the sideboard arranged like an alar. At its centre, where the cross would have been, was a plaque inscribed, "They Hungered for Justice", commemorating the ten hunger strikers who starved themselves to death in the Maze. It was a weird choice for a safe house. It could not have been a more obvious IRA sympathiser's place if Barnie had put a neon sign on the roof saying, "IRA WELCOME HERE".

It wasn't easy to get safe houses, which usually belonged to sympathisers who had no active involvement in the IRA, so we had to use what we could, including Barnie Whelan's. There was always a worry about our safe houses being bugged, but the IRA couldn't do much about it because they didn't have any anti-bugging devices. Towards the end of my time, we all became rather slack anyway, and would use our own flats and houses for meetings. I'm sure a lot of the unit members' houses were bugged, and even my flat may have been wired, but if it was, I was never told about it.

Shorty arrived at Barnie's in great good humour. "Things are definitely picking up now for the RA in Derry. Did you hear about the soldiers the other day?" We nodded.

"We got that police inspector, Duddy, last month as well."

"I know, we heard about it in the Kesh."

"I had to suspend the whole of the Shantallow unit, though, for withholding information. I thought that Duddy was a Catholic, and I had lads going out for weeks to every chapel in Derry trying to find his car to booby-trap it." He paused dramatically.

"So what happened?"

"He was only a fucking Protestant, wasn't he? The Shantallow unit all knew and never bothered to tell me. I had a bloody big row with them and suspended the lot when I found out. Once we knew where to look, it wasn't long before I got him shot ... Anyway, Ray, what was it like inside?"

"It wasn't good, Shorty, that's for sure, and I'll tell you what, those Belfast Provies are nothing but a shower of ignorant cunts."

Shorty was delighted with the answer, slapping his thigh and choking on his pipe as he chortled with laughter. "And do you have plans to come back into the RA?"

"We both want to, but Pat McHugh says he's had enough. He's not coming back."

"Well, as you know, you'll have to be debriefed and given a clearance first, but it shouldn't be a problem. You did well not to admit anything when you were lifted."

Ciaran contacted me again for the debrief a couple of days later. I had to meet him outside the Credit Union office at nine o'clock at night, and he then took me to a flat behind Kells Walk.

Ciaran had already been debriefed, and told me, "You'll be done by old Kevin Caddick and Hugh Porter. Don't worry, Ray, it's a piece of piss."

Despite his reassurances, I was worried. Porter and Caddick were old men, but their eyes missed nothing and they were as cunning as foxes.

Ciaran left me at the door of the flat, which was opened by Hugh Porter. I followed him upstairs, passing the open door of the living-room, where Kevin Caddick was debriefing Pat McHugh, sitting on chairs facing each other about two feet apart. It looked like Pat was being given a pretty tough time.

Porter led me into one of the bedrooms. The only furniture in the room was a double bed and we both sat down on it. Porter came straight to the point.

"Did you have a hard time of it during the police interrogation in Strand Road after your arrest?"

"No, not really. There were a number of different detectives over the couple of days. There was plenty of shouting, the usual crack and the odd slap on the back of the head."

"Did you know any of them?"

"No."

Porter questioned me for half an hour or so, but I didn't get any strong feeling that he was suspicious of me in particular; it was just routine. I told him that reading the Green Book had been a great help to me. "I just studied one place on the wall and kept my mind a blank and didn't react

Porter smiled and nodded.

"I did almost crack once though," I added, emboldened by Porter's warmth into gilding the lily a little.

"Not many people would admit that," said Porter, "but it happens to most men when they get lifted. It gets easier the more times you're in the barracks, though and you will soon find it just the old routine. You know if you say anything at all, you're likely to verbal yourself."

I nodded, "I heard that Christopher Black from the Ardoyne has verballed himself – and other people – in there. He couldn't do his fucking whack without opening his big gob."

I knew the fact that Black was talking to the police was already known to the IRA, but I saw no harm in gaining the credit for reporting the prison gossip.

"We've heard so. He's put a lot of good men at risk. No doubt the SB here will be trying the same trick."

"Maybe, but they'll not get Derrymen to inform."

"I hope you're right."

To my relief, Porter brought the debrief to a close, for the conversation had been straying dangerously close to home.

"Well, Ray, you've all done very well. Usually when three or four get caught, at least one cracks. It's very unusual to get all of you walking out again. That's all I want, but don't go just yet, Kevin may want a word."

When we got downstairs, Pat McHugh was just leaving. Caddick waved me into the living-room and motioned to the chair where Pat had been sitting.

"Now, Ray, there are two types of informers," began Caddick.

I stiffened imperceptibly, then forced myself to relax. His tone was conversational, not inquisitorial.

"There are the ones like Christopher Black," he continued, "the gutless ones who can't do their whack inside. Then there are the others, the boys who get paid for informing on their mates."

I hardly dared to breath, but tried to remain impassive.

"You know that Dympna McGrail was lifted while you were inside and the dump was found?"

"I'd heard that, yes."

"What do you think of Dympna McGrail?"

"I wouldn't trust her once the police had hold of her."

While we were still in Long Kesh, Ciaran had told me that Dympna had named us to the Police.

He nodded, "Do you think she would go to court and give evidence against your unit?"

"I think she might."

"We'll have to send someone up to see her and find out what she intends to do." He gazed moodily into the fire for a moment, then nodded abruptly. "Okay, that's all."

"Am I cleared to resume active service?"

"You are. We'll be assigning you to a new unit shortly."

Two days later, Ciaran and I were again lifted by the police and taken to Strand Road. A series of detectives questioned me about the weapons dump in Dympna McGrail's house. It was the same mixture as before. First came the shouting and aggressive questioning, interspersed with a few stinging slaps and punches from a sour-faced Mr Angry. Then I was left alone for a few minutes' solitary reflection, which was followed by a further session with a soft-voiced, kindly Mr Friendly.

When his honeyed words and offers of tea and cigarettes brought no response, he shook his head sadly in that "this is going to hurt me more than it's going to hurt you" gesture so beloved of schoolmasters. He got up and walked out of the room, handing my back to Mr Angry for a few more slaps and punches. I still refused to answer any of the questions.

I expected Pete to stop by and see me while I was in there, but there was no sign of him and, after a few hours, we were again released without charge. The next evening Ciaran once more summoned me to a debriefing, this time at Hugh Porter's own house in Southend Park. Porter led me into his living-room and settled back on the sofa while I sat on a hard-backed chair. As he began to question me, Charlie Clohessy from Cromore Gardens came in and sat down to listen to my replies.

"This is getting to be a habit, Ray," said Porter, with a wintry smile. "What were you asked this time?"

"The only things they asked me about were the guns at Dympna McGrail's and my membership of the RA. I didn't answer any of the questions."

"Did you find it easier, after your debriefing?"

"Yes, it did me good, it was much easier the second time in the police station."

"So, Charlie," said Porter, turning away from me. "We should have been to see Dympna McGrail before now, but with her trial coming up, it's vital that we go and see her straight away. We need to get her to go over the border and not turn up for her trial."

Clohessy grunted his agreement. "I'll get a couple of fellers together and we'll have a run up there tonight."

Porter turned back to me. "If the police offer her money, do you think she'll give evidence against you?"

I shrugged. "She might."

Clohessy nodded, "I think she might as well."

Porter sat thinking for a moment, then said, "All right, Ray, you're cleared. See yourself out, will you?"

I could hear them talking about Dympna McGrail as I left. I could only hope for her sake that she agreed to go over the border.

I saw Charlie Clohessy again a few days later. He was hanging around the Creggan shops in Central Drive and signaled to me as I was walking past. "Will you take a drink with me, Ray?"

I nodded and thanked him, wary but sensing no immediate danger. He led me over to the shebeen across the street from the shops. It was just a tin shack; people in the Creggan called it the Corned Beef Tin. When we were settled with a drink, Clohessy pursed his lips and said, "Keep an eye out for me on that boy Keenan who lives next door to you, Ray. I think he's a tout for the army."

I knew the man he was talking about, but was surprised he had come under suspicion. He was the sort of timid, anonymous person you could not have described ten seconds after passing him in the street. I could have imagined him collecting stamps, but not information.

Many tip-offs to the Provies were motivated by spite or feuds with neighbours, however, so it was entirely possible that he had been fingered as a tout for not weeding his garden or playing his recordings of steam trains too loud at night.

"I thought he worked in the Free State," I said. "He often seems to be away for a couple of months at a time."

Clohessy tapped his nose. "The next time you see him in the flat, tell me."

"I'll tell you right enough, but I can't believe he's a tout. He seems a nice quiet lad, what I know of him. He keeps himself to himself."

"You may be right, but I'll have him fucking nutted if I find out he's touting."

A week or two later, Clohessy again called me over to him in the street and told me, "Forget about Keenan, Ray, he was the wrong boy."

"Did you find the tout then?"

He nodded grimly and drew a finger across his throat. "He'll not be touting again."

My reward for holding out under RUC interrogation was to be transferred to the most elite unit in Derry – the Brigade Unit. Only the OC in Derry and the Brigade staff themselves knew any of the members of the Brigade Unit. There was a good reason for the secrecy. In the early 1970's, army intelligence on the IRA had been very good, mainly because of all the loose talk and the lack of even rudimentary security. People were lifted and put in prison, and because they had no training in how to resist interrogation, they would get a bit of a hiding and start to talk.

As time went on, however, and volunteers kept falling like autumn leaves, the IRA started to get smarter. First they assured themselves of a steady supply of young recruits, by forming a kind of IRA boy-scouts movement, *Fianna na h'Eireann,* from where you progressed into the Provisional IRA. At one time I was even a member of *Fianna na h'Eireann* myself.

Having made sure of fresh blood, they then tried to make it harder for the army and police to spill it. From being just one big, ramshackle organization, the Provies were restructured into autonomous cells, recruiting members that the security forces did not know and training them to withstand questioning. The Brigade Unit was the most secret of all the cells of the Derry IRA, close to the centre of the spider's web. To be transferred to it showed more clearly than anything else that the Provies still had no suspicions about my loyalty.

The Derry Brigade had a pyramid structure of a large corporation. At the apex was the IRA's equivalent of a company chairman, the Officer Commanding – Shorty McNally – the top man in the city, reporting directly to the Northern Command of the IRA. Immediately below Shorty was the Brigade Command: a dozen senior IRA and Sinn Féin men – the board of directors of this very specialised company.

Each member had specific responsibility for certain areas of operations. Finance, headed by Paul Cleary, oversaw fund-raising in all its myriad forms, from the coins in the pub collection boxes to the protection money extorted from businessmen. Finance also paid the wages to full-time Provisionals and authorised payments to the families of imprisoned volunteers.

The Quartermaster's responsibility was to supply the guns and explosives needed by the active service units, while the Explosives Officers, Vic O'Grady and Eddie McSheffrey, constructed the bombs. Internal Affairs – Eamon Doyle and Dessie Cochrane – hunted down suspected touts and processed the information from the IRA's network of spies and sympathisers.

Like any police state, the Provies had their snitches – spies reporting on everything from the amount of money kept in a shop till to the suspicious stranger who'd just moved in to number 23, or the girl who was suspected of being a soldier doll. Much of it was sparked by malice, jealousy or rows between neighbours, but it was examined and evaluated carefully, because among the dross might be the clue that would give away a tout.

Each of the OCs of the four active service units in the city- Creggan, Bogside, Waterside and Shantallow – was also a member of the Brigade Command. At the next level down were the members of the active service units themselves. Below them, in turn, came the cannon-fodder, used as couriers and look-outs and to plant incendiary bombs in stores, hiding them in racks of clothes or boxes of goods to explode after the shops had closed for the night.

They also carried out hold-ups on shops and post offices, adding another couple of hundred quid to IRA funds with each one. Noel Kavanagh and I had been battered for doing the same thing, but that robbery had been our own initiative; it was a different story if you were working for the Provies.

There was a high attrition rate among the cannon-fodder, who were often lifted or shot, but to the Provies they were utterly expendable. Like taxis, there was always another one coming along, some other snot-nosed kid eager to make his name as a hard-case and pull a few impressionable girls on the strength of his Provie connections.

The bottom tier of the Provie pyramid was made up of the kids who could be organized to throw stones and petrol-bombs or set fire to shops and buildings if a diversion was needed. In theory there was no way that the kids or the cannon-fodder would know the identity of more senior IRA men, but in practice it was impossible to keep such things secret in the tight-knit Catholic communities of Derry. Volunteers were known by the company they kept, and if the kids on the street knew their identities, it was only a matter of time before the security forces knew as well.

When I next saw Shorty, he told me to go to Bernadette Fulcher's flat on Central Drive, at the end of Cromore, that night, where I would meet the members of my new unit. A girl I had never seen before answered the door and led me into the living-room. She curled up on the sofa with her boyfriend and I sat there in silence, waiting for the others to arrive. Mary Cobbe and Ciaran McQuillan had also been transferred, and they arrived together a few minutes later. From the sly looks and smiles they kept darting at each other, I guessed that their relationship continued to be more than simply that of comrades in arms. Brendan McDermott hadn't been allocated to the Brigade Unit, however. I met him on the street a few days later and he told me he'd been assigned to Seamus McQuilkin's unit.

The other members of the unit, Frank O'Neill from Creggan Heights, Barnie McMahon and Con "Dixie" Bingham, drifted in one by one, followed by Ruari Spears, the cell leader and, at thirty-one, the oldest member of the unit. He was a fearsome man in his own right, a ruthless disciplinarian and a member of the Brigade Staff in Derry. His brother, Raymond, was also OC of the Provies in Long Kesh.

Ruari was slightly hump-backed, though it was a brave man who would mention it in his presence. His thinning hair was ash-blond and his skin was so pale that he always looked as if he was on the point of collapsing and dying. It was a misleading impression, for he played squash a lot and was one of the fittest men in the unit.

The other members of the cell were a decidedly motley crew. After

Ruari himself, Dixie Bingham was the most threatening. He had shiny black hair and small moustache that made him look like Adolf Hitler, but it was the cold look in his eyes and his sharp intelligence that made me fear him; not much got past him.

The other two members of the unit were not of the same caliber. Barnie McMahon's face was as pock-marked as a map of the moon. He worked in a bar on the Letterkenny Road, and it surprised me that the landlord let him anywhere near the till, for he had a very shifty air about him. He never looked you in the eye when he was talking to you, and I would never have trusted him to tell a straight tale.

It staged me that Frank O'Neill had managed to rise through the ranks of the IRA to this elite unit, for he was a terrible physical specimen with a distinctly dodgy past. He had a shock of bright red hair but was as gaunt as a skeleton, and his skin beneath the thick layer of freckles was as pallid as skimmed milk. He'd been a wino for years, always swilling one of the syrupy fortified South African wines – Mundie's Wine and Friday's Wine – which were cheap, strong and accordingly popular with Derry alcoholics.

Although only twenty-one, I'd already been an RUC agent for five years. It didn't seem to get any easier. Despite all that experience I was extremely nervous, and when Spears suddenly rapped a question at me, my words dried in my throat to a croak. IRA men are warned to watch out for signs of nervousness and uncharacteristic behaviour which may betray an informer, but my luck was in.

All attention was suddenly focused on the radio news bulletin, which led with a report that Argentinian planes had attacked *HMS Plymouth*, *Sir Galahad* and *Sir Tristram* as they attempted to land British troops on the Falklands. At least fifty British soldiers had been killed.

"That'll teach the Brit bastards. Up the Malvinas!" yelled Mary, who for once was not the only one going orgasmic at the thought of British death. All of them were punching the air in delight.

Spears led us upstairs to a bedroom for the meeting while the girl and her boyfriend remained downstairs. We perched on the bed, the window-sill, the chest of drawers and the floor, as Spears made his formal speech of welcome. "You are all members of the Brigade Unit. That means you are the top cell of the RA in Derry and will be carrying out all the important jobs that the Brigade staff order to be done."

I stole a look at the others. Mary and Ciaran had their chests stuck out as if they would burst with pride.

Spears then asked us about jobs that had been discussed but not carried out by our previous unit. Barnie McMahon piped up straight away. "What about the jobs we had planned, like bombing the Maxol filling station on the Strand Road?"

"That's still on," Spears told him. "We're just waiting for the stuff. As soon as we get the bombs we're on with it. Now, are there any jobs left over from the Brandywell unit that are worth having a crack at?"

Ciaran filled him in on a plan to take over a house in Francis Street an shoot and army patrol as it came to the traffic lights on Northland Road. "The Brits use the road every day. If the lights are at red when the vehicles come along, we'll be in a great position to wipe out every soldier in the patrol, but even if they're at green we'll still have a great chance to kill a few."

"Great," said Spears. "Let's see if we can wipe the smile off that whore Thatcher's face, like the Argies did."

We agreed to carry out the plan the following Thursday. Spears and Bingham would hijack a car from a house they'd identified in the Lone Moor Road. They would then hold the owner hostage while we carried out the shoot. O'Neill, Ciaran McQuillan and McMahon were to do the shooting with three Armalites, while I was to do driver.

With the job set up so far in advance, I had plenty of time to warn Pete. I waited until I had to sign on for my dole, then strolled down into the town, checking behind me as usual for signs that I was being followed. I then called Pete from a pay-phone.

I'd just finished giving him details of the job when there was a rap on the glass behind me. I turned around to see Ciaran staring in at me. Somehow I managed to force a smile to my face and signaled him to wait.

I thought fast. Pete was in mid-sentence but I cut straight across him. "Hold on a minute. Let me get the paper."

"What?" Pete said, but I ignored him as I fumbled for the *Daily Mirror* in my pocket. I found the racing page and ran my finger down the list of runners at Kempton Park. "Got it," I said. "Son of Sam in the two-thirty. Thanks a lot."

By now Pete had worked out what must be going on and just said drily, "Think nothing of it, Ray, just don't put all your money on it."

I hung up and opened the door of the phone box. "Hot tip," I said to Ciaran, "Son of Sam in the two-thirty. Should be about eight to one."

Ciaran nodded eagerly, and said, "Who told you?"

I just smiled cryptically and tapped the side of my nose with my finger. As we walked over to the bookies, I searched his face for any hint of suspicion, scared he might have been listening to my conversation before he tapped on the glass, but I could sense no change in his behaviour towards me.

We both put a fiver on Son of Sam, which duly trailed in a distant seventh out of eight runners. Ciaran wasn't too thrilled at losing his last fiver on a bum tip, but he perked up when I bought him a couple of pints by way of compensation. I was more than happy to buy them. Five quid and the price of a few pints was a small price to pay for getting out of a very dangerous situation.

I had been impressed with the Brigade Unit's planning of the job, which was more detailed and meticulous than in my previous unit, but when it came to the execution of the plan, the potential for cock-ups and black comedy proved to be just as great.

We met on the steps of St Eugene's Cathedral at seven-thirty on a beautiful summer morning. Ruari and Dixie went to hijack the car while Ciaran, Barnie, Frank O'Neill and I walked over to the empty house in Francis Street that Ciaran had earmarked for the shoot. Ciaran had assured us that it was always open, but when he tried the handle, the door didn't budge.

"It's locked," he said superfluously, his face a picture of disbelief.

"Doors often are," Barnie said helpfully. "What about using next door instead?"

We followed his gaze. The house was obviously being renovated by builders, for there was a mound of sand outside the door. Barnie handed out the masks. There were only three balaclavas, so I had to make do with a pair of women's tights. We split up into twos. Barnie, who had a .38 revolver, went to the front door with Ciaran, while Frank and I went round to cover the back door. A few minutes later, Barnie appeared around the corner. "It's locked as well. The lazy fucking builders haven't got here yet."

To avoid arousing suspicion, we wandered round the streets in twos for a quarter of an hour. On the second try, Frank and I only had to wait by the back gate for a couple of minutes before Barnie beckoned us in from the back door. There were three workmen on site and we decided we might as well let them carry on. Two got busy putting in reinforcing rods for the foundations of an extension in the back yard while the third one, allowing nothing to disturb his cherished routine, brewed tea in the kitchen.

Barnie gave me the gun and told me to keep an eye on them while he set off to link up with Ruari and Dixie to collect the other weapons. Frank and Ciaran came downstairs after he'd gone and we all sat around chatting and watching the workmen, who seemed completely unfazed by the presence of three masked, armed men in their midst.

Barnie was back within half an hour, knocking three times on the back door – a pre-arranged signal. When I unlocked it he was standing there with a black guitar case in his hand. "We've hijacked the blue Volkswagen van. It's down at the bottom of the street. I couldn't reverse it up to the gate – can you go and do it?"

"Sure. I'll take it for a spin as well and check it out."

He gave me the keys and I handed over the .38, pulled off my mask and went to look over the van. I drove it round the block a couple of times, then reversed it back to the back gate of the house. It belonged to a TV repair man and still had an old TV and some electrical equipment in the back. I shoved that to one side, away from the side-door. I left the driver's door unlocked and the side-door open, so that we could make a flying getaway after the job – if it happened. I'd warned Pete and was pretty sure that no army vehicles would be passing the house that day, unless the SAS had been told to take out the assassins.

I pulled the tights over my head and went back inside the house. The workers had been given the rest of the day off and were sitting in a row in the upstairs bedroom watching Ciaran, Barnie and Frank preparing their Armalites. They'd pulled the roller blinds down over the windows, leaving a gap through which they could keep watch on the Northland Road. Looking over their shoulders, I had a perfect view of the traffic lights. If Pete's warning hadn't got through there would be some very dead soldiers within an hour.

Barnie and Frank kept listening for the sound of the army Land Rovers approaching, but Ciaran wandered over to the back of the room and started chatting to the workmen. I was on the landing, keeping well out of the firing line, when I heard a knock at the front door. I picked up the .38 and went downstairs.

Still wearing my mask, I opened the door to see a middle-aged man in a smart business suit standing on the doorstep. Holding the gun in one hand, I grabbed him by the lapels and dragged him inside. As soon as I got him through the door, I let him go.

He thought it was a joke at first, but when I told him we were IRA, he stopped laughing and started yelling, "Don't shoot me! Don't shoot me! I'm only a surveyor."

I told him, "No one's going to shoot you," but he sank to his knees, got his rosary beads out and started praying for all he was worth.

The surveyor had come to inspect the builders' work. Ever willing to oblige, I took him out in the back yard, but he couldn't take his eyes off the

.38 in my hand long enough to check what they'd been doing. We went back inside and I took him upstairs to sit with the builders.

Ciaran was still chatting to them. The surveyor immediately latched on to him and started trying to convert him, telling, "Killing is a sin. You should go home and forget all about this evil."

He tried to get Ciaran to join him in a prayer, but Ciaran was too busy telling him, "We're dedicated workers, who have to do this for the cause we believe in."

The builders were creased with laughter at the pair of them and Barnie was shouting, "Shut the fuck up, the lot of youse."

Had the army driven ten Centurion tanks past the windows at that moment, they wouldn't have been heard above the din in the room.

For the next five hours we hung around the house, the builders chatting and joking, the surveyor saying his rosary and the rest of us gazing out at the traffic lights. There wasn't a sniff of an army vehicle. Ciaran kept saying, "I can't understand it, they use this road regularly every day."

Finally, Barnie called the job off. They unloaded the rifles and put them back in the black guitar case. We told the builders and the surveyor not to leave for fifteen minutes and not to say anything to the police, then left by the back door, pulling off our masks as we did so.

Barnie took the guns back to the Brigade dump alone. The Provies had tightened up a lot on access to weapons dumps, for they'd lost a tremendous quantity of both arms and volunteers as police either raided the dumps or planted bugs in the weapons. Once the IRA belatedly realised the RUC were using bugs, they took what precautions they could. Access to the dumps was restricted to a few volunteers, who examined the weapons carefully every time they were taken out of the dump, but bugs still went undetected. One placed inside a ten-pound bomb held by a unit in Derry was only discovered by chance when the Explosives Officer decided to split it into two five-pound bombs instead.

Pete was pressing me hard for information about the Brigade dump.

"We've simply got to find out where that dump is, Ray."

"Do you think I don't know that? You're not asking for Mrs Spears' recipe for potato cakes, you're asking for the most closely-guarded secret in the whole of the Derry Brigade.

Only a couple of members of the unit know where that dump is. I'm trying to find out, Pete, but I can't just go up to Ruari Spears and say,

"Where's the dump?" It just doesn't work like that."

"I know that, but time is absolutely critical. The longer than dump stays undiscovered the more chance there is of a lot of RUC men and soldiers – and civilians – winding up dead."

"I'm doing my best, Pete, I can't do anymore. If it's not enough …"

"Don't go off in a huff. I'm not doubting your ability or the worth of what you've got for us in the past. If I'm pressing you hard on this, it's only because I know how terrible the consequences could be if we don't get those weapons off the streets."

"I understand that, but all I can do is wait. Anything else won't get us any closer to the dump, it'll just get me killed instead. I have to bide my time and wait until I'm trusted enough – or someone else is careless enough – to tell me where it is."

A few days later, we held an inquest into the abortive shooting attempt. The meeting was held in the back bedroom of the safe house in Rathlin Drive, with us perching uncomfortably on the edge of the bed or a trunk at the foot of it. It was even more crowded than usual, for Vic O'Grady, the Brigade Explosives Officer, and Eddie McSheffrey, now also in charge of a bombing team, had come along as well.

Spears started off in the usual way by having us fall in and come to attention, then opened the inquest on the shooting. The usual assortment of gripes and grumbles about bad luck and bad timing was brusquely interrupted by Dixie Bingham. "The army used a different route on the day we set up the ambush, but they went back to using the usual route the next day. Why would they do that, unless they'd been tipped off?" He glared around the room. "I think there's a tout in this unit. How else could they have known?"

Everything seemed to go into slow-motion. There was a stunned silence in the room, the only movement coming from Dixie's head as he swivelled slowly, his stare a challenge to each of us in turn. My heart seemed to have stopped beating. I met his stare with as neutral a look as I could muster, though I was sure my guilt was written all over my face.

As he finally turned away, I couldn't avoid flushing a little and looking guiltily around, but shock was also showing on every other face as we all shot sideways glances at each other. Either I wasn't the only agent in the unit, as Pete had often teased me, or the innocent were reacting in exactly the same way as the guilty.

Ruari knew the havoc that had been created by British disinformation about touts in the past. Innocent men had been tortured and shot and the IRA had almost been destroyed. He squashed the talk immediately. "Don't be stupid, that kind of talk gets us nowhere. You'll sow distrust within the unit and we'll not be able to work together for watching each other. It was just bad luck. The job was a fuck-up from start to finish anyway. While me and Dixie were holding the people we hijacked the car from, the door-bell never stopped ringing all fucking day. It was only a tiny flat, but we started off holding two people and finished up with nine. It was like that scene from the Marx Brothers film, *A Night at the Opera* – if another person had tried to get in, the whole lot of us would have fallen out the door."

We all laughed, defusing the tension. There was no more talk of an informer, though from the expression on Dixie's face, I could see that it wasn't forgotten.

To head off any further comment, Ruari hastily introduced the night's guest speakers. "Vic and Eddie need our help with a job."

Eddie then stood up and explained his plan. It was a pretty familiar one, for he'd already tried to sell it to us several times before when he was leader of the Brandywell unit. He and O'Grady were going to plant three bombs in the small bushes at the front of the Rossville flats across the street from Butcher Gate.

They'd plant them in the middle of the night and run the cortex from the bombs along the corridor to the gable end of the Rossville Flats, facing Pilot's Row Community Centre. When the soldiers opened the Butcher Gate first thing the next morning, McSheffrey or O'Grady would detonate the bombs and the soldiers giving cover spread out around the bushes, as they always did.

Eddie gazed fondly round the room, his face full of the look of bright expectancy that always came over him when talking about bombs. "We need two men to cover us while we're planting the bombs and laying the cortex."

Ruari cleared his throat. "Frank, Ray, you'll do it, all right?" It was a statement, not a question. "Get a couple of Armalites and cover them."

I nodded. "When's the job?"

"Not just yet," said O'Grady. "There's no cortex available."

We all clucked our disapproval, like a bunch of commuters waiting on a platform for a late-running train.

"It'll be in Derry in a week or two's time," said O'Grady. "I'll let Ruari know when the bombs are ready for planting."

I passed a warning to Pete.

"Eddie McSheffrey's favourite job's back on again."

"Which one?"

"Bombing Butcher Gate when the soldiers go to open it."

"When?"

"About a week or so. I don't know exactly. They've no cortex at the moment. Vic O'Grady's going to tip off Ruari when the bombs are ready. He's put me and Frank on to cover them while they plant the bombs, so I'll be able to let you know when it's going to happen."

Once more Eddie's favourite project was fated not to take place, however. A couple of days after the meeting Vic O'Grady's father died, and this put the bombing off for a while. By the time Vic was back on active service, Eddie had disappeared to Buncrana for a holiday with his wife, and when both men were finally back in harness together, M60 mania had swept every other job aside.

As we stood up ready to leave, Ruari halted us. "Wait on, there's one more thing. It's the Derry RA's turn to lead the Bodenstown March this year. Are youse all wanting to go on it?"

The march was held every year to commemorate the death of the father of Irish nationalism, Wolfe Tone, executed in 1798. The way Ruari had phrased the invitation made it clear that it was non-negotiable, but Barnie McMahon was still brave enough to say, "No I can't," though he reddened as he met the full force of Ruari's glare.

"Er, Ruari," said Ciaran hesitantly, "I'm a bit strapped at the moment. Is there any chance we could ..."

"You'll be all right for expenses for the trip," Ruari said patiently.

Ciaran beamed and the rest of us exchanged smiles of anticipation. Unlike their officers, the chance to fiddle some expenses was a rarity for the foot-soldiers in the Republican Army.

"Right. There's training and practice in drilling on Tuesday and Thursday night this week at the Star factory on the Foyle Road," Ruari said, instantly wiping the smiles from our faces. "Eight o'clock sharp, make sure you're there."

On the Tuesday night, Ciaran, Mary and I met up and got to the factory just before eight. It was disused at the time, but the doors were open and someone had obviously switched the power back on, for the lights were blazing. We stood around the echoing, cavernous room as more and more IRA volunteers and sympathisers turned up.

Looking around the people nearest to me, I recognized virtually every face: Ruari Spears, Mary Cobbe, Ciaran McQuillan, Josie Nichol, Paddy Johns, Kevin Balcombe, Frank Friel, Sean McArdle, Seamus McQuilkin, Bobby Sperrin, Eamon Connolly, Chris Bishop, Sean O'Toole, Sean Dennehy, Tam "Stud" McGinty, Tapper McFadden, Johnny Lindsay, Dermot Brody, Sean McGrath (known as "Psycho"), Hugh Porter and Tony Leary. It was like a who's who of the Derry Provisionals.

"Bloody hell," Ciaran said, echoing my thoughts, "if the Brits bombed this place tonight, there wouldn't be an RA in Derry any more."

Ruari was in charge and he called us to order. "It's the turn of the Derry RA to lead the Bodenstown March this year, and I want you to do well and look good. So take the drilling seriously, I don't want anyone pissing about. If they do, they'll answer to me."

He glared challengingly around the room, then ordered us to line up military-fashion, in ranks six long and four deep. Ruari then marched us all around the factory floor for two solid hours. As he was bellowing out the orders in Irish, most of us didn't understand what he was saying, and the confusion was increased by the noise of the George McBrearty and Charlie Maguire memorial band practicing in a corner of the room for their own big moment.

To begin with it was like novice night at a *ceilidh*, with people bumping into each other , turning the wrong way and tripping over their toes, until Ruari was just about demented and close to a thrombosis. In the end we got the hand of it enough to manage a circuit of the room without more than the occasional collision along the way.

When the drilling finally ended, Ruari gave us a withering look and told us, "I want every man-jack of you back here on Thursday and you'd better get it fucking right then."

In the event, Mary ducked out of it, but Ciaran and I dandered over to the Star factory again on the Thursday night. There were even more people there this time, but most of the new ones were strangers to me. I studied their faces carefully, trying to memorise them for future reference.

Ruari was again in charge and it was the same mixture as before, two hours of blundering incompetence with a wafer-thin veneer of sophistication applied only in the last few minutes. Mopping his brown, Ruari finally called a halt. One or two people began sloping off towards the exit, but he halted them in their tracks. "No ones's going anywhere yet awhile. Paul Cleary and Shorty McNally have a few things to say to you. I think you'll find Paul's words particularly interesting."

There was a knowing laugh. Cleary was the money man in the Derry Provisionals and would be handing out the expenses for the Bodenstown weekend. Shorty began the speeches, telling us how we should conduct ourselves in Bodenstown as his eyes misted over with patriotic fervour.

"It's a great honour for Derrymen to be asked to lead this march. You're not just representing yourselves at Bodenstown, you're representing your families, your people, the Derry Provisional IRA and every martyr that has spilled his blood fighting to free Ireland of its British chains."

Moist of eye, he sat down, blushingly acknowledging a congratulatory thump in the back from Ruari. Cleary rose to his feet and gave us more of the same, though delivered in a dry, matter-of-fact monotone, like a solicitor reading a will. We all then filed past him, and after asking our arrangements for travelling, he handed out wads of notes from a bulging black bag. Some said they were going by car, others by bus or train. Ciaran McQuillan, Frank O'Neill and I were travelling together, and told him we'd go by train. Cleary gave us £150 between the three of us to cover our expenses, which suited us fine; we'd already decided to go by bus and split the profits.

When we'd all received our expenses, Cleary snapped the black bag shut with the finality of a police surgeon zipping up a body-bag and handed back to Ruari.

"Pay attention," he bellowed, "this is important. You're to meet at Parnell Mooney's bar in Dublin on Friday at eight p.m. and Saturday at three p.m. You'll be met there and told where you're to be billeted. When you leave here tonight, go down to the cottage in Stanley Walk and collect your uniforms, boots and gloves. Make us proud of you on Sunday; the honour of Derry is in your hands."

I couldn't imagine a worse place for it to be. Ciaran, Frank and I joined the procession down to the Bogside, speculating excitedly on the way about how many pints we could buy with the profits from our expenses. When we got to the cottage, it was already packed with people milling around a stack of boxes piled on the chairs and scattered around the floor.

I fought my way through the crowd, gathering up a full uniform of black boots, green jacket and trousers, black gloves, black beret, white belt and green, white and orange arm flashes. I went into one of the bedrooms and tried it on to make sure it fitted me and then went down to the pub with Ciaran and Frank to make a start on spending our windfall.

On the Friday morning we caught the Dublin bus from Derry. As soon as we got there we went on a pub-crawl. We made the rendezvous at Parnell Mooney's bar all right, but somewhere along the way after that, I lost Frank and Ciaran. I couldn't remember the address of our digs and had to go and stay in a cheap bed-and-breakfast. I met up with them again on the Saturday night at Parnell Mooney's bar and this time I stuck to them like a limpet, but when I got to our digs, I wished I hadn't bothered. It was a cold, dirty and draughty flat on the outskirts and we had to sleep on the floor with only a single blanket each.

The next morning, cold, stiff, hung-over and dog-tired, we caught the bus to Bodenstown. We got off at a big field and changed into our uniforms. Ruari lined us all up in front of the George McBrearty and Charlie Maguire Memorial Band and marched us to the graveside of Wolf Tone, past an admiring crowd and a group of gardai, keeping a discreet watch from a distance. The MP, Owen Carron, made a lengthy speech and then we went back to the field, changed out of our uniforms and straggled off home.

After the weekend break, it was quickly back to business as usual, with Spears desperate to get started on a job using the Brigade's newly-acquired American M60 machine-gun. It was a devastating weapon, one of only three in IRA hands. One had been captured by the army after a Belfast unit had killed SAS Captain Richard Westmacott, and the remaining two were guarded like the crown jewels. This one was on loan from the Belfast Provies, after Martin McGuinness and the Derry Brigade staff had begged for a chance to show what they could do with it.

With the IRA's traditional Republican rivals the Stickies and the INLA moribund, any hatred the Derry Provies' could spare from the Brits and the RUC was channeled into a fierce hostility towards the Belfast Provies. They always thought they were better than the Derry Provies – with good reason, they probably were – and there was tremendous rivalry between them. Martin McGuinness and Kevin Balcombe had boasted to the IRA's Northern Command that the Derry men would show Belfast how to use the M60. It would have been an unbearable loss of face for them to give it back without killing any soldiers or police.

As a result, McGuinness was pushing Shorty, Shorty was pushing Spears, and Spears was pushing us. "Let's get this thing working and show those Belfast bastards what Derrymen can do with it. We don't want to give it back until we've had a big kill with it."

To strengthen the squad for the job, Ruari had brought in Vic O'Grady, Tam McGinty and Tapper McFadden. Vic and Tam were both tall, but that was the only thing they had in common. Tam was the Errol Flynn of the Provies. As well as being tall he was broad-shouldered and had dark, brooding good looks. He absolutely loved himself, but with some justification since most women seemed to share his opinion. When not nuzzling some woman's neck, his black moustache was usually immersed in a pint of stout. His drinking caused him a few problems with the Provies.

If Tam was Errol Flynn, Vic was more like an overweight Worzel Gummidge. His own mother would have been pushed to describe him as good-looking, and although he was stockily-built, it was all fat, not muscle. He always wore scruffy, ill-fitting clothes that looked like they had been rescued from a skip, and he appeared to wash about once a month.

Tapper was on Brigade Staff and was IRA to the core. Pete had already told me to get close to him, which was not hard to achieve, as Tapper liked a drop but never had any money. We'd become drinking buddies and I took him out on sprees just to get information out of him.

I had to sit through a fair amount of gruesome detail about his time on the blanket in the Maze, for he was inordinately proud of that. "You've been in the Kesh, Ray, you know how bad that is, but being in the blanket blocks was something else again. I was bollock-naked apart from the blanket and freezing my treats off every night. There was nothing in the cell but a mattress, a jug of water, a bucket to piss and shit in and a Bible. We'd tear pieces of the foam mattresses and use them to spread the shite from the buckets all over the walls and ceiling. And the smell … Christ almighty, the stench was fucking terrible."

He spoke bitterly, as if it was the warders who'd been smearing shit all over his walls. "The screws would do anything to get at us. You'd hear them stop outside your cell door at night and piss against it, and the food they gave us wasn't fit for pigs. When the screws brought it round they'd tell you that they'd shat in it, and when you tasted it you could well believe it."

I was happy to buy Tapper's beer all night and listen to his interminable reminiscences about life on the blanket, because I got my money's worth out of him in other ways. He was a very good source and got me in closer to the leadership of the Derry IRA. He was actually the one who first told me that Martin McGuinness was a member of the Provisional Irish Republican Army Council in Dublin and the OC of Northern Command – the Chief of Staff of the IRA.

For someone who'd done a lot of time, Tapper was very loose in his talk, though he obviously felt that he had no reason not to trust me. One time he began slagging me about where my money came from.

"Sure, didn't you know, Tapper," I said, "I'm working for the Branch. I mentioned that you were on the Brigade Staff now and they told me to send their congratulations and buy you a pint from them."

Tapper laughed so hard that he almost spilled his drink, and asked me if I could get him a start with them too. He took an appreciative pull at his pint, then said, "You'll like this one, Ray. I heard it from one of the Belfast boys last week. Best of all it's a true story. They had their suspicions about a member of one of their cells; they thought he was touting. Anyway, he was driving along one night when he was stopped at any army checkpoint. One of the guys drags him out of the car and starts shouting, "SAS. We know you're IRA, you're going to fucking die."

"The others are all chiming in as well, yelling, "Shoot the bastard. Shoot the bastard," and yer man just about shits himself. "No, no!" he screams. "You've got it all wrong, I'm army too."

"Prove it," says the soldier, cocking his pistol. "I'm an agent," says the guy. "You've got to believe me. Here's my code number, you can check it with your base." The soldier just looks at him. "Oh, we do believe you," he says. "The trouble is, we're not really what we appear either."

"Yer man stands there staring at them. "What do you mean?" "Provisional IRA. You're fucking dead." When yer man heard that, he really did shit himself."

Tapper was laughing so hard he could hardly get the punchline out.

I forced a smile and asked, "So what happened to him."

"What do you think? He was interrogated, court-martialled and then fucking nutted. They buried the body without telling anyone, so the army'll still be waiting for your man to report in."

He drained his pint in one gulp and I left him sitting at the table, still wiping his eyes and chuckling to himself while I went to get another round. I was glad of the chance to compose myself; for some reason I hadn't found Tapper's tale very funny.

CHAPTER 13

Spear's first plan for a job with the M60 was a shoot on the police outside the Courthouse. At nine o'clock in the morning, he and I were to hijack a Transit van from Doherty's butchers in Rossville Flats, where Martin McGuinness had once worked.

"It'll have to be a van," Ruari said. "A car'll be no good for carrying the M60, three Armalites and a Thompson on the way to the job. I was playing squash yesterday and I've a terrible sore back, so I won't be able to fire the M60 myself. I'll hold the butcher hostage instead. Ray will take the van and pick up Barnie, who'll be firing the M60. Dixie, Ciaran and Frank will fire the Armalites and Vic will use the Thompson."

Once we'd collected the other members of the team, we were to drive past the Diamond and up Bishop Street, parking outside the Dominion Trust building. When the police van passed us, I was to drive up behind it and turn off in the last street before the Courthouse. The guys in the back would then spill out and start firing at the police as they were getting out of their van.

"We need to start using the M60 before she goes back to Belfast." Ruari said. "I don't want to send her back without us doing a job. We need to get a couple of stiffs. There'll be plenty of policemen there. Pick your targets and make sure you don't miss. I want as many dead as you can shoot." He paused for effect, looking round the room in the silence, challenging each of us not to meet his eye. "After the shoot, throw your weapons into the van and jump in. Ray will drive down to the Butcher Gate and stop the van by the Rocking Chair bar, where Tapper and Tam McGinty will have a car waiting. Barnie will take the weapons back to the dump, while the rest of you split up and go home. Right, that's it. Meet at Barnie's sister's house at eight-thirty in the morning, and make it sharp, lads, the Brigade doesn't run on Republican time.

There was a general chorus of "Good plan, Ruari," but the enthusiastic comments seemed very forced. I thought it was a suicide mission, with little or no hope of getting away afterwards. Looking at the eyes of the other members of the unit, I suspected that most of them shared my feelings. Pete certainly did when I phoned him with the news later that night.

Everyone appeared at the rendezvous on time the next morning, apart from Tam McGinty, who was supposed to be hijacking the getaway car with Tapper. He turned up twenty minutes late, claiming that Tapper was supposed to pick him up on the way, but he reeked of drink and his excuses only earned him a mouthful from Ruari. "You lazy bastard, McGinty! If you ever turn up late for one of my jobs again, I'll shoot you myself. Now let's get on with it."

Barnie had brought two revolvers for the double hijacking of the car and van. Ruari told the chastened Tam, Tapper and Ciaran to get a red Mazda belonging to an old man across the road. We watched them from an upstairs window as they masked up and disappeared into the house, but five minutes later they were back, empty-handed.

"That old fucker took a heart attack," said Tam. "He collapsed on the floor when we told him we were taking his car. I searched his pockets for the keys while he was lying on the floor, but I couldn't find them."

"Aw, fuck!" said Ruari, already losing his rag. "The old bastard could be bluffing us. We'll give him fifteen minutes to see if an ambulance comes and then we'll go back for him."

No ambulance came, but by then Ruari had already given up on the Mazda and sent Barnie to drop Ciaran, Tam and Tapper off up the Creggan to find a car. We waited for half an hour, while Ruari paced the room with a face like a bad night in Belfast. Finally he looked at his watch and cursed.

"Too fucking late. The stupid fuckers can't get a car. The job's off."

Five minutes later, a silver Audi pulled up outside and Ciaran came running into the room. "We've got a car."

"Too fucking late," said Ruari. "The job's off."

"Holy Jesus, you're kidding."

"If you'd been a wee bit quicker, the job would still have been on. Where's Tapper and Tam?"

"Holding yer man and his wife in a house up the Circular Road."

"Well take the fucking car back up again and get them out of there."

We all filed out of the house and I walked over to the Creggan shops to get a newspaper. By the time I got to the Telstar Bar, I met Tapper and Tam on their way home.

"What was the crack with the car?" I asked.

"He wouldn't give us the keys at first," said Tam, "and then he set a wee dog on us that nearly ate the fucking leg off me."

There was a second attempt to do the courthouse shoot ten days later. I bumped into Ruari one afternoon and he told me the shoot was on for the next day. "Be there at eight this time. I want plenty of spare time, because I don't want anymore fuck-ups."

I got up early the next morning and caught a taxi down to the house just before eight. I was the last to arrive apart from Tam, who had failed to show up.

"We need him to hijack the car. If he doesn't show, we'll have to get someone else." Ruari's controlled, even tone as he said this was more frightening than his outbursts of rage. We gave Tam half an hour, but he still didn't appear.

"He's been out on the piss again and slept in, the drunken wanker," Ruari said. "Next time I see him, he's fucking dead."

Dixie and Barnie then set off to get Sean McArdle, a member of Paddy Lawler's cell. They arrived back with him in fifteen minutes and Ruari sent Tapper, McArdle and Chris Bishop – another guest from a different unit – to hijack a car.

"Look sharp, boys," said Ruari, "time's getting tight."

Once more, we waited and waited, trying to avoid catching Ruari's eye as he stomped around the room. Finally, an hour later, Tapper, McArdle and Bishop arrived back empty-handed, provoking the most ferocious outburst yet from Ruari as he once more called the whole thing off.

A couple of nights later, Lorraine and I were going out for a night. We dropped off the kids at her mother's, then picked up Paddy "Nelson" Deery – a one-eyed IRA man from Glenowen – and his wife, and drove over to the Derry City Club.

We left the club at eleven o'clock and decided to drive round the Creggan estate and have a look at the bonfires. We cruised around for about an hour and eventually stopped at a bonfire in Carrickreagh Gardens, when we saw Tapper standing there. Paddy got out and talked to him for a few moments and then Tapper came over and got into the passenger seat.

I took him for a spin around the bonfires while Paddy stayed in Carrickreagh talking to a couple of people. Deery's wife didn't even blink when he disappeared, she was well-used to the mysterious comings and goings of IRA men and just carried on chatting to Lorraine in the back seat.

When we got to the Croby at Central Drive, Tapper told me to stop and got out to talk to Dessie Cochrane and Patrick Boyd. What they told him obviously pleased him, for he got back in with a grin from ear to ear, but he just winked and said, "Right, Ray, back to Carrickreagh, if you please."

Deery was still standing chatting and Tapper hopped out and went straight over to him. The next minute, they disappeared into Paddy's sister's flat. There was obviously an arms dump there, for when they came back out of the flat, Deery was carrying a brown guitar case. He got into the front seat with it, while Tapper squeezed into the back alongside Lorraine.

"Where now?" I asked.

"Back to the Croby."

I laughed. "Jesus, the car'll find its own way there before long."

As we drove along, I could hear a rattling sound from inside the guitar case each time we hit a bump.

"What's in the case, Paddy?" I asked, though I knew the answer fine well.

Deery threw an anxious look at his shoulder at the wives in the back seat. Happy that they were still absorbed in their small talk, he muttered, "Two revolvers and a bolt-action rifle."

When we got to the Croby I pulled up beside Cochrane, Eamon Doyle and Boyd. McFadden got out and spoke to them briefly, then got back in and told me to drive around the corner into Creggan Heights.

"Christ alive, Tapper, how long is this magical mystery tour going on?"

He shot me a sharp look, but reassured that I was only joking, he said, "Not much further. This is the end of the line."

After I parked the car, Boyd came around the corner, took the guitar case from Deery and stuffed it into the hedge. He then walked off.

"Right, Ray," said Deery. "You probably think you've earned a few drinks now."

"There's no probably about it."

We drove back to his house and had a skinful, but my hangover the next day wasn't helped by the news report of a shooting in the early hours of the morning, in which an RUC man had been wounded.

Even when they did manage to pull a job off successfully, however, the Derry Provies still couldn't get off a shot from the M60. That night I was on my way down to the Rocking Chair bar when I saw Tapper hanging around by the shops. I asked him if he fancied a pint.

"I can't," said Tapper wistfully, "there's a job on."

As we chatted for a moment, a hijacked car pulled up, with Tam McGinty, Paddy Deery, Dessie Cochrane and Eamon Doyle inside.

I left Tapper climbing into the car and walked on to the Rocking Chair, stopping to phone Pete from a pay-phone. I warned him that there was a job on and gave him the number of the hijacked car, but it was little to go on and I wasn't optimistic that it would do any good.

I'd only been in the bar for a few minutes when there was an army P-check – a personal identity check. A patrol of about eight soldiers burst into the room, shouting at everyone to keep still and keep their hands away from their pockets. One lad made a run for the toilet and was instantly grabbed and dragged off. The rest of us were lined up against the wall, legs and arms spread wide, and roughly searched while a bespectacled soldier sat at one of the tables, taking down our names, addresses and dates of birth.

They could find nothing on anyone else in the bar and withdrew after twenty minutes, their boots thundering on the floor as they went out into the street.

"Drinks on the house?" asked one of the customers hopefully.

"My arse," said the barman. "If you want charity go and beg on the fucking streets."

Half an hour later Tapper and the others all walked in looking as smug as publicans at closing-time.

"You've missed all the excitement, boys," I said. "The army raid's over, though you look like you've had some excitement yourselves. I'd say it was either my round or the job went all right tonight."

"Right on both counts," said Tapper happily.

For once I didn't have to pump Tapper, for they were all gabbing about the job. They'd gone down to the junction of Linsfort and Central Drive and lain in wait for a police patrol. Two police jeeps had driven right into the trap.

"We've shot a peeler dead this night," Deery said proudly.

"How do you know? Did you see the body?"

"We didn't need to. We were firing armour-piercing and we definitely hit one of the jeeps."

"It's a pity they didn't stop though," Tapper said. "We had the M60 lined up to wipe out all the other bastards if they'd got out of the jeeps."

Despite the hit, the Brigade were getting desperate to get a job done with the M60. The next one was no more successful. We met at Bernadette Fulcher's flat at Cromore. Tam McGinty was again there, even though he wasn't in our cell. He floated about from one unit to another.

He produced a short at the meeting, a .38, and put it on top of a cabinet. "It's not the first time I've been in Bernadette Fulcher's bedroom," he bragged, earning a barracking from the rest of us.

"In your dreams maybe," laughed Ciaran.

"More like nightmares," sniggered Mary, never one to recognise good looks in other women.

"Very funny, all of youse," said Ruari, dripping sarcasm, "but if it's no trouble, would it be all right with you if we got down to some RA business now? That's what we're here for, after all."

For the moment, Ruari had run out of plans and Ciaran McQuillan provided one instead. His idea was to shoot a police foot patrol on the Strand Road. "There are usually four to six peelers in the patrol. We could wipe out most of them with a good heavy concentrated attack."

Ruari took over, briskly appropriating the plan. "Frank, Dixie and Ray will hijack a car. We've one earmarked, a Mazda in Rathowen Park."

"What if the car's not there?" Frank asked plaintively. Ruari gave him a withering look.

"We'll find another fucking car then," he snarled. "Christ, I'm not asking a miracle, I just want a fucking car."

"There's an old fellow called Mike O'Rourke from the Bogside. He's got a big mustard-coloured Granada. He's a painter," I added irrelevantly, earning another mouthful from Ruari.

"I don't care if he's fucking Michelangelo. All we want is his car. Barnie, give them a lift down there in the van or we'll be waiting all night. Frank and Dixie'll stay with the owner while Ray drives back here. Ray'll give the keys to Barnie, who'll get the guns from the dump. We'll use the M60 and two Armalite rifles. On the job itself, Ray'll do driver and me, Ciaran and Barnie will do the shooting."

He broke off as he saw Mary's sour expression. "Sorry, Mary, no job for you this time."

She glanced up and gave a weak smile, but relapsed into a scowl as Ruari resumed speaking. "Now then … where was I?"

"Me, you and Barnie will be shooting," supplied Ciaran helpfully.

"Right enough. When Barnie's back with the guns, we'll drive to William Street, park the car and leave the guns in the car while we go to the Gweedore Bar. We'll take it in turns to keep dick outside for a foot patrol coming along Strand Road. As soon as we spot one, we'll run down to the car, get the guns out and blast the shit out of them as they come round the corner. Our main target's peelers, but if the Brits come along, we'll have a shoot at them instead. Any questions?"

"Yes. Why is it always me that misses out?"

"It isn't. Next question," Spears said brutally, not even looking in Mary's direction.

There were none. The plan was simple, though stupid was just as good a description. In their desperation to get a kill with the M60, the unit were running bigger and bigger risks. This job would be carried out practically under the noses of the army sangers on the city walls. If the job went ahead as planned, we could all wind up dead. There was also a good chance of innocent people getting killed. It was a Thursday – pay-day 0 and there was a beauty contest at the Guildhall that night. Duffy's Disco was on as well, so there would be plenty of people on the streets.

Barnie gave Frank a .38 for the hijacking and handed out gloves and masks to everyone. Mary still sat there with a face like Ian Paisley chewing a communion wafer in a Catholic church. Ciaran went over, put a hand on her shoulder and whispered something in her ear, but it didn't have the desired effect. She angrily shrugged off his hand and gave him a gobful, while Ruari glared balefully at the pair of them. Things looked set for another perfect evening of domestic bliss.

Dixie looked from Ruari to Mary and then said, "Listen Ruari, we don't want to be going out on a job in the wrong frame of mind. Let's fight the Brits, not each other. If Mary's wants in on the action that bad, she can take over from me. I'm going to get away home."

Ruari looked as if he was about to start off a fresh row, but instead he swallowed and nodded grumpily. "Right. When you get the car, Ray, bring it up to my place, we'll wait for you there."

Mary's demeanour had changed instantly. She gave Dixie a big smile, squeezed Ciaran's arm and was first in Barnie's van. We went down to the Rathowen Park, but sure enough there was no sign of the Mazda, so we drove on to O'Rourke's house in Glenfadda Park. As we walked up to the door, we pulled our masks on. The door was unlocked and the three of us marched down the hallway and into the living-room. O'Rourke and his wife were watching TV and got the shock of their lives when they looked up and saw us standing there.

"Who the fuck are you?" said his wife, a small, fat woman with grey hair dyed an unlikely strawberry blonde.

"Provisional IRA," I said. "We want the keys for your car."

"You're not getting them," old Mike told me. "I was promised by a man in the IRA that my car wouldn't be taken again."

His wife started in on me as well, yelling, "What do you think you're doing in here? You're not getting my husband's car. Anyway, I've got a bad heart."

"That's funny, so has everyone we want to take a car off," Mary said. Eager to get in on the action, she took the gun from Frank and was brandishing it at them when I saw the car keys on top of the TV. I walked over and lifted them.

"I'm taking the car, it won't come to any harm. The other two will be staying with you while I'm away with it."

I left them still protesting to the other two, took my mask off as I stepped out of the flat and got into the car. I drove up Fahan Street and over Lone Moor Road and was going fairly fast along Melmore when a dog ran out in front of me. I braked, but I hit it hard. As I stopped, the dog – a cocker spaniel – limped away and disappeared between the houses, still trailing one leg. It wasn't a good omen for the evening.

I couldn't do anything about the dog and drove off again, parking by the play area just across from Spears's house. I left the revolver underneath the driver's seat, got out of the car and locked it. I glanced at the front of the car and saw that the number plate was broken. Mike O'Rourke wouldn't agree, but if there was no worse damage to worry about before the night was out, he'd be getting off lightly.

Ruari's wife let me in. I gave Barnie the car keys and told him where it was parked. "If you need it, the .38's under the driver's seat."

"When you've got the guns," Ruari said, "park the car in William Street and meet us in the Gweedore Bar."

As Barnie drove off, the rest of us walked down to Waterloo Street.

"No pints on active service," Ruari growled, reminding us of our duty as we walked through the door.

We had a few drinks of Coke instead. Surrounded by monosyllabic drunks, sinking Guinness with whiskey chasers, we were as inconspicuous as nuns at a strip-show. Barnie arrived after about twenty minutes, but he had an apprehensive look on his face as he reported to Ruari.

"I got the guns in the boot of the car all right, but now I can't get the boot open."

"For fuck's sake!" Ruari shouted.

The whole bar went quiet and everyone turned to look at us. I couldn't believe it; if the shoot went ahead now, there was a bar full of drinkers who could give a description of every single one of us. Under Ruari's fierce stare, most of them quickly dropped their gaze and went back to their pints.

Controlling his temper with visible effort, Ruari lowered his voice and said, "Ray, go with him and get that fucking boot open. If you have to force it though, drive somewhere quieter first. I don't want every peeler in town down on our backs before we start."

Barnie and I exchanged a look; Ruari had already done his personal best to achieve that. We walked over to where he'd parked the car in William Street. I tried to open the boot but it was stuck fast. We drove up to Marlborough Street, where there was no one around, and after banging and kicking it a few times we finally managed to get it open. Barnie opened and closed it a few more times, just to make sure it wouldn't stick again. Then we drove back down to William Street and walked round to the Gweedore Bar.

We took turns at keeping dick for a police foot patrol, watching from near Tracy's Bar on the corner of William Street and Waterloo Street, where we could look right up the Strand Road.

As I'd hoped, Ruari gave me a first watch and I slipped round the corner to a pay-phone, miraculously unvandalised, and put a call through to Pete, staring back towards the corner all the time. I was only on the phone a few seconds, but my heart was beating wildly and my mouth was so dry with fear that I could hardly get the words out to give Pete the information.

"I've no time to talk, but get a message to the uniforms and tell them to recall any foot patrols down the Strand Road tonight. We're in wait for them in William Street."

"Understood," Pete said and the line went dead.

I sidled back to the corner, praying both that none of the unit had noticed my absence and that no foot patrol was already on their way down Strand Road. Both prayers were answered. I took up station outside Tracy's Bar and passed an uneventful half-hour until Ciaran came to relieve me.

We kept up the watch until just before eleven o'clock without a sniff of a patrol, and Ruari, who'd already relaxed discipline enough to have a pint, decided to pack it in. "Another fucking waste of a night. Ray, go along with

Barnie and give him a hand to put the guns back in the dump. The rest of youse get away home. There's a meeting again tomorrow night. I'll get a job done with this M60 if it kills me."

It possibly would. Barnie and I walked back to the car and I drove while he gave me directions to the dump. It was in the Youth Centre at the top of Stewarts Terrace, a dead-end street behind the old people's home. I got the weapons out of the boot while Barnie took out a bunch of keys and unlocked the gate leading into the club.

The two Armalites were in a black plastic guitar case and the M60 was in a long canvas bag, once green, now faded and mildewed with age. I carried them round to the big double doors. Once inside, we walked across the dance-floor to the stage. Barnie shinned up on to it and then took the bag containing the M60 from me. I shoved the Armalites on to the edge of the stage and followed him up. He walked to the back and opened a door on the left-hand side.

Beyond it was a room where they stored the apparatus for the gym. There was a gaping hole in the wall beside the door, just above ground level. It was pitch dark but I could just make out Barnie's shape as he knelt down and pushed the bags with the guns into the hole. He didn't seem to cover the hole with anything. "Christ, Barnie," I said. "It seems a bit insecure for the Brigade dump."

He laughed. "It would be if it was the Brigade dump. It's just a temporary one we always use on night jobs. It's not safe to move weapons straight back to the Brigade dump at this time of night."

As we left the club, Barnie locked the doors behind us, showing me the key for each lock as he did so. "If ever you're coming up on your own, you'll know."

I dropped Barnie off at Westland Street, then drove back to the O'Rourkes' house. I gave the pre-arranged three knocks and, a minute later, Mary, Frank and Ciaran came spilling out. Ciaran had gone over there to wait with them, presumably hoping that the thrill of a job would have got Mary's juices flowing.

It wasn't the smartest thing to do, for he'd worked with O'Rourke painting the Craigavon Bridge. Sure enough, despite Ciaran's mask, old Mike had soon recognized him and gave him a lot of stick.

"Don't worry," Mary said, squeezing his arm. "The old bastard wouldn't dare to go to the peelers. If he does I'll go round there and fucking nut him myself."

Ciaran reacted as if that was the most romantic thing he'd ever heard in his life, and they disappeared into the night, twined around each other.

WHAT PRICE TRUTH?

The Brigade remained equally enamoured of the M60, and kept up their relentless efforts to get a kill with it. When I saw Shorty McNally the following day, he told me there was yet another job on for my unit, and that Ruari would let me know when it was coming off. In fact Ruari called round to see me the next afternoon.

"The wee man's job is on for tomorrow."

I blinked, surprised. "You know the date tomorrow, don't you? It's the Apprentice Boy' march. The place'll be crawling with soldiers."

"All the more reason why they won't be expecting an attack."

I shrugged. "Fair enough. So what's the job?"

"It's a shoot at the army at Glenowen. The army jeeps travel along the Creggan Road and up Shaws Lane every day. If we're hidden in the wee forest at the junction of Shaws Lane and Groarty Road, we'll get a good shot at them as they go past.

Dixie Bingham, Chris Bishop and I were to hijack a car and bring it back to Barnie's sister's house. Barnie would then go down to the dump to get the weapons. He, Frank and I would be firing the Armalites while Ruari used the M60.

Chris and Dixie called for me the next morning at about eight, getting me out of bed. While I was getting dressed, Chris disappeared to get a short for the hijack from a young guy called Gurney, who lived just round the corner in Aranmore Avenue. I heard Chris come back five minutes later. I grabbed my blue balaclava from beneath the floorboards under my bed and ran downstairs. The IRA had very strict rules about keeping incriminating stuff like our balaclavas around the house, but after all, what did I care? Pete had always assured me that the house would only ever be searched under his supervision, and he wouldn't be too surprised to discover that I was a member of the IRA.

I stuffed my mask in my pocket and we walked up the Creggan Heights to get a car. There was a black Cortina parked outside one house. I knew it was a taxi, but we decided to take it anyway. We knocked at the front door and got no reply, but were more successful at the back. As we heard someone coming, we slipped our masks over our faces and Chris pulled a .38 out of his waistband.

A woman in her dressing-gown and carrying a young child opened the door. We all walked past her into the hallway.

"Provisional IRA," Chris said. "We want the keys to the car."

"No way, you're not getting his car."

Chris pulled out the gun and ran up the stairs, looking for her husband. I followed him up. The man was still asleep and Chris tapped him on the shoulder with the gun. He half-opened his eyes blearily, but then woke with a start when he saw the gun.

"Provisional IRA. We want your car – where are the keys?"

"You're not getting them. I pay my money to the Provies. You can't take my car."

I left them arguing and went downstairs, where the man's wife was still haranguing Dixie. I took a look around and found a set of Ford keys lying on the mantelpiece.

The wife saw that I had them and started screaming, "No you're not taking it!", but Chris must have been having more success upstairs by then because the husband shouted down, "It's no good, let them take it," and I walked out, leaving Dixie and Chris to guard them.

I dropped the car off for Barnie and arranged to meet him up at Glenowen, where Ruari and Frank were waiting. Barnie arrived soon after me, saying he'd left the car with the weapons outside Me Da's restaurant. We were a man short, with no one to do driver. When Ruari suggested suggested Paddy Deery, who was a member of another cell in Dery, I had to suppress a smile. If you needed a getaway driver, what could possibly be better than a man with only one eye?

Ruari went to collect him and we then walked down to the car, splitting up into pairs to avoid arousing suspicion. Barnie opened the boot and lifted out the black guitar case containing the Armalites and the green, mildewed canvas bag, which I knew held the M60. Paddy stayed in the car with a handgun, waiting to drive down and pick us up after the shooting. The rest of us set off across the field, carrying the canvas bag and the guitar case down to the clump of trees on the corner just below Glenowen.

A steady, insistent drizzle was falling as we climbed up a small bank and lay down on the wet ground between the trees, inching forward until we could see the road. Barnie handed out the Armalites, giving each of us a spare magazine, apart from Frank, who was not used to handling the weapon. He was given a banana magazine instead, which held more ammunition, to save him from having to re-load. Ruari got the M60 out of the canvas bag and set it up on its stand, loading it with a belt of at least one hundred rounds of ammunition. He told us to spread out a bit and we wriggled sideways, separating from each other by about five yards. Then we lay still in the firing position, our weapons cocked and pointing up Shaws Lane.

There was an awful lot of firepower concentrated on that spot, but, not for the first time, I had the feeling that the Brigade Unit was going to be disappointed. It was just as well, for this one looked even more of a suicide job than the one at the Courthouse. Unless we wiped out every single soldier, Paddy would be a sitting duck when he drove down to pick us up after the shooting, and any surviving soldiers would also wipe us out if we tried to get away in the car or back up the field.

Had I been driver instead of one of the shooters, it was possible that the army or SAS might have been lying in wait, a welcoming committee for Ruari and the boys. I didn't think that the Special Branch would allow them to risk shooting their best agent – at least I hoped they wouldn't – and thought it was more likely that the army patrol would once more just fail to appear. I settled down for a long wait, making myself as comfortable as possible on the hard, wet ground, the smell of metal and machine oil from the Armalite strong in my nostrils.

Soon after we took up position, two police jeeps came up Creggan Hill and then turned up Groarty Road instead of Shaws Lane, travelling very slowly, almost as if taunting us. "Hold your fire," Ruari said, but the warning was superfluous. We all knew not to fire at them. They were armour-plated and we had no armour-piercing ammunition. We were waiting for the army, but the patrol didn't come.

Spears shifted position irritably and grumbled, "They should have been here by now."

Frank look round, "I hope nothing's happened to them."

There was a pause, then Barnie and I burst out laughing.

"What?" asked Frank plaintively, missing the joke as usual.

"Will youse lot shut the fuck up," growled Ruari. "This is supposed to be a job, not a fucking party."

Hours passed. My left hip gradually went numb and the constant drizzle soaked me to the skin, while a cloud of midges kept up an equally constant feeding frenzy on my face and neck.

Every few minutes. Ruari would look at his watch and say, "I can't understand this. We've had this job watched for weeks. The army should be here by now, they've been here every other day."

I said nothing, and just kept staring ahead down the barrel of my Armalite.

As the hours passed, Ruari began to worry that we might be spotted in among the trees and, with no sign of the long-overdue army patrol, he finally called off the job. Barnie went up to get Paddy to drive down to where we were, to save carrying the weapons back up the hill. He parked the car at the bottom of the bank and we handed the weapons down and then jumped down into the road ourselves.

A car drove past as we were finishing loading the weapons into the boot and Ruari became very agitated. He told Barnie to take the weapons back to the dump and asked me to go along and give him a hand. I couldn't believe my luck; I was at last going to discover where the Brigade dump was hidden.

Before we left, Ruari called us all together and said, "There must be a tout. I'm not saying it's one of you, but be very careful who you talk to. There has been too much loose talk and the word has obviously got around that something was planned."

I could feel the fear rising in me once more. Ruari had been the one to slap down Dixie when he began talking about a tout in the unit, but Ruari himself was now convinced of it as well. I left like I was standing on the edge of a black pit. It would only take one little push now to send me tumbling into oblivion.

Luckily I didn't have to expose my face to Ruari's gaze, for we all had our heads down and our eyes averted from each other. I was very glad that we didn't have time to stay and discuss the issue any more.

Instead of heading for the Bogside or the Creggan, as I expected, Barnie drove up Park Avenue and into Templemore Park, a very middle-class area full of big detached houses. We stopped outside a house set back from the road, with a double garage and a large garden. It was a very unlikely-looking place for an IRA arms dump.

"This is it," said Barnie.

I stuck the .38 down my waistband and carried the M60 while Barnie went ahead with the guitar case containing the Armalites. He walked round to the back of the house and opened a sliding glass door, which was unlocked. We carried the weapons into the hall and put them into a cupboard under the stairs. As I went to put the .38 in there as well, Barnie said, "Not the short, that's to go back to young Gumey's place."

After I'd dropped off Barnie, I went back to the Creggan Heights and parked outside the taxi man's house. I rapped twice on the front door to let Chris and Dixie know that it was time to leave, then walked back with them. Chris dropped off the gun at Aranmore Avenue and we went down to the Telstar Bar for a pint.

I was desperate to get off on my own so that I could get in touch with Pete, but I didn't want to do anything to arouse Dixie's suspicions; he was already quite paranoid enough about touts.

We were standing around the bar chatting when Gumey came running in. He was nineteen, but so fresh faced he could have passed for fifteen. He rushed up to Chris and said, "My Ma's found the gun."

"So?" Chris said, taking another pull at his pint.

"So she's threatening to take it straight to the peelers."

Chris sighed and put down his pint. "Then we'd better go and have a little chat with her, hadn't we?"

To my relief, Dixie went with them. As soon as they'd gone, I sank the rest of my pint and hurried off down to the town. I found a pay-phone and got ready to call Pete. Before I dialled his number, however, I stood for a long time, looking out through the scratched perspex windows, daubed with countless IRA slogans.

People shuffled by, their heads hunched down into their shoulders against the cold and damp. A queue of shoppers stood at the army checkpoint, waiting in line as they'd already done at the supermarket checkout. Soldiers crouched on the corners, scanning the streets as the shoppers inched slowly forwards, pausing as other soldiers searched each bag and patted their hands down the people's sides, then sent them on into the dark, wet streets, already emptying of people.

Many of the shop windows were boarded up, as shop-owners sickened by years of bomb damage gave up trying to replace them, but pools of yellow light spilled from the few remaining display windows, throwing the dark mass of the city walls into even sharper relief. The iron cannon jutted defiantly from the ramparts, useless defenders of a city divided against itself. The cannon faced out towards the river, but the barbed wire, the steel and concrete fences and the squat, ugly sangers on the walls all faced the other way, across the city towards the Bogside and the Creggan.

Still I hesitated, staring out as the colour faded from the sky and night fell. These places were all I had ever known, but when I made the call to Pete, my life would change irrevocably, for ever.

Most agents and informants have a very limited shelf-life. The job carries with it an inescapable logic: the more successful you are, the quicker you'll be discovered. The more vital the information you uncover, the greater the temptation for the police to act on it immediately, even though this focuses suspicion directly on the informant. It was mainly down to luck that I'd escaped detection by the Provies this long. Had any IRA man sat down and studied the results of all the jobs I'd been involved in, he would have immediately realised that I was touting. Now I was about to put my head completely into the noose.

Several times I put my hand on the receiver, ready to pick it up and dial, only to snatch it away again as if burned. Finally, deliberately, I picked it up and began to dial. I knew that I had to do it whatever the consequences, but from that moment the clock was running. It was no longer a case of *if* the Provies discovered me, the only question now was *when*.

When Pete answered I told him I had the information for which he'd been waiting since the day I joined the Brigade Unit. We arranged to meet that night. I took even more care than usual on my way to the meeting-place, constantly checking reflections in cars and windows and even doubling back on my tracks once. I was sure that I wasn't being tailed, but I was still very tense and nervous even when safely inside Pete's car. He picked me up on the Strand Road and drove out of town, parking in a quiet road near the army base at Ballykelly. When I told him about the dump he was as excited as a schoolkid.

"That's great work, Ray, great work. There'll be a big bonus for you in a couple of days when we get the M60."

I couldn't share his enthusiasm. "Fuck the bonus, Pete. What about my neck? You can't raid that dump yet. It's the best-kept secret in the Brigade, and I've only just been shown where it is. If you raid it now, you might as well phone up Martin McGuinness and tell him I told you were it was."

"I'm sorry Ray, but we have to have that M60. If they get a chance to use it, they could kill ten or twenty men with it."

"Sorry? Exactly how much use will "sorry" be to me when I'm face-down in a ditch?"

"Have we ever left you exposed in the past?" he asked, immediately answering his own question. "No, we haven't, and we'll protect you again this time."

I was far from convinced. "Exactly how are you going to protect me this time? There's no way the Provies aren't going to point the finger at me over this."

He couldn't answer, and said only, "Give me a minute to think."

I sat there in silence while Pete pondered the options, but his reply, when it finally came, was not especially reassuring. "To throw suspicion away from you, the Special Branch will have no visible involvement in the seizure of the weapons. The RUC will be notified of a suspected break-in at the house, and the weapons will then be found by uniformed constables, backed up by an army patrol."

"It sounds like pretty thin cover for me."

"It's the best we can offer."

I let the silence grow for a minute, then told him, "I want out now,

Pete. From the minute you raid that dump, I'm a dead man. You've got to get me, Lorraine and the kids out of here before it's too late."

Now it was Pete's turn to leave a silence hanging between us. Finally he cleared his throat and said, "Okay. I'll go and talk to my boss about it. Come back to me in a couple of days."

CHAPTER 14

Two days later, I heard on Downtown Radio that the police and army had found an M60, three Armalites, a few pistols and a considerable quantity of ammunition in a house in Templemore Park.

I was both elated and horrified by the news. My information had led to the seizure of the M60, removing one of the IRA's most lethal weapons from its armoury. It was a tremendous coup for the RUC, but the raid would also stir the Provies into a frenzy of recrimination and retribution. As Pete had predicted, a police spokesman claimed that they'd stumbled upon the dump while carrying out a search after an attempted burglary, but that did little to reassure me. The cover story might work for a short while, but even the most naïve IRA man would not take long to put two and two together. The location of the Brigade Unit's weapons dump was one of the most tightly-guarded secrets in the Derry IRA. Within a few days of my being shown the dump, it had been raided.

As luck would have it, I'd already arranged to see Shorty McNally the next day. I'd been buying a car, a gold Cortina Mark IV, for £20 a week from a bloke in the Creggan and had been trying to persuade Shorty to buy it as a staff car for the Provies. A lot of important IRA meetings now took place on the move, because of fears that the SAS or MI5 were planting bugs in the walls of safe houses. A staff car already fitted with listening devices would have yielded some top-grade intelligence.

Tapper and I went to see Shorty about it, but he told me it had been vetoed by Paul Cleary, the money man in Northern Command.

"You're a fairly hot member since your arrest, Ray." said Shorty, "and Paul reckons that the car would come under notice from the army and the police very quickly. But let's have a look at it anyway, now you're here."

When he said it, Shorty whistled through his teeth. "This is some car Ray. Did you buy it with the money you got for the M60?"

I was paralysed with fright for a moment and the colour flooded into my cheeks. I thought frantically. If Shorty really had strong suspicions, he wouldn't have put it to me like that. He'd have sent the boys from Internal Affairs to pick me up and I'd already be making a one-way journey that would end with me lying dead.

Shorty was part-testing, part-teasing me, and attack seemed the only defence. "What the fuck are you talking about? My life's been on the line enough times in jobs for you. I didn't join the RA just to get a fucking car."

"Take it easy, Ray. All I'm saying is that only three people knew where that dump was – Ruari Spears, Barnie McMahon and you. I'm pretty sure that Ruari wouldn't have sold it, so that only leaves you and that bastard Barnie."

"Well, it wasn't me."

Tapper hastily intervened. "Boys, boys, calm down."

Ruari Spears appeared shortly afterwards and I was relieved when Shorty tried the same number on him. "How much did you get for the M60?"

Ruari also reacted angrily and the subject was dropped, for the moment at least.

Although Shorty was clearly unsure about the source of the leak, I had known since the M60 was lifted that the game was as good as up. The cover story of the RUC investigating a burglary had worked initially, but if they thought about it for any length of time, they would realise it was a set-up. It was a very common deception by the security forces; they were always claiming to have stumbled on IRA people or guns by accident.

I phoned Pete again that night from Duffy's Bar, down in the town. "What's happening? When can you lift me out?"

"I've spoken to my boss, Ray, it's all right, but it will take a few days to get everything prepared. We have two options. We can just take you out and give you and your family a new identity, or you can also do what we wanted to do in the first place – get all these guys put away behind bars where they can't kill or maim or do more damage to innocent people. The last thing either of us would want is for someone to get crippled or murdered because we didn't finish the job. We've got to put these guys away for a long time. I can't force you to do that, though, and you'll be well looked after in either case, so the decision is yours."

I'd always known that if I every got to this stage, something like this would happen, but even so, my immediate reaction was to say, "No."

I hung up, but when I thought about it for an hour or so, I realised that I had to see the job through to its conclusion. I phoned Pete back and said, "Okay, we'll got for it."

"Great. Meet me in twenty minutes, the usual spot."

I slipped out of the bar and walked slowly across town to the rendezvous, every sense alert for anything out of the ordinary – a moment, a stillness, someone loitering fractionally too long or taking too much interest in a shop display – that would betray someone watching or following me. Once more I was sure that I was safe, but I still couldn't quell the mounting unease inside me.

Pete's car pulled up dead on time, and as he leaned across to open the passenger door, I sprinted forward, my tracksuit hood pulled up around my head. I'd told Lorraine I was going for a pint with some mates – always keep the alibi as close to the truth as possible – and Pete made for one of the pubs we regularly used.

We drove out towards the coast, heading for Portstewart, thirty miles out of Derry. It was a Protestant town and a popular spot at weekends, but there was little chance of seeing anyone from Derry there on a midweek night. We pulled in the car park of the Edgewater Hotel and wandered into the bar. A fire was blazing in the hearth despite the season, and there was a smattering of solitary male drinkers staring morosely into their pints. Pete rolled his eyes, then bought the first round before we walked across to a table by the window, well away from the other drinkers. We sat for a moment in silence, watching the waves breaking on the rocks below us. Then, keeping a wary eye on the people at the bar, we began to talk through a plan to lift me out and get the others arrested.

The cover story Pete and I prepared, which I'd tell to Shorty and even to Lorraine, was that we needed a holiday and were going over the border to stay at Butlin's for a couple of weeks. I was sure it wouldn't be a hard story for Shorty to swallow. Most of the other members of the unit already had a week or two off to go on their holidays, and he knew that Lorraine and I went to Butlin's every summer. In fact, we'd be meeting Pete and a team of RUC men in our usual spot over the Waterside by the church cemetery. That was the good news; the bad news was that it would take the RUC a fortnight to put the arrangements in place to get me, Lorraine and the kids out of there and prepare for the arrests of everyone else.

Pete dropped me off back in Derry with a few more words of reassurance and I wandered home, my mind buzzing. My time inside the IRA was almost up, but I was now entering its most dangerous phase. It was the most tense period of my whole time as an agent. I couldn't sleep at night and paced about in the dark, doubts and worries preying on my mind. I was convinced that I was being watched and sat in the house staring at the television, too scared to go out in case someone was lying in wait.

Fear had always been with me. I had lived for years in constant terror of discovery, which would inevitably have led to torture and death. But it had always been possible to be optimistic before. Now I knew that there was no escape; it was just a matter of time. The only question was whether I'd be lifted to safety by the RUC before I was killed by the IRA.

Although I trusted Pete completely, that didn't apply to his colleagues. The security forces could be almost as cynical as the IRA in exploiting naïve Creggan kids, putting their lives at risk and, if necessary, sacrificing them without a second thought – pawns in a greater game. Agents could easily be trapped in the no-man's-land of the Dirty War, and I could never be sure that Pete's superiors – or the shadowy men from M15 – wouldn't change the rules of the game at any moment. There was always a thought in the back of my mind that someone in the RUC might decide that it was just too much trouble or expense to look after me, and so they'd throw me to the wolves or betray me in order to divert attention from another, more highly-placed agent in the IRA.

That wasn't just paranoia – they'd done it before and would do it again, with an agent called Joe Fenton, who was told to finger two other informers, Gerard and Catherine Mahon, to divert suspicion from himself. That ploy bought Fenton time, but in the end, in an attempt to conceal yet another agent, he himself was sacrificed by his handlers and executed by the IRA.

These were not comforting thoughts. My nerves and my drinking grew steadily worse. I was swilling Irish whiskey and even poteen, but all the Provies drank fairly heavily and my own boozing did not attract any particular attention. I was always careful not to get too drunk, determined never to give myself away by loose talk, but all the time I felt that the IRA were closing in on me.

It would have been easy for them to interrogate each of the three people who could have told the police where the arms dump was hidden. Shorty had already told me that Internal Affairs – probably Doyle and Cochrane, who were the two main intelligence officers at the time – were likely to have a word with me. I knew exactly what that meant. If they even thought that I might be the culprit, I wouldn't be coming back from the interview. The clock was running. My only hope was that they wouldn't act in haste, but put surveillance on me, pressure me, watch and wait. They would also begin reviewing all the operations in which the three of us had been involved, however. When they did that, there could only be one conclusion.

It wasn't a court of law; they didn't need proof. Strong suspicion would be enough. I'd be whisked across the border to a safe house in the Republic, equipped with more torture equipment than a medieval dungeon. After several agonising days in which I'd tell them everything they wanted to know, I'd be executed in strict accordance with the procedures laid down in the Green Book – just another tout paying the price.

After my interrogation was over, I'd be dressed in a boiler suit so that there would be no forensic traces in the car that transported me. Two executioners would take me to a remote spot and read me the relevant section from the Green Book. A tame priest would also be on hand to give me the last rites and witness the shooting.

My shoes would be removed, my hands tied behind my back and I'd be forced to kneel. The last thing I would see on this earth would be a patch of dirt between my knees as they placed a black cloth hood over my head. Both men would stand behind me and simultaneously fire their pistols into the back of my head, blowing my face off. There'd be a lower jaw and a scalp left; everything in between would have disappeared. There was no way that there would be an open casket at my funeral, for the funeral director had not been born who could put a face back together after two .45 rounds had exited through it.

After I'd pitched forward into the ditch, one of my executioners would push a £20 note into my dead hand, a traditional message to the RUC to show that the Provies knew they'd killed a tout. As a final humiliation, they might attach wires and batteries to the body, to make it look as if it was booby-trapped. When the corpse was found, bomb-disposal men would then have to be called in before it could be taken away. If it was a busy day for the bomb-disposal teams, the body might lie there all day, smothered in flies and bloating in the sun before it could finally be moved.

I had to keep up the appearance that everything was normal, though every instinct was screaming at me to cut and run while I still had time. I knew that the Internal Affairs men were hovering about, watching for any sign of tension or break with routine.

Several times I looked out of the window to see a car with two occupants parked just up the street. The figures inside could have just been two mates having a chat, but when they were there the next day and again the day after that, sitting and staring towards the house for hour upon hour, it was obvious they were watching me. They made no attempt at concealment since visibility was part of the game: crank up the pressure, see if he panics. Hard as I tried to convince myself that Ruari Spears's and Barnie McMahon's houses were probably being watched as well, it was little consolation.

All I could hope was that Internal Affairs remained uncertain of the identity of the tout. As the most recent person to be shown the location of the Brigade dump, I had to be the prime suspect, but in the Byzantine game of bluff and counter-bluff between the security forces and the IRA, Internal Affairs could not be sure that I was not being implicated as a way of concealing the identity of the real traitor. If Barnie McMahon was the tout, his instinct for self-preservation might have led him to wait until he'd shown me the dump before tipping off the Branch.

While Internal Affairs remained uncertain, they would wait. They could act with shocking speed on occasions, but they could also be infinitely patient, increasing the pressure a notch at a time, painstakingly setting the trap that would lure an informer to his death.

I knew that my time was finite, however. Doyle and Cochrane would already be starting to pore over the records of every job in which Barnie, Ruari and I had been involved, and alone of these three suspects, I had never killed or wounded a soldier or a policeman; I had never even fired a shot. If they drew up a list of abandoned or unsuccessful jobs, my name would keep recurring like the ticking of a clock. Once, twice, even three times might be coincidence, but ten, twenty, thirty times could only be deliberate.

The thought increased my fear even more. I skulked around the house, pouring down drink to try and settle my nerves. I knew that my best hope of survival was to stick to my daily routine, but scared shitless, I kept making excuses to myself for staying at home. Once I did set off towards the Creggan shops, but fled home again in a panic when I saw what I thought was a four-man IRA unit reversing up the road towards me.

Finally I had to go out to sign on for my unemployment benefit. I walked down towards the town, checking to see I wasn't being followed. I signed on early, pretending I'd heard about some building work that might be going, and then walked down to Duffy's Bar. I phoned Pete from a pay-phone and asked for a meeting, desperate to explain my fears to someone.

When he picked me up half an hour later I poured everything out.

"Things are really closing in around me, Pete. They're getting more and more suspicious of me and I'm being watched all the time."

Pete was sympathetic but firm. "Might there not be a touch of paranoia in there somewhere?"

I was hurt by his flippancy. "It might be paranoia, but on a few occasions in the past, those feelings have helped me survive. I'm not about to start denying them now."

"I understand that, but you have to hold your nerve, Ray. If you change your routine, they'll only get more suspicious. You've only got a few more days to wait now. Don't let them hear the nerves jangling."

"It's easy for you to say; you're not the one being watched."

"There goes that paranoia again," Pete said, and this time even I had to smile.

"All right, but if you have to pull me out of a ditch tomorrow after they've blown the back of my head off, don't say I didn't warn you."

"I won't. Be sure to mention my name before they do."

"Don't worry, it's the first thing I'll be telling them. They won't even have to torture me to get that."

As black humour goes it was pretty feeble stuff, but as usual I felt better just for talking about things, and after Pete had dropped me off I felt in better spirits than I had for days.

It didn't last long, for as I walked back up William Street, I bumped into Tapper and Ruari. I raised an eyebrow, for it was very unusual to see two prominent IRA men walking about town together so openly.

"You'll be on the march on Sunday, Ray?" Ruari asked, more a statement than a question.

"You know me, Ruari, I'll be there."

We chatted for a few minutes while standing at the side of the road. I was straining to spot any difference in their attitude to me, but could find none. I felt oddly reassured and arranged to go to a dance with Tapper that night. Most of the people there would be IRA men and their wives, and I reasoned it was the last place a guilty man would choose to be.

I went down to the Creggan shops later on to get some shampoo ready for the big night out. As usual Tapper was hanging around outside the shops, and when he saw me getting back into my car, he came straight over and asked me what I was doing.

"Nothing much."

"Would you do a run for me?"

"Aye, where to?"

"Over the Waterside, to collect a short from Vic O'Grady. You won't have to bring it back in the car though, we're meeting a girl over there who'll get it back in a taxi."

He hopped into the car and we drove over to O'Grady's mother's house in the Waterside. Vic's sister let us in and we found him up a step-ladder, papering his mother's ceiling.

"Now, Vic," Tapper said. "We're over for the short."

O'Grady nodded. "We'll have to go and see someone else about it."

We drove up to a bar at the top of the hill, and Tapper and I stood in a laneway beside the bar while O'Grady went inside. A minute later he came out, followed by a boy, James Sheerin, who looked barely old enough for the moustache he was trying to grow.

"Here's yer man," O'Grady said.

"I can get you a short," Sheerin said nervously, "but it's a wee bit light yet. It would be better if it was a bit darker."

Tapper sighed and looked at his watch. "So how long will it take?"

"About three-quarters of an hour."

"How about getting it over the bridge?"

"I'll get the wife to take it across for you."

I shot him another sideways glance; he didn't seem old enough to have a wife, either.

Tapper looked doubtfully at him. "I dunno. Ray, would you take it over in your car?"

I said I would. O'Grady and Sheerin went off to get the gun, while we drove back down to the house and sat around chatting to his mother and his sister, Maureen. Vic eventually came back and told us, "Sorry, lads, it'll be another half-hour. He's a bit scared of moving it before dark."

Tapper muttered, "Christ alive," under his breath, drawing a sharp look from O'Grady's mother, who was evidently quite unmoved by the thought of a gun in her house, but wasn't going to have any blasphemy under her roof, thank you very much.

It was now nine o'clock. I fidgeted for a few minutes and then asked Mrs O'Grady, "Will it be all right if I wash my hair while we're waiting? I'm going out tonight and I won't have time when I get home."

She looked me up and down, checking if I was fit to be let loose in her bathroom, then sighed and nodded. Even after I'd washed my hair and helped myself to some deodorant I found up there, we still had to wait another three-quarters of an hour before Michael McCabe arrived at the house. He and Tapper walked over to a laneway while I got into the car and drove it up level with the entrance.

James Sheerin was standing in the shadows, squinting nervously up and down the lane. He handed something to Tapper and disappeared back down the laneway. Tapper got in the car and showed me the gun, a Ruger revolver with a wooden handle.

"It looks bloody powerful," I said, pushing the barrel away. It had been pointing directly at my head.

Tapper laughed. "It's the one the cop lost a while ago. The Waterside unit knee-capped Culm Michael with it and he bled to death afterwards. What a weapon to knee-cap anybody with, eh, Ray?"

I nodded, for I didn't trust myself to speak for a moment. I was remembering my two brothers being knee-capped. They could have wound up dead just as easily. When I'd got control of my voice again, I asked, "Who was Culm Michael?"

"He was James Sheerin's brother-in-law."

"No wonder he looked so fucking nervous."

Sheerin and McCabe stagged us across the bridge and right over to Iniscarn Road in McCabe's white Mercedes van. They left us there and Tapper told me, "Drive to Rathlin car park, we've two people to meet."

I sighed to myself; my evening out was fast going down the tubes. When I'd parked the car, we left the gun in the glove compartment and walked down Kildrum Gardens, where we met Patrick Boyd and a young lad called Mitch coming towards us. They were both in the Creggan cell.

"I've the short for the job tomorrow morning," Tapper said. "Are you all set?"

"Aye, we've the wigs and everything ready," Boyd said.

When we got back to my car, Tapper took the gun out of the glove compartment and handed it over to Mitch. He and Boyd both cleared off.

I took it they were going to stiff someone in the morning and tried to get out of Tapper what was on, but he wouldn't say much. I didn't dare press him when he was sober and hoped a few drinks might loosen him up. "I've the wife to pick up, Tapper and then we're over to the Bog Inn before the dance, do you want to come along?"

As usual, he needed no encouragement to have a drink. We drove up and collected Lorraine and went to the Bog Inn. I bought him a few pints and tried to pump him again about the job while Lorraine was in the toilet, but he was tight-lipped for once and I couldn't get out of him who the intended victim was. I phoned Pete anyway when I went to the bogs, but without any detail, the tip was virtually useless. The next day I heard on the evening news that a part-time UDR man had been shot dead.

Lorraine was tired and went home early, but I stayed on at the dance with Tapper. Donal Tiernan was still in prison and I walked his wife back to her house in the Creggan Heights after the dance, while Tapper took George McBrearty's widow home. Donal's wife took me in and made me a cup of tea before I went home.

I was still in bed the next morning when Lorraine came in. "There are two men at the front door asking for you."

"Who are they?"

"I don't know. I've never seen them before."

My heart started to pound. Christ, I thought, this is it, they've come to get me. My first thought was to jump out of the window and leg it down the road, but I knew it would be suicide. I had to face it. I put on a pair of trousers and went to the door, scared shitless.

The two guys were standing there, looking very menacing. I vaguely recognized them but couldn't put names to them. I thought to myself, *This is definitely it, and it's too late to run*, but I kept myself under control. "Yeah? What do you want?"

"I'm Donal Tiernan's brother and this is his brother-in-law. I hear you took Donal's wife home last night."

The relief that these were just two relatives keeping an eye on Donal's wife while he was in gaol, rather than two killers from Internal Affairs come to torture and murder me, was almost blinding. I could have kissed the pair of them. Instead I just grunted a surly, "Yeah. What of it?"

"Just this. Do it again and you'll be fucking seen to."

I practically laughed in his face. "Get the fuck away from my door." They turned and walked off.

For the next four days I hung around the house, staring morosely at the television and jumping at every footfall or car passing in the street outside. My nerves were wound to breaking point and I drank steadily, constantly snapping at Lorraine and the kids.

On Sunday I had to go on the march that Ruari had reminded me about. It was to commemorate the first anniversary of the death of Joe McDonnell, one of the ten hunger strikers who had starved themselves to death in Long Kesh the previous year. I was on maximum alert as we milled around before the start of the march, but once again I couldn't detect any difference in the way the guys were with me.

We marched from the Bogside Inn to Creggan Cemetery and then stood dutifully around, pretending to listen to the speeches. I was next to Tapper McFadden, who stood ramrod-straight, apparently following every word with rapt attention, but in fact keeping up a constant conversation with myself and Sean McArdle out of the corner of his mouth.

"We'll be needing a pint after we get through this, Ray," breathed Tapper.

"If we ever do."

Tapper switched to the other side of his mouth and spoke to McArdle. "Did you not get the other bomb into the barracks on Strand Road, Sean?"

I pricked my ears up immediately. For a man who'd been on the blanket in Long Kesh, Tapper's capacity for loose talk never ceased to amaze me.

"Indeed I did," McArdle said in injured tones. "I put it between the corrugated iron and the wall just below the sanger. I can't understand why it didn't go off. It's just like the first one we put there."

"Well the next one had better not fuck up. The wee man's cracking up because none of the bombs are going off. He's threatening court-martials and fucking nuttings if it happens again."

"Sure, if I'd a punt for every time Shorty's threatened to court-martial me," I said, "even you couldn't drink it all, Tapper."

He started to laugh, then remembered where he was and resumed his somber expression.

The march had passed without incident, but as soon as the speeches ended, we were all told to get some rioting going. Our unit went over to Aggro Corner at the junction of William Street and Rossville Street. Over ten years before I'd watched on television as the horror of Bloody Sunday unfolded on this very spot. Today was nothing in comparison. There was some desultory stoning of the troops and a few petrol bombs were thrown, but both the security forces and the rioters seemed jaded and indifferent, as if even the Creggan's bottomless pit of hatred had been temporarily exhausted.

As we stood watching, Ruari called me over and took me to one side. My heart started to pound and my mouth was dry. Not now, surely not now.

"Tomorrow morning," he said. "Be at my house at ten o'clock. No later, Ray, and bring Ciaran McQuillan. We're going on a shoot with a difference."

He chuckled as I vainly tried to understand the joke, my brain a blank and my mouth flapping open lying a dying fish.

"It's a photo shoot, Ray," Ruari said patiently. "*Iris* are sending someone down from Belfast to take photographs. We're doing an armed foot patrol around the Creggan. You'll need to bring masks, but nothing else."

I forced a smile and said, "Great. Shame we'll be wearing masks – my Ma'd love to see her boy in the papers."

Ruari laughed and turned back to watch the riot, which was rapidly petering out. He shook his head wearily and said, "What the hell's the matter with kids these days?", then stumped off grumpily up William Street calling, "See you tomorrow," over his shoulder.

As soon as he was out of sight, I sloped off as well. I badly needed to think. The meeting might be nothing more than he'd said, but it could equally be a set-up. One minute I might be sitting in Ruari's living-room talking about the weather, and the next I could be in the back of a car with a hood over my head, taking a one-way drive into the country with the boys from Internal Affairs.

Yet again I forced myself to be calm, to think it through rationally. If it was a set-up, why not just pick me up today? And why would they want Ciaran McQuillan there? If they were watching me, this could be just another test to see if I'd crack and make a break for it. I had to hold my nerve and turn up at Spears's place as planned.

Iris was a magazine produced by Sinn Féin in which "heroic IRA volunteers" were photographs brandishing their guns and parading through the streets of various different parts of the North. "Armed propaganda" was the description favoured by the Sinn Féin office in Belfast, and Derry was obviously to be honoured in this issue.

The magazine appeared sporadically, but there was always an issue on the streets for the anniversary of internment on the ninth of August. Hundreds of people from the Troops Out movement in Britain and Noraid in America came to Northern Ireland for the anniversary demonstrations, and the Provies and Sinn Féin always liked them to have a souvenir of their visit. It helped with the propaganda effort and, even more crucially, it helped to keep the donations flowing.

I called at Ciaran McQuillan's to tell him about the photo-shoot, then went home to another night on the bottle and another argument with Lorraine. I longed to tell her what was behind my moods, but didn't dare. I'd had years to get used to the pressures, and telling Lorraine now would only put both our lives at risk. In another couple of days I would finally have to tell her everything and then pray she wouldn't reject me. Lorraine went round to her mother's for the evening to get out of the way while I slumped in an armchair, staring blankly at the television and drinking steadily.

The next morning, nursing a hangover, I called for Ciaran and then set off for Ruari's house in Mallan Gardens. The wind blew the dust and the ashes from yesterday's riots into our faces as we walked along, squinting in the bright sunlight. Despite my attempts to apply cool logic to the situation. I was still very nervous. Ciaran was wildly excited about his chance of stardom, albeit wearing a mask. I let him rattle on about it while I pursued my own, rather more gloomy thoughts. Perversly, part of me was also relieved just to be out of the house and doing something, even if it was putting my head on the block.

When we walked into Ruari's living-room, two strangers rose from the sofa to meet us. My heart froze for an instant, but they had Belfast accents and didn't look like hard-faced men from Internal Affairs. If it was a set-up, it was a meticulously staged one, for they also had well-used Nikon cameras and plenty of professional-looking lenses.

"Where's Ruari?" asked Ciaran

"He's upstairs, changing out of his suit," said one them with the ghost of a smile.

Barnie McMahon and Frank O'Neill came in a couple of minutes later. Barnie was carrying a black guitar case. He laid it on the floor by the sofa and took out three Armalites and a Thompson sub-machine gun, each with a loaded magazine.

Ruari appeared a minute later, his hair neatly combed. Barnie and I exchanged a smile as Ruari began barking orders to emphasise his authority.

"Barnie, Frank, take a look out."

They slipped out and went off up the road.

"Ray, Ciaran, grab a gun each. No, not the fucking Thompson," he growled as Ciaran reached for it. "I'm the unit leader, I'm taking that. Get an Armalite."

"Who's the fourth gun for?" I asked.

"Mary Cobbe, if she ever turns up."

"She did a few moments later, red-faced and apologetic.

"Right, let's get to it," said Spears, pulling his mask over his face. He continued issuing orders, but had to repeat them twice because we could hardly hear for the mask muffling his words.

"For fuck's sake," he shouted, tearing his mask off again, "I said, watch yourselves with the fucking guns, they're already loaded. Now this a quick in-and-out job. McMahon and O'Neill are out stagging to see if there are any peelers or army about. When we get the word back from them we're away."

He glared around the room then jammed his mask back over his head.

We picked up our weapons and stood around in silence for a few minutes until the phone rang twice, stopped and then rang twice again.

"That's it," Ruari said. "Let's get the show on the road."

We filed out and walked up Greenwalk and round to Melmore where we struck poses at the side of the road, giving cover while Spears strode imperiously out into the middle of the street, ready to stop the traffic, check the drivers' licences and ask them where they were going.

The effect was somewhat lessened by a complete lack of passing cars, but after an embarrassing hiatus, a battered Ford Escort appeared over the brow of the hill. Ruari held up his hand like a policeman on point duty, then ostentatiously waved the car past with the barrel of the Thompson as the photographers hunched over their cameras, purring with pleasure.

In the ten minutes we were there, we only stopped that one car and eventually Ruari gave up and ran back to the side of the road. He led us down to the Creggan Community Centre, where we once more struck poses with the weapons as a crowd of small boys gathered to watch the free show.

"*Tiocfaidh ar la*" shouted one of the photographers, raising a clenched fist above his head. It was an IRA slogan meaning "Our day will come," and the small boys cheered dutifully, then went back to kicking their ball around the waste ground.

Once the photographers were satisfied, we hurried back to the Spears's house, unloaded the guns and put them back into the guitar case. Barnie and Frank took them back to the dump while the rest of us took off, arranging to meet at a Sinn Féin social that night in aid of the dead hunger-strikers' families.

The photographers also turned up, keen for a big night out in Derry before heading back to Belfast. I shared a few drinks with them, while the singer belted out the usual stuff like "Bloody Sunday" and "Men Behind The Wire", then slipped away. I paused at the door, taking a last look round the room, crowded with people who had been my neighbours, comrades-in-arms and drinking mates. If I ever set eyes on them again it would be in a prison cell or a court-room. I said a silent goodbye to them and to Derry, then turned to leave, passing under the banners festooned with portraits of IRA heroes – every one of them dead.

CHAPTER 15

The next morning, the fifteenth of August, 1982, Lorraine packed the bags for our Butlin's holiday as the kids tore around the house, wild with excitement. We loaded the bags into the car and then I went back inside alone and looked around my home for the last time. As I did, I heard a car driving slowly up the road and instantly began to panic, fearing that having travelled so far I might be discovered right at the last.

I forced myself to breathe slowly and evenly as I came out of the house. The car I had heard had stopped a few yards down the road. Two men were sitting in it, but it was impossible to tell if they were watching me or just waiting for someone. I turned to lock the door, but my hands were shaking and I dropped the keys. I stooped and picked them up, scrabbling frantically in the dirt, my ears pricked for the sound of a car opening and footsteps heading my way.

There was silence. I walked to my car as casually as I could and even managed to wave to a neighbour, though I could feel my heart thumping in my chest. I got into the car and drove off down the hill into Derry, darting nervous glances at the rear-view mirror every couple of seconds to see if the other car would turn and follow us. It hadn't moved by the time we turned the corner, but I kept checking the mirror all the way down the long hill into town. I was so obsessed with the possibility of pursuit that we were out of the Creggan before I noticed it. There would be no time now for a farewell to the place where I'd been born and lived all of my life.

I began to breathe a little easier as we crossed the Craigavon Bridge into Protestant territory. Lorraine shot me a questioning look, because this wasn't the way to Butlin's, but she said nothing, perhaps reluctant to spark another argument by questioning me.

I drove on in silence, lost in my own thoughts, and didn't tell Lorraine our real destination until the last minute. I stopped the car at the side of the road, just short of the rendezvous point with Pete, and turned to face her as I told her for the first time what I'd been doing for so many years. "I've been working for the RUC. I'm a Special Branch agent and I'll be putting people away. The IRA will soon know about it and I have to leave Derry. You have a choice, Lorraine. I want you to go with me, if you want to, but if you want to stay, I'll understand."

She stared at me in disbelief to begin with, but when I told her it was where all the money had been coming from for the groceries, it all dropped into place. She sat staring straight ahead for a moment, gnawing at her lip as she thought it all through, unable to believe that I'd been doing something like this for so long without her knowing. Then she broke down in tears.

As the children played unconcernedly on the back seat, too young to understand the enormity of what was about to happen to their lives, Lorraine began to argue with me. She tried desperately to talk me out of it, saying over and over again, "Let's just go back home. It'll be all right. We can sort it out."

I shook my head. "There's no way I can ever go back."

"But what about the kids?"

"The kids will be fine as long as they're with us. Come away with me."

"And my family? I can't just leave my Ma and Da."

"You'll have to if you want to be with me." I took her hands in mine and pleaded with her. I can't go back, Lorraine. I'll be taken away and killed and you'll be burned out of the house."

She still argued with me, even though she must have known in her heart that I had to leave Derry, but eventually she gave in.

She gave me a long look, her eyes brimming with tears, the look of a widow at her husband's funeral, then she dropped her gaze to her hands knotted in her lap and spoke in a dull, flat voice. "All right, I'll come with you."

As I started the engine she burst into tears, crying as if her heart would break. The kids sat silent as stone in the back. Denise reached forward a hand, gently touching Lorraine's shoulder, then began to cry as well. As Lorraine stifled her own sobs and turned to comfort Denise, our eyes met for an instant. For the first time, I saw hatred for me in my wife's eyes. Things were never to be the same between us again.

I drove on to the meeting place with Pete, who was waiting with a few guys from Special Branch. One of them took my car while we got into the other and were driven up to Lisburn to be debriefed. Pete had never written anything down in any great detail at our regular meetings; he just took down the main points. The detail didn't come out until the debriefing.

I was in a room with the two CID men twelve hours a day for six weeks, giving formal statements. One of the men was Ivor Semple, renewing the acquaintance begun years before when I'd been arrested with Noel Kavanagh for hooding. The last time we'd met, I'd had nothing to say to him, but this time I talked myself hoarse. There was a desperate sense of urgency about the work, for we had something like seven to ten days to finish the preliminary statements and get the guys lifted. If I was away any longer without explanation, the Provies would realise that something was going on and the members of my until might do a runner.

When they'd got my statements, the RUC went to the DPP for warrants, then lifted most of the IRA and INLA people in Derry. They were taken to Castlereagh, Gough Barracks and a number of other barracks around Northern Ireland.

The pre-dawn arrest of around a hundred Derry IRA men and women took place on 25 August, and involved one thousand police and troops. It was the biggest security operation in Derry since Operation Motorman, which had swept away the barricades ten years before. At the same time, a removal van protected by a heavily-armed guard took away all the possessions from our house. It was the first sign to anyone on the Creggan that Ray Gilmour might be a supergrass.

A couple of days later one of my minders brought me a present – a copy of the latest issue of *Iris* magazine. The cover photograph showed two masked figures, Mary Cobbe and Ruari Spears. Mary was kneeling, holding an Armalite in the firing position, Ruari was standing in the middle of the road with the Thompson gun slung casually over his shoulder. The back cover showed Mary, Ciaran McQuillan and me patrolling alongside the iron railings in Greenwalk. It was nice to have a souvenir of my time inside the IRA.

The worst moments for me were when I had to confront each guy in turn in his holding cell. It was the most frightening yet exhilarating feeling. I felt that everything I had been working towards had been achieved, but at the cost of betraying to their faces people who had been my comrades.

I didn't want to do it at all, but it was essential because the RUC were hoping that with me confronting the guys, some would either break and agree to give them information, or at the least say something incriminating in their anger. The police had already told them that I was giving information, but they always say that sort of thing anyway and I'm sure that none of them really believed it until I went in and faced them.

As I walked into each room, a detective read out part of my statement and then asked, "Is this the man?"

I said, "Yes, it is," looking into the once-familiar faces, now contorted with hate.

In the event, the tactic was unsuccessful. Most didn't say anything at all, despite their surprise, though the looks they gave me said more than enough for me. Brendan McDermott made a few remarks, but was smart enough not to make threats, because he knew that was what the RUC wanted. All he said was, "Don't be so stupid, Ray. Think about what you're doing."

Only Dixie Bingham lost control of himself and really abused me, but then he never could keep his mouth shut. Finally I walked into Shorty McNally's cell. When he saw me, he put his face in his hands and shook his head wearily as if to say, "I knew it was you all the time, but I couldn't bring myself to believe it."

All the time we were in Lisburn, we lived in a cold damp pre-fab, guarded twenty-four hours a day by heavily-armed RUC men. Even so, I was always tense, worrying that someone would be able to get into the barracks to have a go at us. On one occasion the RUC changed my minders without letting me know. I saw two strange guys, acting very suspiciously, coming towards our Portakabin. I grabbed a big butcher's knife out of the drawer and stood with my hand behind my back as they approached the door, ready at least to take one of them with me.

They opened the door without knocking and then said, "Hello, we're your new minders."

I nearly blew my top, yelling, "You stupid bastards, you scared me to death!"

Even without the tensions, it was hard to imagine a more miserable environment; I even had nostalgic feelings about the Crum. A big chestnut horse called Chiff-Chaff was stabled in the barracks in Lisburn and the only sane thing we did there was to take the kids up to see him and stroke him every day. As we did so, we couldn't help noticing that the horse's stabling was more solidly built – and warmer – than our Portakabin.

Luckily the kids were really too young to sense what was going on or to pick up on their parents' unhappiness. Lorraine was utterly miserable all the time we were there and missed her family terribly. She also fell ill, needing laser surgery on a cyst on her ovaries. The RUC felt we wouldn't be safe at any hospital in Northern Ireland and flew us all over to the military hospital in Aldershot. Raymond, Denise and I stayed in an army house nearby, still shepherded by minders, until Lorraine was well enough to leave hospital.

Her convalescence wasn't helped when we were immediately returned to the pre-fab in Lisburn, but she was no happier when we were moved, first to an army barracks in Newtownards, and then, after she was recognised by a former employer, to a housing estate in Ipswich.

For four months we lived in a semi-detached police house in Wimborne Avenue, while our four RUC minders – three men and a woman – lived in the other half of the house. Neighbours on the estate assumed we were all on a course at a nearby Suffolk police headquarters, but in fact the local police hated us being there and were constantly agitating to get us moved away.

Living there was a pretty unpleasant experience for all of us. I couldn't get on with the minders I'd been allocated. I didn't feel comfortable around them at all, I expected a bit of respect for what I'd done, but they seemed to look down on me. It may have been my paranoia, but I got the feeling that they weren't classifying me as one of their own, but as just another criminal who'd turned Queen's Evidence to save his hide or make a few quid. That really got to me and I was having arguments with them left, right and centre.

The first thing the minders did when they came over to Ipswich was go to the supermarket and stock up with a case of vodka and loads of beer. They then sat in the house next door to us, getting drunk. Lorraine and I were living on the bare essentials while they seemed to be treating it as a holiday. I rang home and spoke to Brian McVicker, the RUC Inspector who was taking my detailed statements, and told him about the situation. He came over to see for himself a few days later and immediately had the leader of the minders removed. The rest got a kick up the arse from him as well, which did nothing to endear me to them, but my life was at stake.

Lorraine remained very depressed and kept asking me to go back to Derry. Even if we couldn't go home, she wanted us to get away from the minders and police and go away somewhere else to start afresh, but I was adamant that I was going to do the job right and put the IRA men behind bars. I felt under pressure from all sides and was drinking heavily, which didn't help the growing tensions between us. After a few more weeks I was so low that I felt like packing it all in myself.

I was even lower when news came through that my father had been kidnapped. He'd been dragged from his home in Balbane Pass on the night of 17 November by three masked and armed men, taken over the border and held hostage by the Provies. I didn't need the threat spelling out. If I gave evidence against the IRA, my father would be murdered.

As soon s the news of the kidnapping broke, the RUC sent us out to Cyprus. It was supposed to be a holiday, but they were obviously scared that on top of all my other worries, the threat to my father might break me. If so, it would be a lot harder to cut and run from Cyprus than from England. Feuding with my wife and my minders and brooding over the possible fate of my father, I great increasingly depressed. I certainly wasn't in the ideal frame of mind for a holiday, and it didn't lift Lorraine's black mood either. Only the kids seemed excited, still unaware of the growing tension between us.

When we arrived in Cyprus we were taken up to the Troodos Mountains and put into one of the chalets the RAF used for skiing, while our minders, as usual, moved in next door. I went out for a walk the next morning, with the sun reflecting blindingly from the snow. It gave me a savage migraine, the first one I'd ever had.

It lasted several days and, by then, I'd had enough. I am not at all the suicidal type, but I took two packets of little blue tablets – transquillisers that Lorraine had been given by the doctor – and swallowed the whole lot, washing them down with vodka. I don't think I was actually trying to kill myself, but I thought, *If I wake up in the morning, I wake up, and if I don't, I don't; I'm not really bothered one way or the other.*

Lorraine came in shortly afterwards, found the empty packets and told the minders, but they didn't do anything about it. They didn't even come in to look at the packets to find out exactly what I'd taken, and they certainly didn't send for a doctor or an ambulance. Perhaps they were so sick of the sight of me that they were happy to leave it to chance whether I lived or died. In the end Lorraine broke down and begged them to take me to hospital. They took me to a military hospital in Limassol, where the doctors pumped my stomach. I survived, suffering nothing worse than the equivalent of a spectacularly bad hangover, and the experience cured me of any desire to repeat the experiment.

The minders' dislike of me was confirmed after we'd been moved down to the Pissouri Beach hotel on the coast. An army military policewoman had been assigned to us, and one of the minders spent most of his time in bed with her. When I came up to get something from my room one day I heard them talking, sitting up in bed, having obviously just had sex. The minder, who was as nice as pie to my face, was saying what a bastard I was and calling me all the names under the sun, which flipped me out completely.

I tried to kick the door down and was shouting, "Get your arse out here and I'll rip your fucking head off, you two-faced bastard!"

They didn't come out, and after a few minutes another minder came upstairs and calmed me down.

It was an impossible situation for everyone. The minders resented wasting their time looking after someone they saw as a common criminal, and I resented them for their attitude. I also felt they weren't up to their job, and were so busy drinking and screwing that I was a sitting duck for the IRA. I didn't have long to wait for proof.

As Christmas approached, Lorraine grew even more unhappy and whenever I was not around, she kept ringing her parents. There was no direct-dial system from the hotel and when they heard the operator say, "There's a call from a Lorraine Gilmour at the Pissouri Beach Hotel, Cyprus. Do you accept the charges?" they passed the information straight on to the IRA.

It wasn't entirely Lorraine's fault, for there was a policewoman with her at all times who should not have let her do it.

Christmas was a grim affair for all of us, far from home and far from happy. On Boxing Day, Lorraine took the kids to the beach while I went for a drink, with one of my minders, Mike, in attendance as usual. It was then that I spotted the hit-men at the end of the bar. The swarthy one and the pale one, PLO and IRA – whoever they were, it was obvious they were after me. In the adrenaline rush of our escape from the hotel I'd hardly had time to think about how Mike and the others had reacted to the danger, but as the convoy ground to a halt inside the wire of the army base at Dhekelia, I realised I'd spent the entire journey brooding about how our minders had let us down. True, they'd got us out swiftly enough once I'd alerted them to the danger, but if I hadn't spotted the hit team myself, me, Lorraine and the kids could easily have been lying dead by now. I was appalled that a known IRA man had been spotted entering the country and yet we hadn't been warned, and I was sick of the way the minders were treating our protection as little more than an excuse for a holiday.

When they led us to a scabby wooden chalet, I took one look and exploded, "You can fuck off, we're not staying here."

I shrugged off Mike's restraining arm and took off.

I heard Harry say, "Let him go. He'll only go and get pissed. We can pick him up from the bar later on," but I was heading in the other direction, away from the camp. The guard on the gates didn't try to stop me and I strode past him and away down the road towards Limassol. It was about forty miles away but I was so angry, I just kept striding out along the road.

As I walked, the passing taxis kept driving at me and trying to hit me, perhaps a sign of the affection they felt for the British forces. In the end one actually clipped my leg and sent me sprawling into a ditch. I decided the only way I was going to survive was to hire one, so I flagged the next one down and he took me into Limassol. It was a stupid thing to do, but I'd ceased to care. I got drunk and stayed in a small hotel overnight and was walking along the beach the next morning when Mike and Harry pulled up in their car and came sprinting over.

Where the fuck have you been, Ray? We've been searching for you all night."

I ignored the question, "When are we going back to England?"

"Tonight."

"Good."

I got in the car. They drove me back to the base at Dhekelia and that night we flew back to England. We carried on living under false identities, first in Pontefract and then in Newcastle. Meanwhile the IRA kept up the pressure. In mid-January a letter addressed to me, with an Antrim postmark, was delivered to the home of my sister in the Creggan. Inside was a badly-typed letter and two photographs showing my father holding up a recent edition of the *Irish Press* newspaper.

The letter read: "As you can see from the enclosed photos, your father is fine at present. You should know the IRA must protect itself. We are sure you are being told we would not act. It would be a mistake for you to accept that. The IRA give a public guarantee that you will not be harmed if you retract. The choice is yours."

My sister handed the photographs and the letter to the RUC, who passed them on to me. As the Provies intended, it would up the pressure on me another notch, though not all the pressure was coming from the IRA. On Mother's Day, Lorraine and I were allowed out unaccompanied for the first time since we'd gone into exile. The relief of being away from the minders, even if only for a few hours, was overwhelming. We laughed and chatted as we hadn't done for months, but the mood passed quickly. Lorraine phoned her mother before we went home, and when she came out of the call-box her face was once more set and withdrawn. We drove home in silence.

Lorraine kept phoning her parents every couple of days and even actually met them once, in a motorway café on the A1, with RUC minders screening the meeting and making sure that Lorraine wasn't followed afterwards. When she got back, she would say nothing and disappeared into the bedroom, locking the door behind her. She stayed moody and very withdrawn for the next few days, spending a long time sitting on her own, staring out of the window.

At the end of the week she phoned her parents again and then put me on the line to speak to them. I was puzzled until I discovered that my eldest brother, John, my Ma and Martin McGuinness were all at her parents' house, waiting for Lorraine's call. My Ma came on the phone first and told me to come back, then my brother snatched the phone from her and shouted down the line at me, "Get your fucking arse back here, you stupid wee bastard!"

I could hear all sorts of people shouting in the background as well, and Martin McGuinness ordering them to shut up. Then McGuinness himself came on the phone. "Look, Ray, don't be so silly. All these people you've put away are your friends. Come back and it will be okay, nothing will happen to you. No one wants to hurt you, we just want you back here."

I had a bit more savvy than to believe that. McGuinness later made the same promise to a man called Frank "Franko Hegarty, a Special Branch agent who had been an IRA quartermaster in Derry. When a huge arms shipment from Libya was landed, Hegarty told his handlers the locations of three massive dumps of weapons, ammunition and explosives, and was then lifted out.

He went to England under Special Branch guard but was persuaded to return to Derry by McGuinness's promise of immunity. Two weeks after he returned home, he was abducted, tortured and killed. McGuinness had sworn to Hegarty's mother that he'd secure his release and look after him. The next thing she heard was that her son's body had been found by Irish police near Castlederg in County Tyrone. His hands had been tied behind his back and black insulating tape wound around his eyes before he was shot in the back of the head.

I had no intention of ending up like him. McGuinness was a two-faced bastard and I'd never have trusted him. He kept rambling on and on, promising this, that and the other, until finally I just said, "Martin, I'm going now," and put the phone down.

Lorraine had already told her parents where we were. I don't know if she had told them the exact address, but they – and Martin McGuinness – certainly knew we were in Newcastle. It was the last straw. I told her, "You can't keep phoning up and telling your parents where we are. It's being passed straight on to the RA. You're going to get me killed, but you're putting all our lives in danger - not just mine, but your own, the kids and the guys next door.

"When the RA come, they'll be bringing a calling card. They'll come around here shooting and they won't much care who gets hit, as long as I'm among the dead. You have to make a decision now about what you want. It has to be me or your family, you can't have both. If you're going to stay with me, then you're going to have to stop ringing your parents. If not, you're going to have to go home."

"All right, then, I want to go home."

We parted near Newcastle airport a few days later, the Thursday before Easter. I kissed the kids, gave them their Easter eggs and said goodbye to Lorraine, as tears streamed down both our faces. Then she and the kids got in one car with a policewoman and one of the minders, while I and the other two minders drove away in another car. Looking back, I could see the pale faces of Lorraine and the kids, gazing out of the rear window until the car was swallowed up in the traffic.

I had to move out of Newcastle immediately, since Lorraine had given away our location, and for the next few weeks my minders and I just travelled all over the country, never staying more than one night in the same place. We still heard the news from Derry, however. The same day that Lorraine arrived home, the IRA released a video of my father looking frail and ill and pleading with me to recant to save his life. Soon afterwards, Lorraine was attacked and punched in the face by the wife of one of the men who was behind bars as a result of my evidence. I was drunk for the next week, just trying to blot it all out.

After my drunken binge, I began to think a bit more clearly about the situation. The IRA wouldn't allow Lorraine and the kids to be badly hurt, for they needed them alive to keep the pressure on me. The same applied to my parents. I knew in my heart that nothing would happen to my father. The kidnap and the video-tape were just ploys trying to break me and get me to come back, but I had a lot stronger resolve than that. I knew if I went back, I would be dead anyway, if not in the first year, then a bit down the line.

The IRA threat to my father was a bluff, and one in which he might even have been a willing participant. An expenses-paid holiday in Donegal, with a bit of beer money thrown in, would have been all right with him.

If the IRA killed him before I gave evidence, his value was gone, and no purpose would be served by killing him afterwards – it would only further alienate local people from them. I also knew that my mother, who hated the IRA as strongly as ever, would not endanger her husband's or her children's lives by open defiance of McGuinness and the IRA. She would play along with whatever they wanted, but in her heart I knew that she would understand and approve of what I had done.

As it turned out, my father was well looked-after while he was being held, but when the IRA eventually let him go, almost a year later, the relatives of the people who had been rounded up as a result of my evidence were furious. They thought that the IRA would have shot him as punishment for fathering a traitor, or as a warning to other agents. With Sinn Féin's protection of my family lifted, some of them went on the rampage, stoning not only my father's house, but my brothers' and sisters' houses as well.

My father was driven back to Derry by a Dublin priest, Piaras O'Duill, who'd picked him up from an undisclosed location somewhere in the Republic. They arrived at my sister's home at ten at night, and by eleven a mob of fifty or sixty people had gathered outside, jeering and shouting abuse. By one in the morning the mob, now swollen to eighty, began smashing the windows at the front and back of the flat. Half a dozen men kicked in the doors and burst in to confront my father in the living-room. He was badly shaken but unhurt. Eventually the men were persuaded to leave, but the mob stayed outside the house, still screaming abuse, until four-thirty in the morning. Early the next day my father and mother left Derry to stay with my brother Paddy in Liverpool, until it was safe to return.

The IRA kept the pressure up, but I was unmoved. I did return to Northern Ireland, three months after Lorraine had left me, but my journey was to give evidence at the committal hearings. While I was there, Lorraine began divorce proceedings against me.

CHAPTER 16

"All right, Ray, it's time."

Two hulking Special Branch men fell in on either side of me as we began the long walk. We went down a steep flight of stone stairs, ending at the mouth of a dank tunnel that I remembered well. As I peered into the darkness, the glow from the rusting bulkhead lights faintly lit the door of the holding cell in which I'd spent my first night as a prisoner in the Crum. Nothing had changed; the walls of the tunnel were still slimy and wet and the air foul-smelling, but this time I needed no shove in the back from a warder. I strode straight ahead through the dark tunnel, my eyes fixed on the pool of light at the far end.

At the end of the tunnel, another staircase, an iron spiral, led upwards. We paused at the top, on the landing outside a heavy oak door.

"When we get the signal, Ray, we go straight through, down the steps and into the witness box, which is right in front of you. Don't look at the spectators, look straight ahead. We'll be directly in front of you all the time, there's no danger to you whatsoever, but if there is a hint of noise or disturbance, whatever it is, get straight to your feet and head for the door. They're bound to have planned some sort of demonstration to intimidate you, but ignore it. Don't react in any way, just head for the tunnel. We'll be flanking you all the way."

We stood in a row, facing the door separating us from the court, I could hear the magistrate saying: "If there is any disruption by any defendant, relative or member of the public, any person guilty of such disruption or harassment will be excluded from the court for the duration of the trial."

There was a silence and then a brief tap on the door.

"Here we go."

I followed them into the court and was down the few steps and into the witness box in seconds, blinking in the strong sunlight streaming through the windows.

The witness box was in the well of the court, to the right of the magistrate's bench, with tiers of seating rising steeply above it on all sides. The two Special Branch men took up station in front of the box, their backs to me, facing the court. At the benches around me were rows of black-gowned lawyers, frowning in concentration as they studied the bundles of papers stacked in front of them.

There were no jurors and the box for the jury as instead filled with Special Branch men, including Pete, though I gave no sign of recognising him. In the raised dock specially extended for the occasion, were thirty-five defendants, mostly men, with a handful of women, each one standing there because of my evidence. Flanking the dock was a wall of blue-uniformed prison warders staring implacably into the faces of their charges.

Of the one hundred or so people originally arrested, a dozen had jumped bail and another fifty had been released or bailed pending possible prosecution on less serious charges such as membership of a prescribed organisation – the IRA. The ones in the dock today were the most dangerous IRA men in Derry, always excepting the most dangerous of them all, the Sinn Féin and IRA leader Martin McGuinness. He was in court, but not in the dock, for there was only hearsay evidence to link him to the crimes with which the defendants were charged.

Behind and above the dock was the public gallery, packed in equal numbers by relatives and sympathisers of the accused and by green-uniformed RUC men, constantly scanning the benches. They occupied the entire front row and a couple were seated at either end of each of the other rows as well. I glanced up briefly to the gallery. Facing me across the court was my mother. At her side sat McGuinness. It wasn't company my mother would willingly have chosen.

When I was a boy, my mother had been a friend of the mother of an IRA man, Eamon Donegan, who lived next door to the Telstar Bar. McGuinness had often asked Eamon's advice on IRA matters, and whenever he was in the house I'd feel very uneasy. His watery blue eyes seemed to linger on me, and he had a creepy air about him. He was impossible to read, for his face remained absolutely impassive whether he was excited, amused or angry.

We were visiting one afternoon when McGuinness and Donegan were having a heated and interminable argument about the right tactics for keeping the army out of Free Derry – the barricaded Creggan and Bogside. I was cowed into silence for a long time by the anger and intensity of the two men, but finally, thoroughly bored, I began pulling at my mother's sleeve. "Ma, Ma."

McGuinness stopped in mid-flow and turned his baleful stare in my direction. The voice was all the more frightening for being low and expressionless. "Keep the kid quiet or get out," he said.

I shrank behind my mother, frightened but full of fierce hatred for him, a feeling which was never to change. My mother shared my feelings about him, disliking McGuinness himself almost as much as she hated the IRA. Now she was sitting alongside him in court. It was the first time I'd set eyes on her in twelve months, and was to be the last time I would ever see her. My father wasn't with her. He was still being held hostage by the IRA, under threat of death if I didn't retract my evidence. My mother stiffened as she caught my glance, but I looked away again immediately and locked my gaze on to the paneled front of the magistrates' bench, while the Crown Prosecutor laid down the outlines of the case.

At twenty-five past eleven he was ready to start leading me through my evidence. I began a familiar litany: my recruitment into the IRA, my fellow-members, the weapons, the jobs – the bombings and shootings. A defence solicitor quickly interrupted, complaining that he couldn't hear what I was saying and couldn't see my face. I smiled grimly to myself. Sinn Féin obviously didn't want my view of their demonstration to be blocked by Special Branch men. As my two minders moved slightly to one side, opening up the view of the rest of the court-room, I braced myself for whatever McGuinness had arranged.

As I resumed my evidence, the only sound other than my voice was the clack of the stenographer's keys. Then there was a movement on the public benches. My mother had risen from her seat and was picking her way past the RUC men towards the exit door. As she reached it, directly behind me, I heard her voice "Raymond, Raymond, don't you know your mother's here. I can't listen any more to you saying those things about your friends … Your father … God forgive you."

It broke my heart to hear her voice and not even to look at her, but I'd always known what the end result of the path I'd travelled would be. Once begun, it could end only in the loss of my friends, my family and even my wife and children … or in my own death.

I'd felt terribly homesick during the past year in exile and had called my family a few times while I was roaming about the country, but in the end I had to stop. I was doing people I cared about no favours; all I did was bring them heartache and grief. On the day the trial ended, I would cut myself off from the whole of my past – Raymond Gilmour would cease to exist.

Even while my mother was speaking, the Special Branch men were already hustling me to my feet, up the steps and out through the door. It banged shut behind us and we paused, listening to what followed. There was a brief, pregnant silence. I heard the magistrate barring my mother from the proceedings.

Then one of my sisters was on her feet. "Your Honour, can my mother not speak to Raymond? She hasn't seen him for a year. Your Honour, can my mother not speak to Raymond?"

There was a scuffling sound and a yelp of protest from her as the RUC men seized her and shoved her out of the court, but another sister was already on her feet, taking up the refrain, and then a third one. Each one was hustled out of the court, struggling and shouting.

As the noise of their struggles began to fade, I heard my brother, Johnny, shout, "Take your hands off them."

There was another brief silence and then he launched himself at the RUC men with a roar of defiance. There was sound of another more prolonged scuffle, and then he too was led away. There were a few isolated shouts of protest from the dock and the gallery and then silence once more.

Eventually there was a tap on the door and I was led back into court to resume my evidence. I caught a glimpse of Martin McGuinness, now sitting alone in a sea of green uniforms. His face was white with anger as his pale, almost colourless blue eyes drilled into me. It would have been no part of McGuinness's plan to have all my family barred from court. He wanted them in there among all the other relatives, keeping the pressure on me, a sea of reproachful faces staring at me every time I raised my gaze.

When the proceedings resumed, McGuinness himself was soon on his feet, demanding to be allowed to sit in the front row of the public gallery, which was filled by a wall of police. "As Sinn Féin Assemblyman for Derry, I am an elected representative of the people."

"That may entitle you to a seat, but not necessarily a front-row seat, Mr McGuinness," said the magistrate mildly. "There's plenty of room at the back of the public gallery."

McGuinness seemed on the verge of another protest, but then fell silent and sat down again, resigned to pouring out his hatred from a few rows back.

At the end of my evidence I had to stand and identify the people I had named – a moment of drama for which McGuinness would no doubt have preferred my family to wait.

"Please stand and face the dock."

My minders stepped aside and I turned to meet the gaze of my former IRA colleagues for the first time. Thirty-five defendants stared back at me. All were pale, with lank, unwashed hair. They wore T-shirts or worn pullovers, faded jeans and scuffed shoes. I felt acutely conscious of my sun-tan, well-cut hair and sharp new suit, all provided, like my new identity, courtesy of the RUC.

As the prosecutor read out each name in turn, I pointed to the person in the dock. Some I knew almost as well as me own family, others I'd met only once or twice on joint operations with other units.

"Jimmy Costello."

"That man on the left with the yellow T-shirt."

"Mary Cobbe."

"That blonde girl sitting there in the second row, between the two policewomen."

"Brendan "Shorty" McNally."

The wee man, seated in the second row, was almost invisible behind a taller defendant. I glanced up and down the box twice before I spotted him. There was a brief flicker of a smile among some of the defendants, for Shorty's size had always been a standing joke, before the faces resumed their silent outpouring of hatred.

"Brendan McDermott."

I began raking the dock with my eyes from left to right. As I did, I saw McDermott rise from his seat at the right-hand end and stab his finger out at me. We stood there for a long moment, pointing accusingly at each other, and then I said, "That is Brendan McDermott."

I'd identified the first few people in an eerie silence, but now the defendants began to make themselves heard.

"Ruari Spears."

I scanned the line of defendants slowly.

"Is it me your looking for, Gilmour?" said a voice from the end of the dock.

I turned to look at him. "Yes, that's you."

"Frank O'Neill."

He was up on his feet, shouting at me, before I could point to him.

"You're a dirty traitor, Gilmour, selling out your family and your country. You're a gutless, spineless animal."

The judge pounded his gavel and demanded silence, but O'Neill rounded on him and yelled, "Shut yer gob." He was hustled below by the prison warders.

Soon everybody was getting in on the act.

"Niall "Tapper" McFadden."

I pointed him out, provoking Tapper to cry, "Have you no courage left in you? What about your wife and wee 'uns in Derry."

"Joseph Cranney."

As I pointed to him, Cranney yelled, "You've never seen me in your life, you lying bastard!"

"Catch yourself on!" another of them shouted.

The dock was emptying fast and the warders dragged away anyone who shouted, which did at least make the job of identifying the remaining ones easier.

"Niall Blakely."

I identified him, provoking another shout. "You're a liar, you've never seen me before in your life!"

"Con "Dixie" Bingham."

"There's no one lower than you, Gilmour, you cunt!" screamed Dixie. "They'll shoot your Da!"

The warders seized him and took him down as well.

"Liam Taplin."

Before I could identify him, Taplin was also on his feet.

"Gilmour, you yellow bastard. I hope your Da gets stiffed."

He was already turning to go down to the cells before the warders were on him to drag him away. They pushed him out and the door clanged shut behind him. It was the last outburst. The remaining defendants stayed silent as I identified the last few and the court then rose for lunch.

Outside in the street, my mother, brother and sisters, flanked by their grim-faced Sinn Féin minders, held an impromptu press conference. One of the Special Branch guys later told me what had gone on. The plan rehearsed with Martin McGuinness had been that she would wait until I stood up to start identifying the defendants. She should then have stood up herself and said, "Raymond, can you identify me?"

My mother had not kept to the script, however, and was busy apologising to Mr McGuinness for her failure. "I'm sorry, I just couldn't bear it any longer."

My mother knew the realities well enough. Whatever her feelings, she had to play the Sinn Féin game, even though the men standing alongside her were party to the decision to kidnap my father, at the very least. If he died, his blood would be on their hands.

Yet I was sure that my family wouldn't be harmed. Sinn Féin would look after them, not from altruism but from self-interest – keep the pressure on Raymond; if he recants, the boys walk free. Even after the trial was over, my family would be more use to the IRA alive than dead. While they lived, there was always the chance that I would be drawn into a careless disclosure or a clandestine meeting that would give the IRA its chance for revenge.

Sinn Féin protection over the previous few months had saved my mother and family from revenge attacks by the relatives of those I had named, though it didn't prevent Lorraine from being punched in the face by the wife of a prisoner as she sat in a Derry café. McGuinness paid the woman a visit to explain why she shouldn't do it again.

If Lorraine had any doubts about the reason she'd been attacked, the graffiti on a Creggan wall would have answered her: "I knew Raymond Gilmour. Thank fuck he didn't know me."

A further year was to elapse before the cases based on my evidence actually came to trial, during the time I remained in hiding in England with my minders. It was the era of the Diplock courts, where a judge, but no jury, presided over terrorist trials, ostensibly because jurors were so vulnerable to intimidation by the IRA, though many on the Republican side felt that the Diplock courts were really a way of ensuring convictions rather than justice.

When the trial began at the Crumlin Road Courthouse, the number of defendants had swelled to thirty-nine – thirty-six men and three women – after four guys who had skipped bail were recaptured. Bench warrants were issued for another five who were still on the run. Even without them the dock had to be specially extended to make room for all the defendants, taking over seats normally used by the public.

A special bus had been laid on to bring their relatives over from Derry, but unsurprisingly none of my family were to be seen. Most of them had left Derry to stay with Paddy in Liverpool until the trial was over, when they hoped the resentment of them in Derry would begin to fade and the persecution cease.

It took two court clerks working in relays two hours and fourteen minutes just to read out the full list of charges. The defendant showed their contempt for the proceedings in various ways. One was actually smoking a smuggled cigarette in the dock as the judge, Lord Justice McDermott, made his entrance. Two warders descended on the dock and the cigarette was forcibly removed.

Several defendants refused to plead and had formal not-guilty pleas entered on their behalf, and six of them would not identify themselves and had to be pointed out to the judge by their prison warders. When asked how he pleaded to the charges against him, Pat McHugh shouted a defiant – and evidently carefully rehearsed – speech: "I do not believe I will receive any justice in this show trial because I have already been found guilty, so it is irrelevant how I plead."

"Enter a plea of not guilty," the judge ordered impassively. The sitting lasted three and a half hours and the judge then adjourned proceedings for a fortnight. When the trial re-started, it lasted just three days before Lord Justice McDermott disqualified himself for allowing the Crown Prosecutor, John Creaney, to make statements which "could not be sustained by admissible evidence."

Before the trial, Creaney had asked me, "Did you ever, at any time, feel you were going to be prosecuted for the things in which you were involved?"

I answered truthfully, "No, not at any time did I ever think that I would or could be prosecuted for anything I did with the IRA. I asked Pete about it more than once in the early stages and told him, "If you can't protect me, then I won't do this. I don't want to be looked at as an informer or grass, I want to be looked at as a policeman."

"He told me: "You are, Ray, you have a police number at headquarters. Only two or three people know you as Ray Gilmour, the rest know that number. There's no way that you'll be thought of as an informer or a grass. I don't think of you that way." If that hadn't been the case, I would have packed it in."

Creaney nodded, satisfied. When it came to the trial, he made an opening statement saying that he would be using testimony from an agent who had worked for the RUC for several years. "Gilmour's information to the police was reliable and accurate and his evidence will have similar qualities. Once M'Lud hears all the evidence put forward, there will be no doubt in his mind of the guilt of the defendants."

When Creaney finished his opening statement, the defence counsel were immediately on their feet, saying that McDermott had accepted a prosecution statement assuming the guilt of the defendants before he'd even heard the arguments, and he should therefore disqualify himself.

After retiring for the day to think about it, McDermott duly agreed with them. "In the course of h is remarks, Mr Creaney gave a view of the quality of the evidence to be given by Gilmour which could not be sustained by admissible evidence. The primary issue was the credit-worthiness of Gilmour, and if the case had been heard by a jury I would have dismissed that jury and re-commenced with a fresh one.

"A judge sitting alone knows that cases are decided by admissible evidence and nothing else. Judges in the exercise of their discretion have continued hearings confident that the accused would receive a fair trial, and there are strong arguments for me continuing with this case. But on balance, it seems to me that it could appear that an introduction of the assessment of the quality of Gilmour's information might in some way affect my assessment of the quality of his evidence, and I should accede to the application."

It seemed incredible to me, for the whole point of an opening statement was surely to set out what the prosecution intended to prove, and if they didn't believe that they had a witness capable of proving the allegations, they would have been pretty stupid to have brought the cases in the first place.

I personally feel that McDermott did not want anything to do with the case – show trials of the IRA were not good for the health of judges any more than witnesses – and had found a simple way to remove himself from the IRA's firing-line. After a further lengthy delay, the buck stopped with the Lord Chief Justice, Lord Lowry, who decided to take the case himself, even though he'd already been the target of an unsuccessful IRA assassination attempt two years before. Four gunmen had fired at him outside Queen's University, Belfast but he'd escaped unharmed.

I was brought back to Belfast for six weeks while I was giving evidence. All the time I was there I was stuck in the Hilden Road Barracks, except for one very strange evening when I was taken on a strictly unauthorised night out. I was pulling my hair out with boredom and was so pissed off hanging around the barracks that Mike, one of my regular minders, said he'd take me out of there just to give me a change.

Mike turned up with two guys that I knew slightly. I'd seen one of them only once before, when I'd watched him on the television at a Sinn Féin march a few years previously. I watched him warily as we got in the car and drove off. They told me we were going to a bar and discotheque outside Belfast.

They dropped me off at the Groomsport Hotel and told me they'd be back for me later. I was both surprised and alarmed by this stage, but Make waved away my protests and drove off down the road.

As I walked into the bar, I could hear Irish folk music playing. I knew I was in trouble straight away, because Protestant bars don't play that sort of music. I was even more alarmed when I saw the other people in the bar. In the old days back in Derry I'd knocked around with a band called the Diamond Showband, and had even worked as a roadie for them. The members of the band were all in the bar. They spotted me instantly and gave me some very heavy looks and stares.

By now I was convinced I'd been set up by my minders. I kept telling myself, "Mike wouldn't set you up. He wouldn't do that," but I was really worried and don't know what would have happened next had the guy acting as minder to the Crown Prosecutor, John Creaney, not happened to be in the bar as well. He was one of the two guys who stood in front of the witness box while I was testifying and so recognised me instantly and came straight over.

"Christ, Ray, where are your minders? You're not supposed to leave the barracks – what the fuck are you doing here?"

I told him what had happened and he drove me back to the barracks himself. I was so obsessed with the trial at the time that I pushed the incident out of my mind almost as soon as I got back. I mentioned it to Ronnie, the overall boss of the minders, but he was the sort of guy who would just shove it under the carpet, not wanting to make waves about anything. It was only afterwards, back in England, that I sat down and began to wonder just what had really been going on that night.

Mike and I had been the best of friends in the beginning, but towards the end I was increasingly wary of him. I felt he could easily have been manipulated by outsiders. The other minders generally appeared to be more security-conscious, but it seemed to me that if someone got to Mike, I'd be dead.

There were no more excursions out of the barracks before the trial began. It lasted five months – one of the biggest and most expensive cases in British and Irish legal history, involving thirty-five defendants, guarded by a hundred warders and armed policemen, eight QC's, sixteen barristers and 200,000 pages of legal documents. The charges included murder, attempted murder, conspiracy to murder, wounding, hijacking, possession of explosives, guns and ammunition.

After giving my evidence I had to face cross-examination from the defence lawyers, led by Desmond Boal QC. I was not looking forward to the experience one bit, for Pete had warned me that they would throw every piece of mud they could think of in the hope that some of it would stick.

Word had gone out long before that the defence solicitors needed every scrap of rumour, innuendo or gossip to start the character assassination. Eamon Doyle, one of the IRA's Internal Affairs men, who had turned supergrass after being named by me, had been cross-examined in court a few weeks before. I knew from his treatment what I could expect.

Doyle had been reminded that he was in the remedial class at school, accused of beating his wife and taunted in open court that he was not the father of one of his two children. The names of three women he was alleged to have affairs with after his marriage were also thrown at him. The *Irish News* actually printed the names of the women, one of them also married.

Mr Boal unsurprisingly brought up my criminal record, both with the IRA and my conviction for the Post Office robbery with Noel Kavanagh. Among his wilder allegations were claims that I'd deliberately set up Colm McNutt to be killed and that I'd been involved in homosexual acts in the toilet of a city-centre bar when I was seventeen, and had spent the night with a well-known homosexual.

I had no doubt that the judge, Lord Lowry, would be impartial and might even lean towards the prosecution. After the IRA attempt to assassinate him, he could have been expected to be no friend to the Provies. Yet on 18 December 1984, he quashed the case and allowed all the accused to go free, save the nine who were already serving sentences for other offences.

It was the end of the Diplock courts. All the RUC officers were devastated that the evidence had been ignored and all our work had been for nothing. In the eighteen months the defendants had been in gaol, the Derry Brigade had effectively ceased to exist as an operational force. Now the IRA killers were back on the streets.

I was back in England by then and heard that the trial had been stopped on the news. I turned on the television, saw all the people streaming out of the gates of the court and then heard the reporter quote the judge's description of me as being "entirely unworthy of belief".

Lord Lowry felt I was "a selfish and self-regarding man to whose lips a lie invariably comes more naturally than the truth." I had also "unwittingly given a grim and frightening picture of the way that [I] was prepared to give evidence intended to put all these defendants in prison".

According to Lord Lowry, I'd been living a lie for most of my life and therefore couldn't be relied on to know the difference between truth and fiction. He was partly right. Of course I was a liar – on the streets I had to lie to survive. If I hadn't, I would long ago have been lying in a ditch with a bin-bag over my face and a few bullet-holes in the back of my head. But I told the truth in court; that was the whole point of all the years I worked as an agent for the RUC.

I didn't have any trouble under cross-examination. Much was made of the fact that in my answer to the very first question I got my date of birth wrong. One the face of it, that makes me pretty unreliable about anything, but while I'd been on the road I'd had to memorise a complete set of new personal details – including a new date of birth – for the identity I'd assumed. Nervous at the start of what I knew was going to be a grueling session in the witness box, I'd simply confused the two dates.

Lord Lowry also pointed out that my testimony was uncorroborated by anyone, yet he had seen for himself the parade of frightened people, subpoenaed to appear as witnesses, who one after another refused to testify. Each refusal was applauded vigorously by the defendants and their relatives.

The reason for the witnesses' reluctance to testify wasn't hard to pinpoint. As one woman said, "My family is more important to me. I don't want to give evidence."

Four more refused to testify on the same day alone, citing "personal reasons". When Lord Lowry asked one of them to elaborate, he replied, "I live in the area and I have a business there."

I found it hard to work out how Lord Lowry was able to form his opinion that I was an unreliable witness. I'm not used to judges but from where I was sitting I'd swear on my days of the trial he'd close his eyes for a bit after the first hour or so of the proceedings. I sat there in disbelief, wondering why no one made any attempt to wake him. The proceedings just carried on; I suppose they knew he was taking it all in.

My handlers told me that if he asked me if I was feeling unwell, it meant that he wanted to stop for the day. He asked me that a few times, but each time I just said, "Yes, thank you, Your Honour, I'm fine," because I wanted to get the trial over with as quickly as possible.

In the end all of the accused in the supergrass trials were released, but I suspect there was a deeper, darker root to that than the supposed unreliability of evidence from informants. My own feeling is that a deal was done between someone, somewhere, either between the British and Irish governments, or between the British government and the IRA itself.

The British have been talking to the IRA for years – long before the recently – admitted negotiations began. In an interview in 1995, Martin McGuinness told the *Independent* of a meeting as far back as 1972. "I was on the run at the time. Six of us were taken in a blacked-out van from a back road in Derry to a field in which a helicopter landed. We were put in the helicopter and brought to the military end of Aldergrove airport in Belfast. We were then brought on by RAF plane to a military airfield in England, where we were met by a fleet of limousines. We were escorted by the Special Branch through London." That meeting, in Guinness heir Paul Channon's palatial house in Cheyne Walk, ended in deadlock, but contacts between the British government and the IRA were kept up over the years.

It wouldn't surprise me to discover that the ending of the trial in which I was involved was part of another attempt by the British government to win concessions from the IRA. Perhaps it was no coincidence that the Brighton bombing, in which Margaret Thatcher and her Cabinet narrowly escaped with their lives, occurred only two months before Lord Lowry suddenly abandoned the trial.

What happened, happened. If the court chose not to believe that, there was nothing else I could do. The IRA men were back on the streets, free if that was their bent to resume shooting, bombing and killing, but I was now out of the ring and someone else would have to try and bring them to justice. The system had found them innocent of the charges and that's what the record says. The system says "innocent until proved guilty", and the prosecution had failed to find them guilty.

The IRA were not slow to demonstrate that whatever the court verdict, business as usual would continue. Within hours of the acquittal, walls all over the Creggan and Bogside were emblazoned with a straightforward message: "Gilmour will be shot."

They would have to find me first. I was already back in England, and the final episode in my career as an agent came when a senior RUC officer flew over soon after the end of the trial and told me what my pay-off would be. He then went back to Belfast, taking my minders with him. For the first time in two years since I'd been lifted out of Derry, I was now completely on my own.

CHAPTER 17

In this chapter, I will look at, and name some of today's leading Sinn Fein politicians, as well as some hangers-on, and discuss their roles as terrorists and question how and why they became the leading lights on today's political stage both in Northern Ireland and also on the world stage. In particular, I want to question how a man like Martin McGuinness, the former 'Butcher of the Creggan' can possibly be allowed to shake the Queen's hand. On the occasion that he did so, with the same hands that are still red with the blood of Ranger William Best and Joanna Mathers, I hope that she went to an anteroom and washed off the filth that he left on her gloves.

Before I continue, can I refresh the reader's memory with a reminder of two of the foulest murders ever perpetrated by the Republican Movement? On or around May 21, 1972, one of the most controversial killings of the troubles occurred in Derry. Ranger William Best of the Royal Irish Rangers was abducted and murdered by the Official IRA after one of their customary 'kangaroo courts.'

William Best was based with his battalion in Germany and wished to return to his home in the Creggan Estate. His worried parents had contacted the commander of the IRA in the Creggan – Martin McGuinness – and the 'Butcher' gave his permission to his reassured parents that he could return home safely. I understand that the 'usual' caveats were stressed, that he came home in civilian clothes rather than his uniform and that he didn't associate with any other soldiers. He went out drinking with mates and later began walking towards his home in Rathkeele Way. Enroute, he was picked up by armed 'Stickies' (Official IRA) and taken to a safe house near William Street.

He was interrogated and beaten and then tried - with 'full formal IRA judicial ceremony' - by a 'kangaroo court' - but then a decision was made that he would be released. I think that they saw no purpose in killing him. I know that McGuinness was present and he wanted Best dead, but having given Mr & Mrs Best guarantees about their son's safety, he could not be seen, publically at least, to be going back on his word. He spoke to the OIRA 'court' and bullied and cajoled them and eventually shamed them into killing the frightened young soldier. Best was taken to waste ground in William Street and executed in the traditional IRA manner, by having two shots fired from close range into the back of the neck; he was found by a passing nurse, returning from night duty, who tried to help him. The following day, an OIRA spokesman stated: *'Once we had him, there was nothing we could do but execute him.'* There was an outcry in the area and over 400 women in the city attacked the offices of Official Sinn Fein Derry, to protest the murder of the young soldier. It finished the OIRA in the city and moved the Provisionals into the status of 'preferred' guardians of the Nationalist community, which was precisely McGuinness's intention. He didn't pull the trigger, but he engineered the murder, so he might as well have actually done the deed himself.

Let us move forward then to April 7, 1981; on that day, Mrs Joanna Mathers (29), mother of a wee boy called Shane was collecting Census forms on the Gobnascale estate in Derry. She was trying to earn a bit of spending money by collecting the forms and was waiting at a house in Anderson Crescent when a gunman ran up to her and snatched her clipboard and Census forms and then shot her in the neck at point blank range. She died almost immediately. McGuinness and the Provisionals have always denied responsibility, but I am personally aware that the gun – a stolen RUC .357 Magnum - used to kill Mrs Mathers had been previously used by them in punishment shootings, and was part of their armoury and stored by a local quartermaster. The weapon was delivered to the Waterside by Dermott Braney to a local Volunteer called Fergal Grimley. He was the Explosives Officer in the unit which operated in the mainly Protestant Waterside area and he was a ruthless bastard; I am convinced that he killed Mrs Mathers. After the shooting, Braney collected the weapon and took it back to the Creggan armoury. The order to murder a low-profile and soft – even by PIRA's cowardly standards – target can only have been given by somebody senior; that man was McGuinness himself. No one, not even some of the hotheads and pyschos from the Creggan, even those who loved killing would have not dared kill the woman without first clearing it with the top man himself! Someone in the Derry IRA knew who carried out the cowardly and despicable murder of a helpless young woman.

Afterwards, they tried to put around the story that the killing was a mistake, but I know that they were sending a message to other Census-collectors, that they would not tolerate what they saw as 'agents of the Crown' coming into their areas on Government business. Shorty McNally's words still ring in my ears "so what? She's dead now, isn't she? Bleating about it is just wasting breath".

Deputy First Minister McGuinness was challenged to help with a new investigation last year, but like that other 'Teflon man' Gerry Adams, he denied all knowledge. UUP Politician Tom Elliott is quoted as saying: *'It is long past time he came clean about what he knows about the crimes committed by the IRA in Londonderry whilst he was in command.'* As far as I'm concerned McGuinness was responsible for the woman's death, and that everything in Derry went through him; he gave the order for the death of this innocent census-taker. Now, I never heard him give the actual order – he was too clever for that – but his go-between was Shorty McNally and McGuinness was the top man in the IRA's Northern Command. Who else could have made a decision like that but the Butcher himself? I was told that McNally, acting on instructions from McGuinness gave the orders to beat up and generally harass the census-takers, but the order to kill one of them came right from the very top. McNally – also known as the 'wee man' - told me that the order came from McGuinness himself, who was, as I stated, in Operational Command. In fact, I almost died with laughter when I read that McGuinness told the Saville Inquiry that he was Sinn Fein and not IRA! I understand that an Army photographer in the Rossville Flats area actually took a photo of McGuinness carrying and aiming an sub-machine gun, standing on a wall on the morning of 'Bloody Sunday.' I didn't see him on the morning, but I remember him and other Provies coming into the Telstar Bar, actually carrying weapons, including sub-machine guns on many occasions. Out the back of the pub in Dunore Gardens and Fanad Drive is where the IRA used to take people for punishment beatings or knee-capping. I wish to state here and now, that I was never personally involved in punishment shootings or beatings. I was on a job once which involved keeping an old man and his son hostage, whilst the local unit carried out an operation. It was above a fish shop close to the Cathedral and whilst there, a member of my unit stole money out of the till which came to light at a later hearing, attended by Shorty McNally and he was sentenced to be knee-capped. Two local volunteers, Eddie McSheffrey – my unit commander at the time - and Paddy Deery – who were both killed when a bomb they were transporting through the Creggan on October 28, 1987 exploded –volunteered to shoot him. Of all the weapons they could be given they were handed a .357 Magnum. Now that could blow a big hole in anything so can you imagine what it would do to a leg; it would blow it straight off. Anyway, they shot him in the muscle instead and although he was left in agony he lived.

I encountered the Derry Brigade's 'nutting squad' a number of times and I came across Dermott Braney and Arthur Patterson who were leading lights in that feared and loathed section of the IRA. I was starting to come to their attention, because a lot of the jobs which either had my name on them or where I was scheduled to participate were going wrong; mainly, of course, because I was leaking information to my Special Branch handler.
Examples would be that a foot patrol which was to be shot up in a certain location would either not show, or approach from a different direction or an off-duty UDR soldier would suddenly be moved to another location along with his family. I had moved up the hierarchy a little bit and certain events in which I was involved had brought me to the positive attention of the Brigade.

Anyway, we got the weapons to the dump and it was a very well hidden dump, but very quickly compromised because I told my handler where it was. The Derry Internal Security Unit or 'nutting squad' were called in and they knew that only a finite number of people were aware of its existence, including McQuillan, Cobbe, McSheffrey and myself and the owner of the house where the dump was. They knew that the householder would be too shit-scared to inform, so that narrowed it down a bit. I think that the incident which finished me was when our unit 'borrowed' the awesome M60 from the Belfast Brigade and it was to be used in a shoot in our area. This was the weapon which was used to kill the SAS Captain on the Antrim Road, Belfast in 1980. I let my handlers know and a break-in was contrived and the RUC came. Naturally the weapon was found and questions were raised immediately. I was called in for a meeting with Shorty and at the time, I had just bought a new car with my Special Branch payments. When I arrived in my car at his house, he looked out of the window and the first question was 'how did you pay for that?' I explained that I was buying it on the 'never, never' and that I got it from a friend who sold cars. He said to me: '*How much did you get for the M60?*' I can tell you that I nearly shit myself, because I could tell that he was only half joking. The earth could have opened up and just swallowed me and I wouldn't have minded. Just at that moment one of the 'nutting squad' – Dermott Braney – walked into the room and I'm thinking 'Ah, Jesus, I'm going to get nutted!' How I walked away from that one, I'll never know. The rest, as they say, is history.

During what the Provies called the 'armed struggle,' many of their volunteers fled across the border, because they knew that the Gardaí would always turn a blind eye. They knew that it was safe over in the Republic as they could live it up, knowing that the Brits couldn't get them, although they were shit-scared of the SAS sneaking over the border and stiffing them as they slept. They more or less took over the town of Dundalk and although they were meant to lie low until they could be sent back into the North to continue the struggle, many of them drank themselves silly and whored it with the local Colleens who would drop their knickers for these glamorous 'freedom fighters.' These men were known as OTRs – on the run – and many would eventually go back into the North where they might be killed, be captured or just go on shooting and bombing. In recent weeks, prior to the publication of this book, the press has been full of leaked stories about these OTRs receiving letters of amnesty and even the most hardened killers have been given a 'get out of jail free' card. The British Government in my opinion has betrayed the troops and the police and the innocent civilians murdered by bullet and bomb over nearly 40 years of the troubles. How the devil can the Brits just look the other way, when they know that these men have caused so much misery, made so many orphans and so many widows? I blame Blair for being the first to turn a blind eye, but now Cameron is doing the same thing; not fit to govern, any of them. I tell you this: the Brits are so shit-scared of the troubles being reborn and all the economic damage that would result in, that they will do anything – and I mean anything – to prevent this, even to the extent of kissing Republican ass!

How can these men get away with murder and live into old age, which is something that they denied to all the people that they slaughtered? I know that I did some crimes and I know also that the IRA who sentenced me to death will go on looking for me until they finally catch me or I curl up my toes and die naturally. The thing I mean is that I know that I have a life sentence, and must keep looking over my shoulder, or sleep with one eye open, or stare at every stranger in the room as I did back those many years at a bar in Cyprus.

I was given an extract of a book by a soldier-author and he claimed that many of the IRA/INLA were able to use the Troubles as an outlet for their psychopathic tendencies. He claimed that they would have been paedophiles, rapists or cut-throats had the Troubles not happened. Sure that's right enough, even though neither of us are psychiatrists. I met some rum blokes when I was in the Derry Provies. Some of them were quiet lads when they came into the movement but once they had been green-booked and given a handgun, they were keen to get out and kill. I saw those same lads after a kill and there was a definite sexual excitement about taking a life. Many of them wanted to get up close before they pulled the trigger and see that look of terror in their victim's eyes as they knew their life was over. I wonder how many of them thought of their wives, their kids, even where they were going for a drink that night, in the split second before the flash of light then blackness? I have spoken to shooters after a kill, and they were bubbling and shaking with excitement. I don't know, but maybe that author was right. There was never a shortage of volunteers to go to some policeman's house and shoot him down in front of his wife and children. I wonder if McGuinness gave a thought to the scene in the dead man's home as the RUC told a wife that her husband would not be home, or the kids that their daddy wouldn't be taking them to the seaside again or out for sweets or walking in the park with them anymore?

Me? Well my conscience is a lot clearer than most of them, because I know that the information I got to 'Pete' who was my Special Branch handler, saved lives. I remember them stiffing a young soldier called Shenton in January, 1981 whilst he was closing the security gates at Castle Gate in Derry. The Provies had tried to set up a kill multiple times over the previous 8 or 9 months, but I got the intelligence to 'Pete' and saved several lives, because at the last minute, the regular closing of the gates would not go ahead. I knew about the intended hit and Shorty McNally passed on the orders to us that they were setting up the kill from a house in Waterloo Street, I told my handlers but they did fuck-all about it and the result was a grieving mother in Stoke-on-Trent. It was around that time that I felt that I was under a bit of suspicion especially from an old IRA man called Paddy McQuirk. What I can say is that all orders at this stage of troubles, for hits and bombings were issued by Martin McGuinness. He was responsible for all operations.

There were at the time rumours, and even today, these rumours still persist that McGuinness was in the pay of the RUC Special Branch and/or British Intelligence. I know that in the late 70s, early 80s, he was in meetings with the Secretary of State for Northern Ireland and there didn't seem any difficulty with the NIO talking to him. I did, I must confess, have my suspicions about him, but given that I was working for Special Branch, I had to be very careful in case he found out and 'leaked' it to local Unit commanders and I was paid a visit by the 'nutting squad.'

I have been asked just how I was able to pass any info onto my SB handler and I can tell you it was difficult; very difficult at times; in those days there were no mobile phones and every phone on the Creggan was smashed beyond repair. At the time, there was a shop called Jacksons and there was a phone out the back and I used to call from there. But it looked suspicious me nipping out time after time and there's only so many times that you can go out for fags or a loaf of bread. Sometimes I had to nip into town which was a couple of miles from the Creggan and if an operation was happening there and then, it made it all the more urgent.

One of the incidents which turned my stomach was the murder of Mountbatten in 1979. This man served his country, fought in wars and he had a genuine love for Ireland and the Irish people. He was no enemy of Ireland. He sailed often at Mullaghmore, Co Sligo and the IRA knew that even though he was high-profile, he was the softest of soft targets and he had declined Gardaí protection. They knew that he often had his family with him and they knew that he had some Irish crew members. In God's name, how did the killing of a young Irish cabin boy further the cause of Irish unity? Paul Maxwell was 15 years old at the time. Mountbatten was an easy target and the Provies and their even more twisted counterparts in INLA knew that because of the lack of security, they could plant the bomb in safety and be well away by the time that the explosion ripped the *Shadow V* to pieces of matchwood. Maybe they had men watching the blast and then melting away to drink to their success, knowing that the Gardaí couldn't – or wouldn't – touch them.

On the day in question, having been previously invited by Padraig Mullaine, a PIRA explosives' expert, I was on what I thought was a camping holiday in Bundoran with a number of junior members of the Provisional IRA. Judging by the way a few of them were talking and raising issues about 'high-profile targets' I was very suspicious and convinced that something major was happening. Then a day or so later, it was announced that Mountbatten had been blown up; now, one thing I remember very vividly, was that when I was Green-Booked by Mullaine, that it was forbidden to conduct any military action inside the Republic. Now, I must confess to only flicking through their 'military manual' and just picking up bits and pieces, but I do remember the section about shitting on our own doorstep, so to speak. During the time we were in the camp, a Belfast Provisional called Rory Stanley came and joined us. He had long blond hair. He also had an English accent, which I know was put on, we were told that he was going to teach us survival tactics, so that if we were taking the war to the Brits in the countryside, we would be able to function and survive in the open. Stanley got me on my own, and began questioning me about my activities. I was very suspicious of him as I thought that I might be in the process of being set up, in order to protect either him or another informer within the group. It was not unknown that in this very dirty war, there might be one or two informers, agents, call them what you may, within the same Provie group, and if the Special Branch handlers thought that their favoured agent was close to being rumbled, information would be leaked to the Provies to the effect that such and such was a tout. He would then be watched, or simply just handed over to the nutting squad for torture and questioning. Believe you me, those boys enjoyed their torture and they were good at it. This would divert suspicions away from the other agent. I have to confess here, that when he (Stanley) was asking me these questions, I was shitting myself because I was sure that he knew something that I didn't and he was trying to trip me up.

During the time that I was in this camp, which was basically a terrorist training unit, Stanley and Mullaine would disappear from time to time. The night before the explosion, Stanley left in the early hours and I recall that Mullaine, the explosives' expert, and another man called Fred Davey also left with him. Although it was a long time ago, I remember that they suddenly weren't there. I believe that they were headed for Mullaghmore where Mountbatten's boat was moored.

Once the news of Mountbatten's murder filtered through, I put two and two together and came up with the correct answer! Mullaine, Stanley and Davey acted suspiciously throughout and their disappearance just hours before the Mountbatten bomb was planted and given the camp's close, very close proximity to the murder scene, leads me to conclude that all three were heavily involved. The camp was in a country village 5 or 6 miles from Bundoran and Mullaghmore was not that far away, maybe a few miles or so, and it was an easy drive down the main road from where we were. Who killed Mountbatten? Mullaine, Stanley and Davey were very much involved and I will maintain that they killed the Queen's cousin on that August day in 1979.

EPILOGUE

The title of this book, as the reader will know is 'What Price Truth?' I have told the truth and I have named names and I have given the British Government and the Security Services the names of people who have committed murders and who have escaped any form of punishment for what any decent society would consider the ultimate crime.

So what price have I, Raymond Gilmour, former Provisional IRA and Irish National Liberation Army member paid? I am now living under an assumed identity, in an unknown location under penalty of death. In return for destroying the IRA in Derry, I live my life constantly looking over my shoulder. I can barely survive on benefits and suffer from chronic Post Traumatic Stress Disorder. The NHS has refused to treat me, informing me that because of my background as a former agent, it is the Security Services who are responsible for my welfare. But the Security Services for whom I spied, for whom I saved the lives of soldiers and policemen have deserted me.

My Special Branch handlers assured me that, in return for informing on the terror groups, saving lives and property and at the same time, losing my family, my friends and my home I would be given financial support for the rest of my life including a lump sum payment, in order that I could settle somewhere, away from the reach of the tentacles of Martin McGuinness' IRA.

That promise has been broken. The Chief Constable of the PSNI - Matt Baggott CBE, QPM, BA (Hons) - doesn't even have the common courtesy to answer my solicitor's letters. I am an almost broken individual; I went through hell for my country and am now alone and penniless. I have gone through 4 marriages and have no hope of returning safely to Derry to see my family again. On one occasion, my own father was abducted and held hostage by the Provisionals – on the orders of McGuinness and his life was threatened if I didn't return to face them.

On the other hand, the man who passed the death sentence on me is now the Deputy First Minister in Her Majesty's Assembly in Northern Ireland. What an irony it is that the man who many believe fired the first shots on 'Bloody Sunday' should now share power with the followers of his avowed enemy Ian Paisley. Effectively, he and his party run the state with impunity and have the full backing of the pusillanimous Westminster administration. Whilst he glad hands leaders across the globe including several US Presidents and the late Nelson Mandela, I have lived in near destitution. Sinn Féin and the IRA call the tune at Stormont and have a massive influence on policing. Some of his followers, convicted and/or suspected murderers who have been on the run from justice have been welcomed back into the British state with letters of amnesty. At the time of writing no such amnesty has been granted to me.

The Troubles ended, not because the Army and police ground the life out the IRA – which they nearly did – but because of the massive financial losses caused by bombs in the Barbican and Canary Wharf which were estimated in the billions. The British will give the Provies anything to avoid another Canary Wharf.

Before giving evidence at Belfast Crown Court I was questioned for over six weeks by Special Branch. I was always steered away from mentioning McGuinness. As far as I am concerned, nothing happened in respect of IRA operations, without the initiation and direct order from the same man. He was at the top of the Provies' hierarchy and he was involved directly or indirectly in the Mountbatten bomb, in the murder of Mrs Mathers and the murder of Franko Heggarty. McGuinness gave personal assurances to the Heggarty family, as with the family of Ranger Best that Franko could come safely home and then either ordered his assassination or did it himself. I have been given similar assurances, but I have no faith in them.

This book is my story, it is not about revenge or apportioning blame. It is about putting the record straight and reminding people about the past. I will never see my family again. I will never set foot on Irish soil again. I am alone. Such is the price of truth.

Raymond Gilmour
2015

APPENDIX

Verbatim excerpt from Lecture 4(b) of the IRA's Green Book - conclusion to section on arrest and anti-interrogation techniques.

Conclusion

The best protection against interrogation is not to get arrested. In order to avoid arrest Volunteers must at all times, "amongst friends" be fully conscious of their own security. In order to be security conscious Volunteers should trust no-one, this includes other Volunteers as well as the general public. It had been a practice in the past for Volunteers to discuss operations with each other, this practice has now stopped. Volunteers should not discuss their exploits with other Volunteers because other Volunteers need not from a military point of view and should not from a security point of view, have knowledge of operations in which they were not personally involved.

British Law

British law requires "in order to get a conviction":

1. A material witness
2. Concrete forensic evidence.
3. A verbal or written statement, signed or unsigned.

WHAT PRICE TRUTH?

British law requires from an arrested person, his name, address, date of birth, fingerprints and photographs. British law also requires that all "terrorist activity" be reported to the "security forces". All Volunteers when arrested have no knowledge of terrorist activity committed or about to be committed. Suspects under interrogation have the legal right – TO REFUSE TO ANSWER ALL QUESTIONS AND TO SEEK A SOLICITOR AND A DOCTOR.

Under the Prevention of Terrorism Act the "security forces", the Brits, can apply for a 28 day extension order. The threat of using this is quite common but it has been used only once – in the Miami Showband case.

We have already seen and examined some of the many techniques employed by the police and army while interrogating suspects, it would be quite unrealistic to write all of them into a short lecture but broadly speaking the techniques are threefold and always in combination with one another: these involve:

1. Humiliation.
2. Physical Torture.
3. Psychological Torture.

So Volunteers can expect treatment of this nature if arrested and when being interrogated. A technique at present being practised by the Brits and the Police is one of shock aimed psychologically. This involves exposing blown up photographs, usually of dead bomb victims, dead soldiers and policemen and more often than not the corpses of the suspects comrades. The technique behind this tactic is to arouse emotions of hysteria in the suspect and by doing so to disorientate him temporarily. All Volunteers must understand and be fully aware of the anxiety, the shock and the hysteria it can arouse in the unprotected suspect. By understanding this technique and by looking at it logically and the tactic behind it, Volunteers should be ready to meet the situation of that nature, with confidence in the knowledge that it's purpose is to shock the Volunteer into confession. Another tactic of this nature is throwing the limb or limbs of a corpse into the cell of a suspect.

The best protection while being interrogated is LOYALTY to the Movement. This implies LOYALTY to all YOUR COMRADES and PROTECTION of all members of the Movement. Again, commitment to the aims and objectives of the Movement, a deep and unmoving POLICITICAL COMMITMENT to the ideas of the Socialist Republic, CONSTANT AWARENESS that you are a REVOLUTIONARY with a found POLICITAL base, NOBLE and JUSTIFIABLE CAUSE, and a deep and firm belief that those holding you and interrogating you are MORALLY WRONG, that you are SUPERIOR in all respects, because your cause is RIGHT and JUSTIFIED.

WHAT PRICE TRUTH is the astonishing story of a man who spent years as an undercover police agent inside the IRA. It exposes the reality of the dark, claustrophobic world of the Provisionals: the iron grip they hold over their communities: their ruthless and cynical disregard for human life; the single-minded professionalism of some IRA volunteers – and the rank incompetence of others.

Raymond Gilmour learned the brutal facts of life in Northern Ireland at an early age. Beatings, murders and knee-capping were common currency on the dead-end Derry estate where he grew up, and despite the omnipresence of British soldiers no one way in any doubt about who really held the balance of power. Many young Catholics, with few options and fewer jobs open to them, joined the terrorists as volunteers. So, at the age of sixteen, did Ray Gilmour – but his recruitment had a vital and deadly difference: his brief to infiltrate the IRA, sabotage their activities, and report back to his Special Branch contact.

So began nearly a decade of life in no-man's land, an impossibly dangerous double life where every day brought with it a new and potentially terminal threat. Gilmour relates in gripping style the hazards of playing along with the shootings and bombings while secretly trying to subvert them; the constant fear of exposure, torture and execution by his IRA 'comrades' – and the tension of wondering when he might out-live his usefulness and be sacrificed by the shadowy men from MI5.

Incredibly, Gilmour not only avoided exposure and sacrifice, he also became one of the RUC's most valued agents, foiling countless terrorist attacks and helping the police seize huge quantities of arms and explosives. As one RUC source admitted: "He kept Derry clean for us."

Gilmour's career as an agent came to an abrupt and spectacular end when he uncovered one of the IRA's most prized arms caches, forcing him and his family – who until then had known nothing of his double life – to go on the run before the IRA's notorious Internal Affairs men caught up with them.

But even escape has its penalties: Gilmour has not seen his wife and children for over thirty years, and he now lives in permanent exile, flitting from safe house to safe house under a sentence of death unrevoked by peace-talks amnesties.

What Price Truth is Gilmour's story: a narrative of heart-stopping tension and unrelenting human drama which makes a mockery of fictionalised accounts of terrorism in Northern Ireland.

OTHER PUBLICATIONS

A Long Long War: Voices from the British Army in Northern Ireland, 1969-1998. Helion and Company. (2008)

Bullets, Bombs and Cups of Tea: Further Voices of the British Army in Northern Ireland, 1969-98. Helion and Company. (2009)

Bloody Belfast: An Oral History of the British Army's War Against the IRA. The History Press Ltd. (2010)

The Bloodiest Year: British Soldiers in Northern Ireland 1972, *in Their Own Words.* The History Press Ltd. (2011)

Sir, They're Taking the Kids Indoors: The British Army in Northern Ireland, 1973/74. Helion and Company. (2012)

Wasted Years, Wasted Lives: Vol 1 *The Troubles* 1975/7. Helion and Company (2013)

Wasted Years, Wasted Lives: Vol 2 *The Troubles* 1978/9. Helion and Company (Spring 2014)

Northern Ireland 1980-83: An Agony Continued. Helion and Company Due for publication in 2015

Another Bloody Chapter in An Endless Civil War; Northern Ireland and the troubles 1984-1989. Due for publication in 2016

Northern Ireland:- A Guide to Atrocity (Jackdaw 2014).

Printed in Great Britain
by Amazon.co.uk, Ltd.,
Marston Gate.